FOUR REVENGE TRAGEDIES

THE SPANISH TRAGEDY By THOMAS KYD

THE REVENGER'S TRAGEDY By THOMAS MIDDLETON

THE REVENGE OF BUSSY D'AMBOIS By GEORGE CHAPMAN

THE ATHEIST'S TRAGEDY By CYRIL TOURNEUR

A Digireads.com Book
Digireads.com Publishing

Four Revenge Tragedies (The Spanish Tragedy, The Revenger's Tragedy, The Revenge
    of Bussy D'Ambois, and The Atheist's Tragedy)
By Thomas Kyd, Thomas Middleton, George Chapman, Cyril Tourneur
ISBN 10: 1-4209-4936-5
ISBN 13: 978-1-4209-4936-0

Please visit *www.digireads.com*

CONTENTS

4

THE SPANISH TRAGEDY

OR, HIERONIMO IS MAD AGAIN,

By THOMAS KYD

CONTAINING THE LAMENTABLE END OF DON HORATIO,
AND BEL-IMPERIA; WITH THE PITIFUL DEATH OF HIERONIMO.

NEWLY CORRECTED, AMENDED, AND ENLARGED WITH NEW
ADDITIONS OF THE PAINTERS PART, AND OTHERS,
AS IT HATH OF LATE BEEN DIVERS TIMES ACTED.

DRAMATIS PERSONAE

GHOST OF ANDREA
REVENGE
KING OF SPAIN
DON CYPRIAN, *Duke of Castile, his brother*
LORENZO, *the Duke's son*
BEL-IMPERIA, *Lorenzo's sister*
PEDRINGANO, *Bel-imperia's servant*
LORENZO'S PAGE
VICEROY OF PORTUGAL
DON PEDRO, his brother
BALTHAZAR, *the Viceroy's son*
SERBERINE, *Balthazar's servant*
HIERONIMO, *Marshal of Spain*
ISABELLA, *his wife*
HORATIO, *their son*
ISABELLA'S MAID
SPANISH GENERAL
DEPUTY
PORTUGUESE AMBASSADOR
PORTUGUESE NOBLEMEN
ALEXANDRO
VILUPPO
BAZULTO, *an old man*
CHRISTOPHIL, *Bel-imperia's Janitor*
HANGMAN
MESSENGER
THREE WATCHMEN
TWO PORTUGUESE

In Hieronimo's Play:

SOLIMAN, *Sultan of Turkey (by Balthazar)*
ERASTUS, *Knight of Rhodes (by Lorenzo)*
THE BASHAW *(by Hieronimo)*
PERSEDA *(by Bel-imperia)*

In First Dumb Show:

THREE KINGS
THREE KNIGHTS
IN SECOND DUMB SHOW
HYMEN
TWO TORCH BEARERS

In the Additions to the Play:

BAZARDO, *a painter*
PEDRO, JACQUES, *Hieronimo's servants.*
ARMY, ROYAL SUITES, NOBLES, OFFICERS, HALBERDIERS, SERVANTS
&C.

SCENE: *Spain and Portugal*

No early Quarto contains Dramatis Personae. Dodsley's list of 1744 was copied by later editors till Schick, from whose list the above varies in tome details, and in adding the characters in Hieronimo's play.

THE SPANISH TRAGEDY

ACT I.

SCENE I. *Induction.*

[*Enter the* GHOST *of Andrea, and with him* REVENGE.]

GHOST. When this eternal substance of my soul
    Did live imprisoned in my wanton flesh,
    Each in their function serving others need,
    I was a Courtier in the Spanish Court.
    My name was *Don Andrea*; my descent,
    Though not ignoble, yet inferior far
    To gracious fortunes of my tender youth:
    For there in prime and pride of all my years,
    By duteous service and deserving love,
    In secret I possessed a worthy dame,
    Which hight sweet *Bel-imperia* by name.
    But in the harvest of my summer joys,
    Deaths winter nipped the blossoms of my bliss,
    Forcing divorce betwixt my love and me.
    For in the late conflict with Portugal
    My valour drew me into dangers mouth,
    Till life to death made passage through my wounds.
    When I was slain, my soul descended straight,
    To pass the flowing stream of *Acheron*;
    But churlish *Charon*, only boatman there,
    Said that my rites of burial not performed,
    I might not sit amongst his passengers.
    Ere *Sol* had slept three nights in *Thetis* lap,
    And slaked his smoking chariot in her flood,
    By *Don Horatio*, our Knight Marshals son,
    My funerals and obsequies were done.
    Then was the Ferryman of Hell content
    To pass me over to the slimy strand
    That leads to fell *Auernus* ugly waves.
    There, pleasing Cerberus with honeyed speech,
    I past the perils of the foremost porch.
    Not far from hence, amidst ten thousand souls,
    Sate *Minos*, *Eacus*, and *Rhadamant*,
    To whom no sooner gan I make approach,
    To crave a passport for my wandering Ghost,
    But *Minos*, in graven leaves of Lottery,
    Drew forth the manner of my life and death.
    This Knight (quoth he) both lived and died in love,
    And for his love tried fortune of the wars,

And, by wars fortune, lost both love and life.
Why then, said *Eacus*, convey him hence,
To walk with lovers in our fields of love,
And spend the course of everlasting time
Under green myrtle trees and Cypress shades.
No, no, said *Rhadamant*, it were not well
With loving souls to place a Martialist:
He died in war, and must to Martial fields,
Where wounded Hector lives in lasting pain,
And *Achilles* Mermedons do scour the plain.
Then *Minos*, mildest censor of the three,
Made this device to end the difference:
Send him (quoth he) to our infernal King,
To dome him as best seems his Majesty.
To this effect my passport straight was drawn.
In keeping on my way to *Plutos* Court,
Through dreadful shades of ever glooming night,
I saw more sights then thousand tongues can tell,
Or pens can write, or mortal hearts can think.
Three ways there were: that on the right hand side
Was ready way unto the foresaid fields,
Where lovers live and bloody Martialists;
But either sort contained within his bounds.
The left hand path, declining fearfully,
Was ready downfall to the deepest hell,
Where bloody furies shakes their whips of steel,
And poor *Ixion* turns an endless wheel;
Where usurers are choked with melting gold,
And wantons are embraced with ugly Snakes,
And murderers groan with never killing wounds,
And perjured wightes scalded in boiling lead,
And all foul sins with torments overwhelmed.
Twixt these two ways I trod the middle path,
Which brought me to the fair Elizian green,
In midst whereof there stands a stately Tower,
The walls of brass, the gates of adamant.
Here finding *Pluto* with his *Proserpine*,
I showed my passport humbled on my knee;
Whereat fair *Proserpine* began to smile,
And begged that only she might give my doom.
Pluto was pleased, and sealed it with a kiss.
Forthwith, *Revenge*, she rounded thee in th' ear,
And bad thee lead me through the gates of Horn,
Where dreams have passage in the silent night.
No sooner had she spoke, but we were here,
I won't not how, in twinkling of an eye.
REVENGE. Then know, *Andrea*, that thou art arriv'd
    Where thou shalt see the author of thy death,

Don Balthazar, the Prince of *Portugal*,
Deprived of life by *Bel-imperia*.
Here sit we down to see the mystery,
And serve for *Chorus* in this Tragedy.

SCENE II.

[*Enter Spanish* KING, GENERAL, CASTILE, HIERONIMO.]

KING. Now say, Lord General, how fares our Camp?
GENERAL. All well, my sovereign Liege, except some few
    That are deceased by fortune of the war.
KING. But what portends thy cheerful countenance,
    And posting to our presence thus in hast?
    Speak, man, hath fortune given us victory?
GENERAL. Victory, my Liege, and that with little loss.
KING. Our Portugals will pay us tribute then?
GENERAL. Tribute and wonted homage therewithal.
KING. Then blest be heaven, and guider of the heavens,
    From whose fair influence such justice flows.
CASTILE. *Oh multum dilecte Deo, tibi militat aether,*
    Et coniuratae curuato poplite gentes
    Succumbunt: recti soror est victoria iuris.
KING. Thanks to my loving brother of Castile.
    But, General, unfold in brief discourse
    Your form of battle, and your wars success,
    That, adding all the pleasure of thy news
    Unto the height of former happiness,
    With deeper wage and greater dignity,
        We may reward thy blissful chivalry.
GENERAL. Where *Spain* and Portugal do jointly knit
    Their frontiers, leaning on each others bound,
    There met our armies in their proud array:
    Both furnished well, both full of hope and fear,
    Both menacing alike with daring shows,
    Both vaunting sundry colours of device,
    Both cheerly sounding trumpets, drums, and fifes,
    Both raising dreadful clamors to the sky,
    That valleys, hills, and rivers made rebound,
    And heaven itself was frighted with the sound.
    Our battles both were pitched in squadron form,
    Each corner strongly fenced with wings of shot;
    But ere we joined and came to push of Pike,
    I brought a squadron of our readiest shot
    From out our rearward to begin the fight:
    They brought another wing to encounter us.
    Meanwhile, our Ordinance played on either side,
    And Captains strove to have their valours tried.

Don Pedro, their chief Horsemen's Colonel,
Did with his Cornet bravely make attempt
To break the order of our battle ranks:
But *Don Rogero*, worthy man of war,
Marched forth against him with our Musketeers,
And stopt the malice of his fell approach.
While they maintain hot skirmish too and fro,
Both battles join and fall to handy blows,
Their violent shot resembling th' oceans rage,
When, roaring loud, and with a swelling tide,
It beats upon the rampiers of huge rocks,
And gapes to swallow neighbour bounding lands.
Now while Bellona rageth here and there,
Thick storms of bullets ran like winters hail,
And shivered Launces dark the troubled air.
     Pede pes et cuspide cuspis,
    Arma sonant armis vir petiturque viro.
On every side drop Captains to the ground,
And Soldiers, some ill maimed, some slain outright:
Here falls a body scindred from his head,
There legs and arms lye bleeding on the grass,
Mingled with weapons and unbowed steeds,
That scattering over spread the purple plain.
In all this turmoil, three long hours and more,
The victory to neither part inclined,
Till Don *Andrea* with his brave Launders
In their main battle made so great a breach
That, half dismayed, the multitude retired:
But *Balthazar*, the Portugals young Prince,
Brought rescue and encouraged them to stay.
Here-hence the fight was eagerly renewed,
And in that conflict was *Andrea* slain,
Brave man at arms, but weak to *Balthazar*.
Yet while the Prince, insulting over him,
Breathed out proud vaunts, sounding to our reproach,
Friendship and hardy valour, joined in one,
Pricked forth *Horatio*, our Knight-Marshals son,
To challenge forth that Prince in single fight:
Not long between these twain the fight endured,
But straight the Prince was beaten from his horse,
And forest to yield him prisoner to his foe.
When he was taken, all the rest they fled,
And our Carbines pursued them to the death,
Till, *Phoebus* waving to the western deep,
Our Trumpeters were chargde to sound retreat.
KING. Thanks, good Lord General for these good news;
    And for some argument of more to come,
    Take this, and wear it for thy Sovereigns sake.

[*Gives him his Chain.*]

But tell me now, hast thou confirmed a peace?
GENERAL. No peace, my Liege, but peace conditional,
    That, if with homage tribute be well paid,
    The fury of your forces will be stayed:
    And to this peace their *Viceroy* hath subscribed,

[*Gives the* KING *a paper.*]

And made a solemn vow that, during life,
    His tribute shall be truly paid to *Spain*.
KING. These words, these deeds, become thy person well.
    But now, Knight Marshall, frolic with thy King,
    For 'tis thy Son that wins this battles prize.
HIERONIMO. Long may he live to serve my Sovereign liege,
    And soon decay unless he serve my liege.

[*A tucket afar off.*]

KING. Nor thou nor he shall dye without reward:
    What means this warning of this trumpets sound?
GENERAL. This tells me that your graces men of war,
    Such as wars fortune hath reserved from death,
    Come marching on towards your royal seat,
    To show themselves before your Majesty;
    For so I gave in charge at my depart.
    Whereby by demonstration shall appear,
    That -all (except three hundred or few more)
    Are safe returned, and by their foes enriched.

[*The Army enters*; BALTHAZAR, *between* LORENZO *and* HORATIO, *captive.*]

KING. A gladsome sight: I long to see them here.

[*They enter and pass by.*]

Was that the war-like Prince of *Portugal*
    That by our Nephew was in triumph led?
GENERAL. It was, my Liege, the Prince of *Portugal*.
KING. But what was he that on the other side
    Held him by the arm, as partner of the prize?
HIERONIMO. That was my son, my gracious sovereign;
    Of whom, though from his tender infancy
    My loving thoughts did never hope but well,
    He never pleased his father's eyes till now,
    Nor filled my heart with over flowing joys.

KING. Go, let them march once more about these walls,
    That, staying them, we may confer and talk
    With our brave prisoner and his double guard.
    Hieronimo, it greatly pleaseth us
    That in our victory thou have a share,
    By virtue of thy worthy sons exploit.

[*Enter again.*]

Bring hither the young Prince of *Portugal*:
The rest marched on, but ere they be dismissed,
We will bestow on every soldier
Two duckets and on every leader ten,
That they may know our largesse welcomes them.

[*Exeunt all but* BALTHAZAR, LORENZO, *and* HORATIO.]

    Welcome *Don Balthazar*; welcome Nephew;
    And thou, *Horatio*, thou art welcome too.
    Young prince, although thy fathers hard misdeeds,
    In keeping back the tribute that he owes,
    Deserve but evil measure at our hands,
    Yet shalt thou know that *Spain* is honorable.
BALTHAZAR. The trespass that my father made in peace
    Is now controlled by fortune of the wars;
    And cards once dealt, it boots not ask, why so?
    His men are slain, a weakening to his Realm;
    His colours ceased, a blot unto his name;
    His Son distressed, a cursive to his heart:
    These punishments may clear his late offence.
KING. I, *Balthazar*, if he observe this truce,
    Our peace will grow the stronger for these wars.
    Mean while live thou, though not in liberty,
    Yet free from bearing any servile yoke;
    For in our hearing thy deserts were great,
    And in our sight thy self art gracious.
BALTHAZAR. And I shall study to deserve this grace.
KING. But tell me (for their holding makes me doubt)
    To which of these twain art thou prisoner?
LORENZO. To me, my Liege.
HORATIO. To me, my Sovereign.
LORENZO. This hand first took his courser by the reins.
HORATIO. But first my launce did put him from his horse.
LORENZO. I ceased his weapon and enjoyed it first.
HORATIO. But first I forc'd him lay his weapons down.
KING. Let go his arm, upon our privilege.

[*Let him go.*]

Say, worthy Prince, to whether didst thou yield?
BALTHAZAR. To him in curtsey, to this perforce:
    He spake me fair, this other gave me strokes;
    He promised life, this other threatened death;
    He want my love, this other conquered me:
    And truth to say, I yield myself to both.
HIERONIMO. But that I know your grace for just and wise,
    And might seem partial in this difference,
    Enforced by nature and by law of arms
    My tongue should plead for young *Horatio's* right.
    He hunted well that was a Lyons death,
    Not he that in a garment wore his skin:
    So Hares may pull dead Lyons by the beard.
KING. Content thee, Marshall, thou shall have no wrong;
    And, for thy sake, thy Son shall want "ho right.
    Will both abide the censure of my doom?
LORENZO. I crave no better then your (grace awards.
HORATIO. Nor I, although I sit beside my-right.
KING. Then by my judgment thus your strife shall end:
    You both deserve, and both shall have reward.
    Nephew, thou tookst his weapon and his horse:
    His weapons and his horse are thy reward.
    Horatio, thou didst force him first to yield:
    His ransom therefore is thy valor's fee;
    Appoint the sum, as you shall both agree.
    But, Nephew, thou shalt have the Prince in guard,
    For thine estate best fitteth such a guest.
    Horatios house were small for all his train;
    Yet, in regard thy substance passeth his,
    And that just guerdon may befall desert,
    To him we yield the armour of the Prince.
    How likes *Don Balthazar* of this device?
BALTHAZAR. Right well, my Liege, if this proviso were,
    That Don *Horatio* bear us company,
    Whom I admire and love for chivalry.
KING. *Horatio*, leave him not that loves thee so.
    Now let us hence to see our soldiers paid,
    And feast our prisoner as our friendly guest.

    [*Exeunt.*]

SCENE III.

[*Enter* VICEROY, ALEXANDRA, VILLUPPO.]

VICEROY. Is our Ambassador dispatched for *Spain*?
ALEXANDRO. Two days, my Liege, are past since his depart.
VICEROY. And tribute payment gone along with him?
ALEXANDRO. I, my good Lord.
VICEROY. Then rest we here a while in our unrest,
 And feed our sorrows with some inward sighs,
 For deepest cares break never into tears.
 But wherefore sit I in a Regal throne?
 This better fits a wretches endless moan:
 Yet this is higher then my fortunes reach,
 And therefore better then my state deserves.
 Falls to the ground. I, I, this earth, Image of melancholy,
 Seeks him whom fates adjudge to misery:
 Here let me lye; now am I at the lowest.
   Qui iacet in terra non habet vnde cadat.
  In trie consumpsit vires fortuna nocendo,
   Nil superest ut iam possit obesse magis.
 Yes, Fortune may bereave me of my Crown:
 Here, take it now; let Fortune do her worst,
 She will not rob me of this sable weed.
 Oh no, she envies none but pleasant things.
 Such is the folly of despiteful chance.
 Fortune is blind, and sees not my deserts;
 So is she deaf, and hears not my laments;
 And could she hear, yet is she willful mad,
 And therefore will not pity my distress.
 Suppose that she could pity me, what then?
 What help can be expected at her hands,
 Whose foot (is) standing on a rolling stone,
 And mind more mutable then fickle winds?
 Why wail I then, wheres hope of no redress?
 Oh yes, complaining makes my grief seem less.
 My late ambition hath distained my faith;
 My breach of faith occasioned bloody wars;
 Those bloody wars have spent my treasure;
 And with my treasure my peoples blood;
 And with their blood, my joy and best beloved,
 My best beloved, my sweet and only Son.
 Oh wherefore went I not to war myself?
 The cause was mine; I might have died for both:
 My years were mellow, his but young and green,
 My death were natural, but his was forced.
ALEXANDRO. No doubt, my Liege, but still the prince survives.

VICEROY. Survives? I, where?
ALEXANDRO. In *Spain*, a prisoner by mischance of war.
VICEROY. Then they have slain him for his fathers fault
ALEXANDRO. That were a breach to common law of arms. I:
VICEROY. They wreck no laws that meditate revenge.
ALEXANDRO. His ransoms worth will stay from foul revenge.
VICEROY. No; if he lived the news would soon be here.
ALEXANDRO. Nay, evil news fly faster still than good.
VICEROY. Tell me no more of news, for he is dead.
VILLUPPO. My Sovereign, pardon the author of ill news,
    And He bewray the fortune of thy Son.
VICEROY. Speak on. He guerdon thee what ere it be:
    Mine ear is ready to receive ill news,
    My heart grown hard against mischiefs battery.
    Stand up, I say, and tell thy tale at large.
VILLUPPO. Then hear that truth which these mine eyes have seen.
    When both the armies were in battle joined,
    Don Balthazar, amidst the thickest troupes,
    To win renown did wondrous feats of arms:
    Amongst the rest I saw him, hand to hand,
    In single fight with their Lord General;
    Till *Alexandro*, that here counterfeits
    Under the colour of a duteous friend,
    Discharged his Pistol at the Princes back,
    As though he would have slain their General:
    And therewithal *Don Balthazar* fell down;
    And when he fell, then we began to fly:
    But, had he lived, the day had sure been ours.
ALEXANDRO. Oh wicked forgery: Oh traitorous miscreant.
VICEROY. Hold thou thy peace. But now, *Villuppo*, say,
    Where then became the carcasses' of my Son?
VILLUPPO. I saw them drag it to the Spanish tents.
VICEROY. I, I, my nightly dreams have told me this.
    Thou false, unkind, unthankful, traitorous beast,
    Wherein had *Balthazar* offended thee,
    That thou shouldst thus betray him to our foes?
    Wast Spanish gold that bleared so thine eyes, So
    That thou couldst see no part of our deserts?
    Perchance, because thou art *Terseraes* Lord,
    Thou hadst some hope to wear this Diadem,
    If first my Son and then myself were slain.
    But thy ambitious thought shall break thy neck.
    I, this was it that made thee spill his blood,

[*Takes the crown and puts it on again.*]

    But He now wear it till thy blood be spilt.
ALEXANDRO. Vouchsafe, dread Sovereign, to hear me speak.

VICEROY. Away with him; his sight is second hell.
 Keep him till we determine of his death:
 If *Balthazar* be dead, he shall not live.
 Villuppo, follow us for thy reward.

[*Exit Viceroy.*]

VILLUPPO. Thus have I with an envious, forged tale
 Deceived the King, betrayed mine enemy,
 And hope for guerdon of my villany.

[*Exit.*]

SCENE IV.

[*Enter* HORATIO *and* BEL-IMPERIA.]

BEL-IMPERIA. Signior *Horatio*, this is the place and hour,
 Wherein I must entreat thee to relate
 The circumstance of *Don Andreas* death,
 Who, living, was my garlands sweetest flower.
 And in his death hath buried my delights.
HORATIO. For love of him, and service to yourself,
 I nill refuse this heavy doleful charge;
 Yet tears and sighs, I fear, will hinder me.
 When both our Armies were enjoyed in fight,
 Your worthy chevalier amidst the thickest,
 For glorious cause still aiming at the fairest,
 Was at the last by Young *Don Balthazar*
 Encountered hand to hand: their fight was long,
 Their hearts were great, their clamours menacing,
 Their strength alike, their strokes both dangerous.
 But wrathful Nemesis, that wicked power,
 Envying at Andreas praise and worth,
 Cut short his life to end his praise and worth.
 She, she herself, disguised in armor's mask,
 (As Pallas was before proud *Pergamus*)
 Brought in a fresh supply of Halberdiers,
 Which paunched his horse and dinged him to the ground,
 Then Young *Don Balthazar* with ruthless rage,
 Taking advantage of his foes distress,
 Did finish what his Halberdiers begun,
 And left not till Andreas life was done.
 Then, though too late, incensed with just remorse,
 I with my hand set forth against the Prince,
 And brought him prisoner from his Halberdiers.
BEL-IMPERIA. Would thou hadst slain him that so slew my love.
 But then was *Don Andreas* carcass lost?

HORATIO. No, that was it for which I chiefly strove,
 Nor stept I back till I recovered him:
 I took him up, and wound him in mine arms;
 And welding him unto my private tent,
 There laid him down, and dewed him with my tears,
 And sighed and sorrowed as became a Friend.
 But neither Friendly sorrow, sighs, nor tears,
 Could win pale death from his usurped right.
 Yet this I did, and less I could not do:
 I saw him honored with due funeral.
 This scarf I plucked from off his lifeless arm,
 And wear it in remembrance of my Friend.
BEL-IMPERIA. I know the scarf: would he had kept it still;
 For had he lived he would have kept it still,
 And worn it for his *Bel-imperias* sake:
 For 'twas my favor at his last depart.
 But now wear thou it both for him and me,
 For after him thou hast deserved it best.
 But for thy kindness in his life and death,
 Be sure while *Bel-imperias* life endures,
 She will be Don *Horatios* thankful Friend.
HORATIO. And (Madame) Don *Horatio* will not slack
 Humbly to seem fair *Bel-imperia*.
 But now, if your good liking stand thereto,
 He crave your pardon to go seek the Prince,
 For so the Duke, your father, gave me charge. [*Exit.*]
BEL-IMPERIA. I, go, *Horatio*, leave me here alone,
 For solitude best fits my cheerless mood.
 Yet what avails to wail *Andreas* death,
 From whence *Horatio* proves my second love?
 Had he not loved *Andrea* as he did,
 He could not sit in *Bel-imperias* thoughts.
 But how can love find harbour in my breast,
 Till I revenge the death of my beloved?
 Yes, second love shall further my revenge:
 He love *Horatio*, my *Andreas* Friend,
 The more to spite the Prince that wrought his end.
 And where *Don Balthazar* that slew my love,
 Himself now pleads for favor at my hands,
 He shall, in rigour of my just disdain,
 Reap long repentance for his murderous deed:
 For what wast else but murderous cowardice,
 So many to oppress one valiant knight,
 Without respect of honor in the fight?
 And here he comes that murdered my delight.

[*Enter* LORENZO *and* BALTHAZAR.]

LORENZO. Sister, what means this melancholy walk?
BEL-IMPERIA. That for a while I wish no company.
LORENZO. But here the Prince is come to visit you.
BEL-IMPERIA. That argues that he lives in liberty.
BALTHAZAR. No, Madame, but in pleasing servitude.
BEL-IMPERIA. Your prison then, belike, is your conceit.
BALTHAZAR. I, by conceit my freedom is enthralled.
BEL-IMPERIA. Then with conceit enlarge yourself again.
BALTHAZAR. What, if conceit have laid my heart to gage?
BEL-IMPERIA. Pay that you borrowed and recover it.
BALTHAZAR. I die, if it return from whence it lies.
BEL-IMPERIA. A heartless man and live? A miracle.
BALTHAZAR. I, Lady, love can work such miracles.
LORENZO. Tush, tush, my Lord, let go these ambages,
    And in plain terms acquaint her with your love.
BEL-IMPERIA. What boots complaint, when there's no remedy?
BALTHAZAR. Yes, to your gracious self must I complain,
    In whose fair answer lies my remedy;
    On whose perfection all my thoughts attend;
    On whose aspect mine eyes find beauties bower;
    In whose translucent breast my heart is lodged.
BEL-IMPERIA. Alas, my Lord, these are but words of course,
    And but devise to drive me from this place.

    [*She in going in, lets fall her glove which* HORATIO *coming out takes up.*]

HORATIO. Madame, your Glove.
BEL-IMPERIA. Thanks, good *Horatio*, take it for thy pains.
BALTHAZAR. Signior *Horatio* stooped in happy time.
HORATIO. I reaped more grace then I deserved or hoped.
LORENZO. My Lord, be not dismayed for what is past;
    You know that women oft are humorous:
    These clouds will over blow with little wind;
    Let me alone, He scatter them myself.
    Meanwhile let us devise to spend the time
    In some delightful sports and reveling.
HORATIO. The King, my Lords, is coming hither straight,
    To feast the *Portugal* Ambassador;
    Things were in readiness before I came.
BALTHAZAR. Then here it fits us to attend the King,
    To welcome hither our Ambassador,
    And learn my Father and my Countries health.

SCENE V.

[*Enter the banquet, Trumpets, the* KING, *and* AMBASSADOR.]

KING. See, Lord Ambassador, how *Spain* entreats
    Their prisoner *Balthazar*, thy Viceroys son:
    We pleasure more in kindness then in wars.
AMBASSADOR. Sad is our King, and *Portugal* laments,
    Supposing that *Don Balthazar* is slain.
BALTHAZAR. So am I slain, by beauties tyranny.
    You see, my Lord, how *Balthazar* is slain:
    I frolic with the Duke of *Castiles* Son,
    Wrapt every hour in pleasures of the Court,
    And graced with favors of his Majesty.
KING. Put off your greetings, till our feast be done;
    Now come and sit with us, and taste our cheer.

[*Sits to the Banquet.*]

    Sit down, young Prince, you are our second guest:
    Brother, sit down; and, Nephew, take your place.
    Signior *Horatio*, wait thou upon our Cup,
    For well thou hast deserved to be honored.
    Now, Lordings, fall too; *Spain* is *Portugal*
    And *Portugal* is *Spain*; we both are Friends;
    Tribute is paid, and we enjoy our right.
    But where is old *Hieronimo*, our Marshall?
    To He promised us, in honor of our guest,
    To grace our banquet with some pompous jest.

[*Enter* HIERONIMO *with a Drum, three Knights, each his Scutcheon; then he
    fetches three Kings; they take their Crowns and them captive.*]

    Hieronimo, this mask contents mine eye,
    Although I sound not well the mystery.
HIERONIMO. The first arm'd knight that hung his Scutcheon up,

[*He takes the Scutcheon, and gives it to the King.*]

    Was English Robert, Earle of Gloucester,
    Who, when King *Stephen* bore sway in Albion,
    Arrived with five and twenty thousand men
    In *Portugal*, and by success of war
    Enforced the King, then but a Sarasin,
    To bear the yoke of the English Monarchic
KING. My Lord of *Portugal*, by this you see
    That which may comfort both your King and you,

And make your late discomfort seem the less.
But say, *Hieronimo*, what was the next?
HIERONIMO. The second knight that hung his Scutcheon up,

[*He doth as he did before.*]

Was *Edmund*, Earle of Kent in Albion,
When English *Richard* wore the Diadem.
He came likewise, and razed Lisbon walls,
And took the King of *Portugal* in fight;
For which, and other such like service done,
He after was created Duke of York.
KING. This is another special argument,
    That *Portugal* may deign to bear our yoke,
    When it by little England hath been yoked:
    But now, *Hieronimo*, what were the last?
HIERONIMO. The third and last, not least in our account,

[*Doing as before.*]

Was, as the rest, a valiant Englishman,
Brave John of Gaunt, the Duke of Lancaster,
As by his Scutcheon plainly may appear.
He with a puissant Army came to *Spain*,
And took our King of Castile prisoner.
AMBASSADOR. This is an argument for our *Viceroy*
    That *Spain* may not insult for her success,
    Since English warriors likewise conquered *Spain*,
    And made them bow their knees to Albion.
KING. *Hieronimo*, I drink to thee for this devise,
    Which hath pleased both the Ambassador and me.
    Pledge me, *Hieronimo*, if thou love the King.

[*Takes the Cup of* HORATIO.]

My Lord, I fear we sit but over long,
Unless our dainties were more delicate:
But welcome are you to the best we have.
Now let us in, that you may be dispatched:
I think our council is already set.

[*Exeunt omnes.*]

SCENE VI.

ANDREA. Come we for this from depth of underground,
  To see him feast that gave me my deaths wound?
  These pleasant sights are. sorrow to my soul:
  Nothing but league, and love and banqueting.
REVENGE. Be still, *Andrea*; ere we go from hence,
  I'll turn their Friendship into fell despite;
  Their love to mortal hate, their day to night;
  Their hope into despair, their peace to war;
  Their joys to pain, their bliss to misery.

ACT II.

SCENE I.

[*Enter* LORENZO *and* BALTHAZAR.]

LORENZO. My Lord, though *Bel-imperia* seem thus coy,
  Let reason hold you in your wonted joy:
  In time the savage Bull sustains the yoke,
  In time all haggard Hawks will stoop to lure,
  In time small wedges cleave the hardest Oak,
  In time the Flint is pierced with softest shower,
  And she in time will fall from her disdain,
  And rue the sufferance of your Friendly pain.
BALTHAZAR. No, she is wilder, and more hard withal,
  Then beast, or bird, or tree, or stony wall.
  But wherefore blot I *Bel-imperias* name?
  It is my fault, not she that merits blame.
  My feature is not to content her sight,
  My words are rude, and work her no delight.
  The lines I send her are but harsh and ill,
  Such as do drop from *Pan* and *Marsias* quill.
  My presents are not of sufficient cost,
  And being worthies, all my labours lost.
  Yet might she love me for my valiancy:
  I, but that's slandered by captivity.
  Yet might she love me to content her sire:
  I, but her reason masters his desire.
  Yet might she love me as her brother's Friend:
  I, but her hopes aim at some other end.
  Yet might she love me to up-rear her state:
  I, but perhaps she hopes some nobler mate.
  Yet might she love me as her beauties thrall:
  I, but I fear she cannot love at all.
LORENZO. My Lord, for my sake leave this ecstasy,

And doubt not but we'll find some remedy.
Some cause there is that lets you not be loved:
First that must needs be known, and then removed.
What, if my Sister love some other Knight?
BALTHAZAR. My summers day will turn to winters night.
LORENZO. I have already found a stratagem,
To sound the bottom of this doubtful theme.
My Lord, for once you shall be ruled by me;
Hinder me not what ere you hear or see.
By force, or fair means will I cast about,
To find the truth of all this question out.
Ho, *Pedringano.*
PEDRINGANO. *Signior.*
LORENZO. *Vien qui presto.*

[*Enter* PEDRINGANO.]

PEDRINGANO. Hath your Lordship any service to command me?
LORENZO. I, *Pedringano*, service of import:
And not to spend the time in trifling words,
Thus stands the case: it is not long, thou knowest,
Since I did shield thee from my father's wrath,
For thy conveyance in *Andreas* love,
For which thou wert adjudged to punishment:
I stood betwixt thee and thy punishment;
And since, thou knowest how I have favored thee.
Now to these favors will I add reward,
Not with fair words, but store of golden coin,
And lands and living joined with dignities,
If thou but satisfied my just demand:
Tell truth, and have me for thy lasting Friend.
PEDRINGANO. What ere it be your Lordship shall demand,
My bounden duty bids me tell the truth,
If case it lye in me to tell the truth.
LORENZO. Then, *Pedringano*, this is my demand:
Whom loves my sister *Bel-imperial*
For she reposeth all her trust in thee.
Speak, man, and gain both Friendship and reward:
I mean, whom loves she in *Andreas* place?
PEDRINGANO. Alas, my Lord, since *Don Andreas* death,
I have no credit with her as before,
And therefore know not if she love or no.
LORENZO. Nay, if thou dally, then I am thy foe,

[*Draws his sword.*]

And fear shall force what Friendship cannot win:
Thy death shall bury what thy life conceals;

Thou diest for more esteeming her then me.
PEDRINGANO. Oh stay, my Lord.
LORENZO. Yet speak the truth, and I will guerdon thee,
    And shield thee from whatever can ensue,
    And will conceal what ere proceeds from thee;
    But if thou dally once again, thou diest.
PEDRINGANO. If Madame *Bel-imperia* be in love—
LORENZO. What, Villain, ifs and ands?

[*Offers to kill him.*]

PEDRINGANO. Oh stay, my Lord, she loves *Horatio.*

[BALTHAZAR *starts back.*]

LORENZO. What, Don *Horatio,* our Knight Marshals son?
PEDRINGANO. Even him, my Lord.
LORENZO. Now say but how knowest thou he is her love,
    And thou shalt find me kind and liberal:
    Stand up, I say, and fearless tell the truth.
PEDRINGANO. She sent him letters which myself perused,
    Full fraught with lines and arguments of love,
    Preferring him before Prince *Balthazar.*
LORENZO. Swear on this cross that what thou sayest is true,
    And that thou wilt conceal what thou hast told.
PEDRINGANO. I swear to both, by him that made us all.
LORENZO. In hope thine oath is true, here's thy reward:
    But if I prove thee perjured and unjust,
    This very sword whereon thou tookst thine oath,
    Shall be the worker of thy tragedy.
PEDRINGANO. What I have said is true, and shall, for me,
    Be still concealed from *Bel-imperia.*
    Besides, your Honors liberalize
    Deserves my duteous service, even till death.
LORENZO. Let this be all that thou shalt do for me:
    Be watchful when and where these lovers meet,
    And give me notice in some secret sort.
PEDRINGANO. I will, my Lord.
LORENZO. Then shalt thou find that I am liberal:
    Thou knowest that I can more advance thy state
    Then she; be therefore wise, and fail me not.
    Go and attend her, as thy custom is,
    Least absence make her think thou dost amiss.

[*Exit* PEDRINGANO.]

Why so: *Tam armis quam ingenio:*
Where words prevail not, violence prevails;

But gold doth more then either of them both.
How likes Prince *Balthazar* this stratagem?
BALTHAZAR. Both well and ill: it makes me glad and sad:
  Glad, that I know the hinderer of my love;
  Sad, that I fear she hates me whom I love:
  Glad, that I know on whom to be revenged;
  Sad, that she'll fly me, if I take revenge.
  Yet must I take revenge, or dye myself,
  For love resisted grows impatient.
  I think *Horatio* be my destined plague:
  First, in his hand he brandished a sword,
  And with that sword he fiercely waged war, no
  And in that war he gave me dangerous wounds,
  And by those wounds he forced me to yield,
  And by my yielding I became his slave:
  Now, in his mouth he carries pleasing words,
  Which pleasing words do harbour sweet conceits,
  Which sweet conceits are limed with sly deceits,
  Which sly deceits smooth *Bel-imperias* ears,
  And through her ears dive down into her heart,
  And in her heart set him where I should stand.
  Thus hath he ta'en my body by his force,
  And now by sleight would captivate my soul:
  But in his fall I'll tempt the destinies,
  And either loose my life, or win my love.
LORENZO. Let's go, my Lord; your staying stays revenge.
  Do you but follow me, and gain your love:
  Her favor must be won by his remove.

  [*Exeunt.*]

SCENE II.

[*Enter* HORATIO *and* BEL-IMPERIA.]

HORATIO. Now, Madame, since by favor of your love
  Our hidden smoke is turned to open flame,
  And that with looks and words we feed our thoughts
  (Two chief contents, where more cannot be had);
  Thus in the midst of loves fair blandishments,
  Why show you sign of inward languishments?

  [PEDRINGANO *showeth all to the* PRINCE *and* LORENZO, *placing them in* secret.]

BEL-IMPERIA. My heart (sweet Friend) is like a ship at sea:
  She wisheth port, where riding all at ease
  She may repair what stormy times have worn,

And leaning on the shore may sing with joy
That pleasure follows pain, and bliss annoy.
Possession of thy love is th' only port,
Wherein my heart, with fears and hopes long tossed,
Each hour doth wish and long to make resort,
There to repair the joys that it hath lost,
And, sitting safe, to sing in Cupids Quire
That sweetest bliss is crown of loves desire.

[BALTHAZAR *and* LORENZO *above.*]

BALTHAZAR. Oh sleep, mine eyes, see not my love profaned;
    Be deaf, my ears, hear not my discontent;
    Dye, heart: another joys what thou deservest.
LORENZO. Watch still, mine eyes, to see this love disjoined;
    Hear still, mine ears, to hear them both lament;
    Live, heart, to joy at fond *Horatios* fall.
BEL-IMPERIA. Why stands *Horatio* speechless all this while?
HORATIO. The less I speak, the more I meditate.
BEL-IMPERIA. But whereon doost thou chiefly meditate?
HORATIO. On dangers past, and pleasures to ensue.
BALTHAZAR. On pleasures past, and dangers to ensue.
BEL-IMPERIA. What dangers, and what pleasures doost thou mean?
HORATIO. Dangers of war, and pleasures of our love.
LORENZO. Dangers of death, but pleasures none at all.
BEL-IMPERIA. Let dangers go, thy war shall be with me,
    But such a war, as breaks no bond of peace.
    Speak thou fair words, I'll cross them with fair words;
    Send thou sweet looks, I'll meet them with sweet looks;
    Write loving lines, I'll answer loving lines;
    Give me a kiss, I'll countercheck thy kiss:
    Be this our warring peace, or peaceful war
HORATIO. But, gracious Madame, then appoint the field,
    Where trial of this wane shall first be made.
BALTHAZAR. Ambitious Villain, how his boldness grows.
BEL-IMPERIA. Then be thy fathers pleasant bower the field,
    Where first we vowed a mutual amity:
    The Court were dangerous, that place is safe.
    Our hour shall be when *Vesper* 'gins to rise,
    That summons home distressful travelers.
    There none shall hear us but the harmless birds;
    Happily the gentle Nightingale
    Shall carol us asleep, ere we be ware,
    And, singing with the prickle at her breast,
    Tell our delight and mirthful dalliance:
    Till then each hour will seem a year and more.
HORATIO. But, honey sweet and honorable love,
    Return we now into your fathers sight:

Dangerous suspicion waits on our delight.
LORENZO. I, danger mixed with jealous despite
 Shall send thy soul into eternal night.

 [*Exeunt.*]

SCENE III.

 [*Enter* KING *of Spain, Portugal* AMBASSADOR, *Don* CIPRIAN, *&c.*]

KING. Brother of Castile, to the Princes love
 What says your daughter *Bel-imperia*?
CIPRIAN. Although she coy it as becomes her kind,
 And yet dissemble that she loves the Prince,
 I doubt not, I, but she will stoop in time.
 And were she forward, which she will not be,
 Yet herein shall she follow my advice,
 Which is to love him, or forgo my love.
KING. Then, Lord Ambassador of *Portugal*,
 Advise thy King to make this marriage up,
 For strengthening of our late confirmed league;
 I know no better means to make us Friends.
 Her dowry shall be large and liberal:
 Besides that she is daughter and half heir
 Unto our brother here, *Don Ciprian*,
 And shall enjoy the moiety of his land,
 He grace her marriage with an uncles gift;
 And this it is: in case the match go forward,
 The tribute which you pay shall be released,
 And if by *Balthazar* she have a Son,
 He shall enjoy the kingdom after us.
AMBASSADOR. He make the motion to my Sovereign liege,
 And work it if my counsel may prevail.
KING. Do so, my Lord, and if he give consent,
 I hope his presence here will honor us,
 In celebration of the nuptial day;
 And let himself determine of the time.
AMBASSADOR. Wilt please your grace command me ought beside?
KING. Commend me to the king, and so farewell.
 But wheres Prince *Balthazar* to take his leave?
AMBASSADOR. That is performed already, my good Lord.
KING. Amongst the rest of what you have in charge,
 The Princes ransom must not be forgot:
 That's none of mine, but his that took him prisoner,
 And well his forwardness deserves reward.
 It was *Horatio*, our Knight Marshals Son.
AMBASSADOR. Between us there's a price already pitched,
 And shall be sent with all convenient speed.

KING. Then once again farewell, my Lord.
AMBASSADOR. Farewell, my Lord of Castile, and the rest. [*Exit.*]
KING. Now, brother, you must take some little pains
 To win fair *Bel-imperia* from her will:
 Young virgins must be ruled by their Friends.
 The Prince is amiable and loves her well;
 If she neglect him and forgo his love,
 She both will wrong her own estate and ours.
 Therefore, whiles I do entertain the Prince
 With greatest pleasure that our Court affords,
 Endeavor you to win your daughters thought:
 If she give back, all this will come to naught.

 [*Exeunt.*]

SCENE IV.

 [*Enter* HORATIO, BEL-IMPERIA, *and* PEDRINGANO.]

HORATIO. Now that the night begins with sable wings
 To over-cloud the brightness of the Sun,
 And that in darkness pleasures may be done,
 Come, *Bel-imperia*, let us to the bower,
 And there in safety pass a pleasant hour.
BEL-IMPERIA. I follow thee, my love, and will not back,
 Although my fainting heart controls my soul.
HORATIO. Why, make you doubt of *Pedringanos* faith?
BEL-IMPERIA. No, he is as trusty as my second self.
 Go, *Pedringano*, watch without the gate,
 And let us know if any make approach.
PEDRINGANO. In steed of watching, I'll deserve more gold
 By fetching Don *Lorenzo* to this match.

 [*Exit* PEDRINGANO.]

HORATIO. What means my love?
BEL-IMPERIA. I know not what myself:
 And yet my heart foretells me some mischance.
HORATIO. Sweet, say not so; fair fortune is our Friend,
 And heavens have shut up day to pleasure us.
 The stars, thou seest, hold back their twinkling shine,
 And Luna hides herself to pleasure us.
BEL-IMPERIA. Thou hast prevailed; I'll conquer my misdoubt,
 And in thy love and council drown my fear:
 I fear no more; love now is all my thoughts.
 Why sit we not? for pleasure asketh ease.
HORATIO. The more thou sit'st within these levy bowers,
 The more will *Flora* deck it with her flowers.

BEL-IMPERIA. I, but if *Flora* spy *Horatio* here,
    Her jealous eye will think I sit too near.
HORATIO. Hark, Madame, how the birds record by night,
    For joy that *Bel-imperia* sits in sight.
BEL-IMPERIA. No, *Cupid* counterfeits the Nightingale,
    To frame sweet music to *Horatios* tale.
HORATIO. If *Cupid* sing, then *Venus* is not far;
    I, thou art *Venus*, or some fairer star.
BEL-IMPERIA. If I be *Venus*, thou must needs be *Mars*;
    And where *Mars* reigneth there must needs be wars.
HORATIO. Then thus begin our wars: put forth thy hand,
    That it may combat with my ruder hand.
BEL-IMPERIA. Set forth thy foot to try the push of mine.
HORATIO. But first my looks shall combat against thine.
BEL-IMPERIA. Then ward thy self: I dart this kiss at thee.
HORATIO. Thus I retort the dart thou threwst at me.
BEL-IMPERIA. Nay then, to gain the glory of the field,
    My twining arms shall yoke and make thee yield.
HORATIO. Nay then, my arms are large and strong withal:
    Thus Elms by vines are compassed till they fall.
BEL-IMPERIA. Oh let me go, for in my troubled eyes
    Now may'st thou read that life in passion dies.
HORATIO. Oh stay a while, and I will die with thee;
    So shalt thou yield, and yet have conquered me.
BEL-IMPERIA. Whose there, *Pedringano*? We are betrayed.

[*Enter* LORENZO, BALTHAZAR, SERBERINE, PEDRINGANO *disguised.*]

LORENZO. My Lord away with her, take her aside.
    Oh sir, forbear: your valour is already tried.
    Quickly dispatch, my masters.

[*They hang him in the Arbor.*]

HORATIO. What, will you murder me?
LORENZO. I thus, and thus: these are the fruits of love.

[*They stab him.*]

BEL-IMPERIA. Oh, save his life, and let me dye for him.
    Oh, save him, brother; save him, *Balthazar*:
    I loved *Horatio*, but he loved not me.
BALTHAZAR. But *Balthazar* loves *Bel-imperia*.
LORENZO. Although his life were still ambitious proud,
    Yet is he at the highest now he is dead.
BEL-IMPERIA. Murder, murder: help, *Hieronimo*, help.
LORENZO. Come, stop her mouth; away with her.

[*Exeunt.*]

SCENE V.

[*Enter* HIERONIMO *in his shirt, &c.*]

HIERONIMO. What out-cries pluck me from my naked bed,
  And chill my throbbing heart with trembling fear,
  Which never danger yet could daunt before?
  Who calls *Hieronimo*? speak, here I am.
  I did not slumber; therefore 'twas no dream.
  No, no, it was some woman cried for help,
  And here within this garden did she cried,
  And in this garden must I rescue her.
  But stay, what murderous spectacle is this?
  A man hanged up and all the murderers gone:
  And in my bower, to lay the guilt on me.
  This place was made for pleasure, not for death.

[*He cuts him down.*]

  Those garments that he wears I oft have seen:
  Alas, it is *Horatio*, my sweet son.
  Oh no, but he that whilom was my son.
  Oh was it thou that call'dst me from my bed?
  Oh speak, if any spark of life remain.
  I am thy Father; who hath slain my son?
  What savage monster, not of human kind,
  Hath here been glutted with thy harmless blood,
  And left thy bloody corpse dishonored here,
  For me amidst these dark and deathful shades,
  To drown thee with an ocean of my tears?
  Oh heavens, why made you night to cover sin?
  By day this deed of darkness had not been.
  Oh earth, why didst thou not in time devour
  The wild profaner of this sacred bower?
  Oh poor *Horatio*, what hadst thou misdone,
  To lease thy life ere life was new begun?
  Oh wicked butcher, what so ere thou wert,
  How could thou strangle virtue and desert?
  Ay me most wretched, that have lost my joy,
  In leasing my *Horatio*, my sweet boy.

[*Enter* ISABELLA.]

ISABELLA. My husband's absence makes my heart to throb:—
  Hieronimo.
HIERONIMO. Here, *Isabella*, help me to lament;

For sighs are stopt, and all my tears are spent.
ISABELLA. What world of grief; my son *Horatio!*
    Oh, where's the author of this endless woe?
HIERONIMO. To know the author were some ease of grief,
    For in revenge my heart would find relief.
ISABELLA. Then is he gone? and is my son gone too?
    Oh, gush out tears, fountains and floods of tears;
    Blow sighs, and raise an everlasting storm;
    For outrage fits our cursed wretchedness.

FIRST PASSAGE OF ADDITIONS.

Aye me, *Hieronimo*, sweet husband, speak.
HIERONIMO. He supped with us to-night, frolic and merry,
    And said he would go visit *Balthazar*
    At the Dukes Palace: there the Prince doth lodge.
    He had no custom to stay out so late:
    He may be in his chamber; some go see.
    Roderigo, ho.

    [*Enter* PEDRO *and* JAQUES.]

ISABELLA. Aye me, he raves, sweet *Hieronimo*.
HIERONIMO. True, all *Spain* takes note of it
    Besides, he is so generally beloved;
    His Majesty the other day did grace him
    With waiting on his cup: these be favors
    Which do assure me he cannot be short lived.
ISABELLA. Sweet *Hieronimo*.
HIERONIMO. I wonder how this fellow got his clothes:
    Sirrah, sirrah, He know the truth of all:
    Jaques, run to the Duke of Castiles presently,
    And bid my son *Horatio* to come home.
    I and his mother have had strange dreams to night.
    Do ye hear me, sir?
JAQUES. I, sir.
HIERONIMO. 'Well sir, begone.
    Pedro, come hither; knowest thou who this is?
PEDRINGANO. Too well, sir.
HIERONIMO. Too well, who? who is it? Peace, *Isabella*:
    Nay, blush not, man.
PEDRINGANO. It is my Lord *Horatio*.
HIERONIMO. Ha, ha, Saint James, but this doth make me laugh,
    That there are more deluded then myself.
PEDRINGANO. Deluded?
HIERONIMO. I: I would have sworn myself, within this hour,
    That this had been my soon *Horatio*:
    His garments are so like. Ha, are they not great persuasions?

ISABELLA. Oh would to God it were not so.
HIERONIMO. Were not, *Isabella*! doest thou dream it is?
    Can thy soft bosom entertain a thought,
    That such a black deed of mischief should be done
    On one so pure and spotless as our son?
    Away, I am ashamed.
ISABELLA. Dear *Hieronimo*, Cast a more serious eye upon thy grief:
    Weak apprehension gives but weak belief.
HIERONIMO. It was a man, sure, that was hanged up here;
    A youth, as I remember. I cut him down.
    If it should prove my son now after all.
    Say you? say you? Light, lend me a Taper;
    Let me look again. Oh God,
    Confusion, mischief, torment, death and hell,
    Drop all your stings at once in my cold bosom,
    That now is stiff with horror; kill me quickly:
    Be gracious to me, thou infective night,
    And drop this deed of murder down on me;
    Gird in my wast of grief with thy large darkness,
    And let me not survive, to see the light
    May put me in the mind I had a Son.
ISABELLA. Oh sweet *Horatio*, Oh my dearest son.
HIERONIMO. How strangely had I lost my way to grief.

END OF ADDITIONS.

HIERONIMO. Sweet lovely Rose, ill plucked before thy time;
    Fair worthy son, not conquered, but betrayed;
    He kiss thee now, for words with tears are stayed.
ISABELLA. And I'll close up the glasses of his sight,
    For once these eyes were only my delight.
HIERONIMO. Seest thou this handkerchief besmeared with blood?
    It shall not from me, till I take revenge.
    Seest thou those wounds that yet are bleeding fresh?
    He not entombed them, till I have revenged.
    Then will I joy amidst my discontent;
    Till then my sorrow never shall be spent.
ISABELLA. The heavens are just, murder cannot be hid:
    Time is the author both of truth and right,
    And time will bring this treachery to light.
HIERONIMO. Mean while, good *Isabella*, cease thy plaints,
    Or, at the least, dissemble them awhile:
    So shall we sooner find the practise out,
    And learn by whom all this was brought about.
    Come *Isabel*, now let us take him up,

    [*They take him up.*]

And bear him in from out this cursed place.
He say his dirge, singing fits not this case.
Oh aliquis mihi quas pulchrum ver educat herbas,

[HIERONIMO *sets his breast unto his sword.*]

Misceat, & nostro detur medicina dolori:
Aut si qui faciunt annorum obliuia, succos
Prebeat; ipse metam magnum quaecunque per orbem
Gramina Sol pulchras effert in luminis oras;
Ipse bibam quicquid meditatur saga veneni,
Quicquid & herbarum vi caeca nenia nectit:
Omnia perpetiar, ktkum quoque, dum semel omnis
Noster in extincto moriatur pectore sensus.
Ergo tuos oculos nunquam (mea vita) videbo,
Et tua perpetuus sepeliuit lumina somnus?
Emoriar tecum: sic, sic iuuat ire sub umbras.
At tamen absistam properato cedere letho,
Ne mortem vindicta tuam tam nulla sequatur.

[*Here he throws it from him and bears the body away.*]

SCENE VI.

ANDREA. Broughtst thou me hither to increase my pain?
I looked that *Balthazar* should have been slain:
But 'tis my Friend *Horatio* that is slain,
And they abuse fair *Bel-imperia*,
On whom I doted more then all the world,
Because she loved me more then all the world.
REVENGE. Thou talkest of harvest, when the come is green:
The end is crown of every work well done;
The Sickle comes not, till the come be ripe.
Be still; and ere I lead thee from this place;
He show thee *Balthazar* in heavy case.

ACT III.

SCENE I.

[*Enter* VICEROY *of Portugal*, NOBLES, ALEXANDRO, VILLUPPO.]

VICEROY. Unfortunate condition of Kings,
Seated amidst so many helpless doubts.
First we are placed upon extremest height,
And oft supplanted with exceeding hate;
But ever subject to the wheel of chance;
And at our highest never joy we so,

As we both doubt and dread our overthrow.
So striveth not the waves with sundry winds,
As Fortune toileth in the affairs of Kings,
That would be feared, yet fear to be beloved,
Sith fear or love to Kings is flattery:
For instance, Lordings, look upon your King,
By hate deprived of his dearest son,
The only hope of our successive line.
NOBLES. I had not thought that Alexandros heart
    Had been envenomed with such extreme hate:
    But now I see that words have several works,
    And there's no credit in the countenance.
VILLUPPO. No; for, my Lord, had you beheld the train,
    That feigned love had coloured in his looks,
    When he in Camp consorted *Balthazar*,
    Far more inconstant had you thought the Sun,
    That hourly coasts the center of the earth,
    Then *Alexandros* purpose to the Prince.
VICEROY. No more, *Villuppo*, thou hast said enough,
    And with thy words thou stayest our wounded thoughts;
    Nor shall I longer dally with the world,
    Procrastinating *Alexandros* death:
    Go, some of you, and fetch the traitor forth,
    That, as he is condemned, he may die.

[*Enter Alexandro with a Noble man and Halberts.*]

ALEXANDRO. But in extremes what patience shall I use?
    Nor discontents it me to leave the world,
    With whom there nothing can prevail but wrong.
NOBLES. Yet hope the best.
ALEXANDRO. 'tis heaven is my hope.
    As for the earth, it is too much infect
    To yield me hope of any of her mould.
VICEROY. Why linger ye? bring forth that daring fiend,
    And let him die for his accursed deed.
ALEXANDRO. Not that I fear the extremity of death,
    (For Nobles cannot stoop to servile fear)
    Doo I (Oh King) thus discontented live.
    But this, Oh this, torments my labouring soul,
    That thus I die suspected of a sin,
    Whereof, as heavens have known my secret thoughts,
    So am I free from this suggestion.
VICEROY. No more, I say: to the tortures, when!
    Bind him, and burn his body in those flames,

[*They bind him to the stake.*]

That shall prefigure those unquenched fires,
    Of Phlegethon prepared for his soul.
ALEXANDRO. My guiltless death will be avenged on thee,
    On thee, *Villuppo*, that hath maliced thus,
    Or for thy meed hast falsely me accused.
VILLUPPO. Nay, *Alexandro*, if thou menace me,
    He lend a hand to send thee to the lake,
    Where those thy words shall perish with thy works:
    Injurious traitor, monstrous homicide.

[*Enter* AMBASSADOR.]

AMBASSADOR. Stay, hold a while,
    And here, with pardon of his Majesty,
    Lay hands upon *Villuppo*.
VICEROY. Ambassador,
    What news hath urged this sudden entrance?
AMBASSADOR. Know, Sovereign Lord, that *Balthazar* doth Hue.
VICEROY. What sayest thou? liveth *Balthazar* our son?
AMBASSADOR. Your highness son, Lord *Balthazar* doth live;
    And, well entreated in the Court of *Spain*,
    Humbly commends him to your Majesty.
    These eyes beheld, and these my followers;
    With these, the letters of the Kings commends

[*Gives him Letters.*]

Are happy witnesses of his highness health.
    The King looks on the Letters, and proceeds.
VICEROY. *Thy son doth live, your tribute is received;*
    Thy peace is made, and we are satisfied.
    The rest resolve upon as things proposed
    For both our honors and thy benefit.
AMBASSADOR. These are his highness farther articles.

[*He gives him more Letters.*]

VICEROY. Accursed wretch, to intimate these ills
    Against the life and reputation
    Of noble Alexandra. Come, my Lord, unbind him:
    Let him unbind thee that is bound to death,
    To make a quintal for thy discontent.

[*They unbind him.*]

ALEXANDRO. Dread Lord, in kindness you could do no less,
    Upon report of such a damned fact:
    But thus we see our innocence hath saved

The hopeless life which thou, *Villuppo*, sought
By thy suggestions to have massacred.
VICEROY. Say, false *Villuppo*, wherefore didst thou thus
    Falsely betray Lord *Alexandros* life?
    Him, whom thou knowest that no unkindness else,
    But even the slaughter of our dearest son,
    Could once have moved us to have misconceived.
ALEXANDRO. Say, treacherous *Villuppo*, tell the King:
    Wherein hath Alexandra used thee ill?
VILLUPPO. Rent with remembrance of so foul a deed,
    My guilty soul submits me to thy doom:
    For not for Alexandra injuries,
    But for reward and hope to be preferred,
    Thus have I shamelessly hazarded his life.
VICEROY. Which, Villain, shall be ransomed with thy death,
    And not so mean a torment as we here
    Devised for him, who thou saidst slew our Son,
    But with the bitterest torments and extremes
    That may be yet invented for thine end.

[ALEXANDRO *seems to entreat.*]

Entreat me not; go, take the traitor hence.

[*Exit* VILLUPPO.]

        And, *Alexandro*, let us honor thee
With public notice of thy loyalty.
To end those things articulated here
By our great Lord the mighty King of *Spain*,
We with our Council will deliberate.
Come, *Alexandro*, keep us company.

[*Exeunt.*]

SCENE II.

[*Enter* HIERONIMO.]

HIERONIMO. Oh eyes, no eyes, but fountains fraught with tears;
    Oh life, no life, but lively forum of death;
    Oh world, no world, but masse of public wrongs,
    Confused and filed with murder and misdeeds.
    Oh sacred heavens, if this unhallowed deed,
    If this inhumane and barbarous attempt,
    If this incomparable murder thus
    Of mine, but now no more my son,
    Shall unrevealed and unrevenged pass,

How should we term your dealings to be just,
If you unjustly deal with those, that in your justice trust?
The night, sad secretary to my moans,
With direful visions wake my vexed soul,
And with the wounds of my distressful son
Solicit me for notice of his death.
The ugly fiends do sally forth of hell,
And frame my steps to unfrequented paths,
And fear my heart with fierce inflamed thoughts.
The cloudy day my discontents records,
Early begins to register my dreams,
And drive me forth to seek the murderer.
Eyes, life, world, heavens, hell, night and day,
See, search, show, send some man, some mean, that may—

[*A Letter falleth.*]

What's here? a letter? tush, it is not so:
A letter written to *Hieronimo*.

[*Red ink.*]

> For want of ink receive this bloody writ:
> Me hath my hapless brother hid from thee;
> Revenge thy self on Balthazar and him,
> For these were they that murd(e)red thy son.
> Hieronimo, revenge Horatios death,
> And better fare then Bel-imperia doth.

What means this unexpected miracle?
My Son slain by *Lorenzo* and the Prince.
What cause had they *Horatio* to maligne?
Or what might move thee, *Bel-imperia*,
To accuse thy brother, had he been the mean?
Hieronimo, beware, thou art betrayed,
And to entrap thy life this train is laid.
Advise thee therefore, be not credulous:
This is devised to endanger thee,
That thou by this *Lorenzo* shouldst accuse,
And he, for thy dishonor done, should draw
Thy life in question and thy name in hate.
Dear was the life of my beloved Son,
And of his death behooves me be revenged:
Then hazard not thine own, *Hieronimo*,
But live t'effect thy resolution.
I therefore will by circumstances try,
What I can gather, to confirm this writ;
And harkening near the Duke of *Castiles* house,

Close, if I can, with *Bel-imperia*,
To listen more, but nothing to bewray.

[*Enter* PEDRINGANO.]

HIERONIMO. Now, *Pedringano*.
PEDRINGANO. Now, *Hieronimo*.
HIERONIMO. Where's thy Lady?
PEDRINGANO. I know not; here's my lord.

[*Enter* LORENZO.]

LORENZO. How now, whose this? *Hieronimo*?
HIERONIMO. My Lord.
PEDRINGANO. He asketh for my Lady *Bel-imperia*.
LORENZO. What to doo, *Hieronimo*? The Duke, my father, hath
    Upon some disgrace a while removed her hence;
    But if it be ought I may inform her of,
    Tell me, *Hieronimo*, and I'll let her know it.
HIERONIMO. Nay, nay, my Lord, I thank you, it shall not need.
    I had a suit unto her, but too late,
    And her disgrace makes me unfortunate.
LORENZO. Why so, *Hieronimo*, use me.
HIERONIMO. Oh no, my Lord; I dare not; it must not be:
    I humbly thank your Lordship.

SECOND PASSAGE OF ADDITIONS.

    Who? you, my Lord?
    I reserve your favor for a greater honor;
    This is a very toy, my Lord, a toy.
LORENZO. All's one, *Hieronimo*, acquaint me with it.
HIERONIMO. Y' faith my Lord, 'tis an idle thing I must confess,
    I ha' been too slack, too tardy, too remiss unto your honor.
    LORENZO. How now, *Hieronimo*?
HIERONIMO. In troth, my Lord, it is a thing of nothing:
    The murder of a Son, or so—
    A thing of nothing, my Lord.

END OF ADDITIONS.

LORENZO. Why then, farewell.
HIERONIMO. My grief no heart, my thoughts no tongue can tell. [*Exit.*]
LORENZO. Come hither, *Pedringano*, seest thou this?
PEDRINGANO. My Lord, I see it, and suspect it too.
LORENZO. This is that damned villain *Serberine*,
    That hath, I fear, revealed *Horatios* death.
PEDRINGANO. My lord, he could not, 'twas so lately done;

And since he hath not left my company.
LORENZO. Admit he have not, his conditions such,
    As fear or flattering words may make him false.
    I know his humour, and therewith repent
    That ere I used him in this enterprise.
    But, *Pedringano*, to prevent the worst,
    And cause I know thee secret as my soul,
    Here, for thy further satisfaction, take thou this.

    [*Gives him more gold.*]

    And harken to me, thus it is devised:
    This night thou must, and prithee so resolve,
    Meet *Serberine* at S. *Luigis* Parke—
    Thou knowest 'tis here hard by behind the house—
    There take thy stand, and see thou strike him sure;
    For dye he must, if we do mean to live.
PEDRINGANO. But how shall *Serberine* be there, my Lord?
LORENZO. Let me alone; I'll send to him to meet
    The Prince and me, where thou must do this deed.
PEDRINGANO. It shall be done my Lord, it shall be done;
    And I'll go arm myself to meet him there.
LORENZO. When things shall alter, as I hope they will,
    Then shalt thou mount for this; thou knowest my mind.

    [*Exit* PEDRINGANO.]

    Che le Ieron.

    [*Enter* PAGE.]

PAGE. My Lord.
LORENZO. Go, sirrah, to *Serberine*,
    And bid him forthwith meet the Prince and me
    At S. *Luigis* Parke, behind the house;
    This evening, boy. *Page.* I go, my Lord.
LORENZO. But, sirrah, let the hour be eight a clock:
    Bid him not fail.
PAGE. I fly, my Lord. [*Exit.*]
LORENZO. Now to confirm the complot thou hast cast
    Of all these practices, He spread the Watch,
    Upon precise commandment from the King,
    Strongly to guard the place where *Pedringano*
    This night shall murder hapless *Serberine*.
    Thus must we work that will avoid distrust;
    Thus must we practise to prevent mishap,
    And thus one ill another must expulse.
    This sly inquiry of *Hieronimo*

For *Bel-imperia* breeds suspicion,
And this suspicion bodes a further ill.
As for myself, I know my secret fault,
And so do they; but I have dealt for them.
They that for coin their souls endangered,
To save my life, for coin shall venture theirs:
And better its that base companions dye,
Then by their life to hazard our good haps.
Nor shall they live, for me to fear their faith:
He trust myself, myself shall be my Friend;
For dye they shall, slaves are ordained to no other end. [*Exit.*]

SCENE III.

[*Enter* PEDRINGANO *with a Pistol.*]

PEDRINGANO. Now, *Pedringano*, bid thy Pistol hold;
And hold on, Fortune, once more favor me,
Give but success to mine attempting spirit,
And let me shift for taking of mine aim.
Here is the gold, this is the gold proposed;
It is no dream that I adventure for,
But *Pedringano* is possessed thereof.
And he that would not strain his conscience
For him that thus his liberal purse hath stretched,
Unworthy such a favor may he fail,
And, wishing, want, when such as I prevail.
As for the fear of apprehension,
I know, if needs should be, my noble Lord
Will stand between me and ensuing harms:
Besides, this place is free from all suspect.
Here therefore will I stay, and take my stand.

[*Enter the* WATCH.]

FIRST WATCH. I wonder much to what intent it is
That we are thus expressly charged to watch.
SECOND WATCH. 'tis by commandment in the Kings own name.
THIRD WATCH. But we were never wont to watch and ward
So near the Duke his brothers house before.
SECOND WATCH. Content yourself, stand close, there's somewhat in 't.

[*Enter* SERBERINE.]

SERBERINE. Here, *Serberine*, attend and stay thy pace,
For here did Don Lorenzos *Page* appoint
That thou by his command shouldst meet with him.
How fit a place, if one were so disposed,

Me thinks this corner is to close with one.
PEDRINGANO. Here comes the bird that I must cease upon;
    Now, *Pedringano*, or never play the man.
SERBERINE. I wonder that his Lordship stays so long,
    Or wherefore should he send for me so late?
PEDRINGANO. For this, *Serberine*, and thou shalt ha' t.

    [*Shoots the Dag.*]

So, there he lies; my promise is performed.
FIRST WATCH. Hark, Gentlemen, this is a Pistol shot.
SECOND WATCH. And here's one slain; stay the murderer.
PEDRINGANO. Now by the sorrows of the souls in hell,

    [*He strives with the* WATCH.]

Who first lays hand on me, I'll be his Priest.
THIRD WATCH. Sirrah, confess, and therein play the Priest,
    Why hast thou thus unkindly killed the man?
PEDRINGANO. Why? because he walked abroad so late.
THIRD WATCH. Come sir, you had been better kept your bed,
    Then have committed this misdeed so late.
SECOND WATCH. Come to the Marshals with the murderer.
FIRST WATCH. On to *Hieronimos*: help me here
    To bring the murdered body with us too.
PEDRINGANO. *Hieronimo*? carry me before whom you will:
    What ere he be, I'll answer him and you;
    And do your worst, for I defy you all.

    [*Exeunt.*]

SCENE IV.

    [*Enter* LORENZO *and* BALTHAZAR.]

BALTHAZAR. How now, my Lord, what makes you rise so soon?
LORENZO. Fear of preventing our mishaps too late.
BALTHAZAR. What mischief is it that we not mistrust?
LORENZO. Our greatest ills we least mistrust, my Lord,
    And inexpected harms do hurt us most.
BALTHAZAR. Why tell me, *Don Lorenzo*, tell me, man,
    If ought concerns our honor and your own?
LORENZO. Nor you, nor me, my Lord, but both in one:
    For I suspect, and the presumptions great,
    That by those base confederates in our fault,
    Touching the death of *Don Horatio*,
    We are betrayed to old *Hieronimo*.
BALTHAZAR. Betrayed, *Lorenzo*? tush, it cannot be.

LORENZO. A guilty conscience, urged with the thought
 Of former evils, easily cannot err:
 I am persuaded, and dissuade me not,
 That alls revealed to *Hieronimo*.
 And therefore know that I have cast it thus—

[*Enter* PAGE.]

 But here's the *Page*—how now, what news with thee?
PAGE. My Lord, *Serberine* is slain.
BALTHAZAR. Who? *Serberine*, my man?
PAGE. Your Highness man, my Lord.
LORENZO. Speak, *Page*, who murdered him?
PAGE. He that is apprehended for the fact.
LORENZO. Who?
PAGE. *Pedringano*.
BALTHAZAR. Is *Serberine* slain, that loved his Lord so well?
 Injurious Villain, murderer of his Friend.
LORENZO. Hath *Pedringano* murdered *Serberine*?
 My Lord, let me entreat you to take the pains
 To exasperate and hasten his revenge
 With your complaints unto my Lord the King.
 This their dissention breeds a greater doubt.
BALTHAZAR. Assure thee, *Don Lorenzo*, he shall dye,
 Or else his Highness hardly shall deny.
 Mean while I'll haste the Marshall Sessions:
 For die he shall for this his damned deed.

[*Exit* BALTHAZAR.]

LORENZO. Why so, this fits our former policy,
 And thus experience bids the wise to deal.
 I lay the plot: he prosecutes the point;
 I set the trap: he breaks the worthies twigs,
 And sees not that wherewith the bird was limed.
 Thus hopeful men, that mean to hold their own,
 Must look like fowlers to their dearest Friends.
 He runs to kill whom I have hope to catch,
 And no man knows it was my reaching fatch.
 'Tis hard to trust unto a multitude,
 Or any one, in mine opinion,
 When men themselves their secrets will reveal.

[*Enter a* MESSENGER *with a Letter.*]

LORENZO. Boy.
PAGE. My Lord.
LORENZO. What's he?

MESSENGER. I have a letter to your Lordship.
LORENZO. From whence?
MESSENGER. From *Pedringano* that's imprisoned.
LORENZO. So he is in prison then?
MESSENGER. I, my good Lord.
LORENZO. What would he with us? He writes us here,
    To stand good L(ora) and help him in distress.
    Tell him, I have his letters, know his mind;
    And what we may, let him assure him of.
    Fellow, be gone; my boy shall follow thee.

    [*Exit* MESSENGER.]

    This works like wax; yet once more try thy wits.
    Boy, go, convey this purse to *Pedringano*;
    Thou knowest the prison, closely give it him,
    And be advised that none be there about:
    Bid him be merry still, but secret;
    And though the Marshall Sessions be today,
    Bid him not doubt of his delivery.
    Tell him his pardon is already signed,
    And thereon bid him boldly be resolved:
    For were he ready to be turned off—
    As 'tis my will the uttermost be tried—
    Thou with his pardon shalt attend him still.
    Show him this box, tell him his pardons, in 't;
    But open 't not, and if thou lovest thy life;
    But let him wisely keep his hopes unknown:
    He shall not want while *Don Lorenzo* Hues:
    Away.
PAGE. I go, my Lord, I run.
LORENZO. But, Sirra, see that this be cleanely done.

    [*Exit* PAGE.]

    Now stands our fortune on a tickle point,
    And now or never ends *Lorenzos* doubts.
    One only thing is unaffected yet,
    And that's to see the Executioner,
    But to what end? I list not trust the Air
    With utterance of our pretence therein,
    For fear the privy whispering of the wind
    Convey our words amongst unfriendly ears,
    That lye too open to advantages.
    Et quel che voglio io, nessun lo sa;
    Intendo to: quel mi bastera. [*Exit.*]

SCENE V.

[*Enter* BOY *with the Box.*]

BOY: My master hath forbidden me to look in this box; and, by my troth, 'tis likely, if he had not warned me, I should not have had so much idle time: for we men's-kind, in our minority, are like women in their uncertainty: that they are most forbidden, they will soonest attempt: so I now. —By my bare honesty, here's nothing but the bare empty box: were it not sin against secrecy, I would say it were a piece of gentleman-like knavery. I must go to Pedringano, and tell him his pardon is in this box; nay, I would have sworn it, had I not seen the contrary. I cannot choose but smile to think ...how the villain will flout the gallows, scorn the audience, and descant on the hangman; and all presuming of his pardon from hence. Will't not be an odd jest for me to stand and grace every jest he makes, pointing my finger at this box, as who would say, 'Mock on, here's thy warrant.' Is't not a scurvy jest that a man should jest himself to death? Alas, poor Pedringano, I am in a sort sorry for thee; but if I should be hanged with thee, I cannot weep. [*Exit.*]

SCENE VI.

[*Enter* HIERONIMO *and the Deputy.*]

HIERONIMO. Thus must we toil in other men's extremes,
    That know not how to remedy our own;
    And do them justice, when unjustly we,
    For all our wrongs, can compass no redress.
    But shall I never Hue to see the day,
    That I may come (by Justice of the heavens)
    To know the cause that may my cares allay?
    This toils my body, this consumeth age,
    That only I to all men just must be,
    And neither Gods nor men be just to me.
DEPUTY. Worthy *Hieronimo*, your office asks
    A care to punish such as do transgress.
HIERONIMO. So is't my duty to regard his death,
    Who, when he lived, deserved my dearest blood:
    But come, for that we came for: let's begin,
    For here lies that which bids me to be gone.

[*Enter Officers, Boy, and* PEDRINGANO, *with a letter in his hand, bound.*]

DEPUTY. Bring forth the Prisoner, for the Court is set.
PEDRINGANO. Gramercy, boy, but it was time to come;
    For I had written to my Lord anew
    A nearer matter that concerneth him,
    For fear his Lordship had forgotten me.
    But sith he hath remembered me so well,

Come, come, come on, when shall we to this gear?

HIERONIMO. Stand forth, thou monster, murderer of men,
And here, for satisfaction of the world,
Confess thy folly, and repent thy fault;
For there's thy place of execution.

PEDRINGANO. This is short work: well, to your marshalship
First I confess, nor fear I death therefore,
I am the man, 'twas I slew *Serberine*.
But, sir, then you think this shall be the place,
Where we shall satisfy you for this gear?

DEPUTY. I, *Pedringano*.

PEDRINGANO. Now I think not so.

HIERONIMO. Peace, impudent, for thou shalt find it so:
For blood with blood shall, while I sit as judge,
Be satisfied, and the law discharged.
And though myself cannot receive the like,
Yet will I see that others have their right.
Dispatch: the faults approved and confessed,
And by our law he is condemned to die.

HANG-MAN. Come on, sir, are you ready?

PEDRINGANO. To do what, my fine officious knave?

HANG-MAN. To go to this gear.

PEDRINGANO. Oh sir, you are to forward: thou wouldst feign furnish me with a halter, to disfurnish me of my habit. So I should go out of this gear, my raiment, into that gear, the rope. But, Hang-man, now I spy your knavery, He not change without boot, that's flat. Hang. Come, sir.

PEDRINGANO. So, then, I must up?

HANG-MAN. No remedy.

PEDRINGANO. Yes, but there shall be for my coming down.

HANG-MAN. Indeed, here's a remedy for that.

PEDRINGANO. How? be turned off?

HANG-MAN. I truly; come, are you ready? I pray, sir, dispatch; the day goes away.

PEDRINGANO. What, do you hang by the hour? if you doo, I may chance to break your old custom.

HANG-MAN. Faith, you have reason; for I am like to break your Young neck.

PEDRINGANO. Dost thou mock me, hang-man? pray God, I be not preserved to break your knaves pate for this.

HANG-MAN. Alas, sir, you are a foot too low to reach it, and I hope you will never grow so high while I am in the office.

PEDRINGANO. Sirrah, dost see yonder boy with the box in his hand?

HANG-MAN. What, he that points to it with his finger?

PEDRINGANO. I, that companion.

HANG-MAN. I know him not; but what of him?

PEDRINGANO. Dost thou think to Hue till his old doublet will make thee a new truss?

HANG-MAN. I, and many a fair year after, to truss up many an honester man then either thou or he.

PEDRINGANO. What hath he in his box, as thou thinkest?

HANG-MAN. Faith, I cannot tell, nor I care not greatly. Methinks you should rather hearken to your souls health.

PEDRINGANO. Why, sirrah Hangman, I take it that that is good for the body is likewise good for the soul: and it may be, in that box is balm for both.

HANG-MAN. Well, thou art even the merriest piece of mans flesh that ere groaned at my office door.

PEDRINGANO. Is your roguery become an office with a knaves name?

HANG-MAN. I, and that shall all they witness that see you seal it with a knave's name.

PEDRINGANO. I prithee, request this good company to pray with me.

HANG-MAN. I, marry, sir, this is a good motion: my masters, you see here's a good fellow.

PEDRINGANO. Nay, nay, now I remember me, let them alone till some other time; for now I have no great need.

HIERONIMO. I have not seen a wretch so impudent.
Oh monstrous times, where murders set so light,
And where the soul, that should be shrined in heaven,
Solely delights in interdicted things,
Still wand'ring in the thorny passages
That intercepts itself of happiness.
Murder, Oh bloody monster, God forbid
A fault so foul should scape unpunished.
Dispatch, and see this execution done:—
This makes me to remember thee, my son.

[*Exit* HIERONIMO.]

PEDRINGANO. Nay, soft, no hast.

DEPUTY. Why, wherefore stay you? have you hope of life?

PEDRINGANO. Why, I.

HANG-MAN. As how?

PEDRINGANO. Why, Rascal, by my pardon from the King.

HANG-MAN. Stand you on that? then you shall off with this.

[*He turns him off.*]

DEPUTY. So, Executioner; convey him hence:
But let his body be unburied:
Let not the earth be choked or infect
With that which heaven condemns, and men neglect.

[*Exeunt.*]

SCENE VII.

[*Enter* HIERONIMO.]

Where shall I run to breath abroad my woes,
My woes, whose weight hath wearied the earth?
Or mine exclaims, that have surcharged the air

With ceaseless plaints for my deceased son?
The blustering winds, conspiring with my words,
At my lament have moved the leafless trees,
Disrobed the meadows of their flowered green,
Made mountains marsh with spring tides of my tears,
And broken through the brazen gates of hell.
Yet still tormented is my tortured soul
With broken sighs and restless passions,
That winged mount, and, hovering in the air,
Beat at the windows of the brightest heavens,
Soliciting for justice and revenge:
But they are placed in those empyreal heights,
Where, countermurde with walls of diamond,
I find the place impregnable; and they
Resist my woes, and give my words no way.

[*Enter* HANG-MAN, *with a letter.*]

HANG-MAN. Oh Lord, sir: God bless you, sir: the man, sir, *Petergade*, sir, he that was
    so full of merry conceits—
HIERONIMO. Well, what of him?
HANG-MAN. Oh Lord, sir, he went the wrong way; the fellow had a fair commission to
    the contrary. Sir, here is his passport; I pray you, sir, we have done him wrong.
HIERONIMO. I warrant thee, give it me.
HANG-MAN. You will stand between the gallows and me?
HIERONIMO. I, I.
HANG-MAN. I thank your Lord worship.

[*Exit* HANG-MAN.]

HIERONIMO. And yet, though somewhat nearer me concerns,
    I will, to ease the grief that I sustain,
    Take truce with sorrow while I read on this.
        My Lord, I write as mine extremes required,
        That you would labour my delivery;
        If you neglect, my life is desperate,
        And in my death I shall reveal the troth.
        You know, my Lord, I slew him for your sake,
        And was confederate with the Prince and you;
        Won by rewards and hopeful promises,
        I help to murder Don Horatio too.
    Hope he to murder mine *Horatio*?
    And actors in th' accursed Tragedy
    Wast thou, *Lorenzo*, *Balthazar* and thou,
    Of whom my Son, my Son deserved so well?
    What have I heard, what have mine eyes beheld?
    Oh sacred heavens, may it come to pass
    That such a monstrous and detested deed,

So closely smothered, and so long concealed,
Shall thus by this be venged or revealed?
Now see I what I durst not then suspect,
That *Bel-imperias* Letter was not feigned,
Nor feigned she, though falsely they have wronged
Both her, myself, *Horatio*, and themselves.
Now may I make compare twixt hers and this,
Of every accident I near could find
Till now, and now I feelingly perceive
They did what heaven unpunished would not leave.
Oh false *Lorenzo*, are these thy flattering looks?
Is this the honor that thou didst my Son?
And *Balthazar*, bane to thy soul and me,
Was this the ransom he reserved thee for?
Woe to the cause of these constrained wars:
Woe to thy baseness and captivity:
Woe to thy birth, thy body, and thy soul,
Thy cursed father, and thy conquered self:
And band with bitter execrations be
The day and place where he did pity thee.
But wherefore waste I mine unfruitful words,
When naught but blood will satisfy my woes?
I will go plain me to my Lord the King,
And cry aloud for justice through the Court,
Wearing the flints with these my withered feet;
And either purchase justice by entreats,
Or tire them all with my revenging threats. [*Exit.*]

SCENE VIII.

[*Enter* ISABELLA *and her* MAID.]

ISABELLA. So that you say, this herb will purge the eye,
And this the head?
Ah, but none of them will purge the heart.
No, there's no medicine left for my disease,
Nor any physic to recur the dead.

[*She runs lunatic.*]

Horatio, Oh, where's *Horatio*!
MAID. Good Madam, affright not thus yourself
With outrage for your son *Horatio*:
He sleeps in quiet in the *Elisian* fields.
ISABELLA. Why, did I not give you gowns and goodly things,
Bought you a whistle and a whip-stalk too,
To be revenged on their villainies?
MAID. Madame, these humors do torment my soul.

ISABELLA. My soul— poor soul, thou talks of things
    Thou knowest not what—my soul hath silver wings,
    That mounts me up unto the highest heavens;
    To heaven: I, there sits my *Horatio*,
    Backed with a troop of fiery Cherubins,
    Dancing about his newly healed wounds,
    Singing sweet hymns and chanting heavenly notes:
    Rare harmony to greet his innocence,
    That died, I, died a mirror in our days.
    But say, where shall I find the men, the murderers,
    That slew *Horatio*? whether shall I run
    To find them out that murdered my Son?

    [*Exeunt.*]

SCENE IX.

    [BEL-IMPERIA, *at a window.*]

BEL-IMPERIA. What means this outrage that is offered me?
    Why am I thus sequestered from the Court?
    No notice:—Shall I not know the cause
    Of these my secret and suspicious ills?
    Accursed brother, unkind murderer,
    Why bends thou thus thy mind to martin me?
    Hieronimo, why writ I of thy wrongs?
    Or why art thou so slack in thy revenge?
    Andrea, Oh *Andrea*, that thou sawest,
    Me for thy Friend *Horatio* handled thus,
    And him for me thus causeless murdered.
    Well, force perforce, I must constrain my self
    To patience, and apply me to the time,
    Till heaven, as I have hoped, shall set me free.

    [*Enter* CHRISTOPHILL.]

CHRISTOPHILL. Come, Madame *Bel-imperia*, this may not be.

    [*Exeunt.*]

SCENE X.

    [*Enter* LORENZO, BALTHAZAR, and the PAGE.]

LORENZO. Boy, talk no further; thus far things go well.
    Thou art assured that thou sawest him dead?
PAGE. Or else, my Lord, I live not.
LORENZO. That's enough. As for his resolution in his end,

Leave that to him with whom he sojourns now.
Here, take my Ring, and give it *Christophill*,
And bid him let my Sister be enlarged,
And bring her hither straight.

[*Exit* PAGE.]

This that I did was for a policy,
To smooth and keep the murder secret,
Which, as a nine days wonder, being ore-blown,
My gentle Sister will I now enlarge.
BALTHAZAR. And time, *Lorenzo*: for my Lord the Duke,
You heard, enquired for her yester-night.
LORENZO. Why, and my Lord, I hope you heard me say
Sufficient reason why she kept away.
But that's all one. My Lord, you love her?
BALTHAZAR. I.
LORENZO. Then in your love beware, deal cunningly;
Salve all suspicions, only sooth me up;
And if she hap to stand on terms with us,
As for her sweet heart, and concealment so,
Jest with her gently: under feigned jest
Are things concealed that else would breed unrest.—
But here she comes.

[*Enter* BEL-IMPERIA.]

Now, Sister—
BEL-IMPERIA. Sister? no;
Thou art no brother, but an enemy;
Else wouldst thou not have used thy Sister so:
First, to affright me with thy weapons drawn,
And with extremes abuse my company;
And then to hurry me, like whirlwinds rage,
Amidst a crew of thy confederates,
And clap me up where none might come at me,
Nor I at any, to reveal my wrongs.
What madding fury did possess thy wits?
Or wherein is't that I offended thee?
LORENZO. Advise you better, *Bel-imperia*,
For I have done you no disparagement;
Unless, by more discretion then disserved,
I sought to save your honor and mine own.
BEL-IMPERIA. Mine honor? why, *Lorenzo*, wherein is't
That I neglect my reputation so,
As you, or any, need to rescue it?
LORENZO. His Highness and my father were resolv'd
To come confer with old *Hieronimo*,

Concerning certain matters of estate,
That by the *Viceroy* was determined.
BEL-IMPERIA. And wherein was mine honor touched in that?
BALTHAZAR. Have patience, *Bel-imperia*; hear the rest.
LORENZO. Me, next in sight, as messenger they sent,
To give him notice that they were so nigh:
Now when I came, consorted with the Prince,
And unexpected, in an arbour there,
Found *Bel-imperia* with *Horatio*—
BEL-IMPERIA. How than?
LORENZO. Why, then, remembering that old disgrace
Which you for *Don Andrea* had endure,
And now were likely longer to sustain,
By being found so meanly accompanied,
Thought rather, for I knew no readier mean,
To thrust *Horatio* forth my fathers way.
BALTHAZAR. And carry you obscurely somewhere else,
Least that his Highness should have found you there.
BEL-IMPERIA. Even so, my Lord? and you are witness,
That this is true which he entreateth of?
You (gentle brother) forged this for my sake,
And you, my Lord, were made his instrument:
A work of worth, worthy the noting too.
But what's the cause that you concealed me since?
LORENZO. Your melancholy, Sister, since the news
Of your first favourite *Don Andreas* death,
My Fathers old wrath hath exasperate.
BALTHAZAR. And better wast for you, being in disgrace,
To absent yourself, and give his fury place.
BEL-IMPERIA. But why had I no notice of his ire?
LORENZO. That were to add more fuel to your fire,
Who burnt like *Ætne* for *Andreas* loss.
BEL-IMPERIA. Hath not my Father then enquired for me?
LORENZO. Sister, he hath, and thus excused I thee.

[*He whispereth in her ear.*]

But, *Bel-imperia*, see the gentle Prince;
Look on thy love, behold Young *Balthazar*,
Whose passions by thy presence are increased;
And in whose melancholy thou mayest see
Thy hate, his love; thy flight, his following thee.
BEL-IMPERIA. Brother, you are become an Orator—
I know not, I, by what experience—
Too politic for me, past all compare,
Since last I saw you; but content yourself:
The Prince is meditating higher things.
BALTHAZAR. 'tis of thy beauty, then, that conquers Kings;

Of those thy tresses, *Ariadnes* twines,
Wherewith my liberty thou hast surprised;
Of that thine ivory front, my sorrows map,
Wherein I see no haven to rest my hope.
BEL-IMPERIA. To love and fear, and both at once, my Lord,
In my conceit, are things of more import
Then women's wits are to be busied with.
BALTHAZAR. 'Tis I that love.
BEL-IMPERIA. Whom?
BALTHAZAR. *Bel-imperia.*
BEL-IMPERIA. But I that fear.
BALTHAZAR. Whom?
BEL-IMPERIA. *Bel-imperia.*
LORENZO. Fear yourself?
BEL-IMPERIA. I, Brother.
LORENZO. How?
BEL-IMPERIA. As those,
That what they love, are loath, and fear to loose.
BALTHAZAR. Then, fa ire, let *Balthazar* your keeper be.
BEL-IMPERIA. No, *Balthazar* doth fear as well as we.
  Et tremulo metui pauidum iunxere timorem,
   Et vanum stolidae proditionis opus. [*Exit.*]
LORENZO. Nay, and you argue things so cunningly,
We'll go continue this discourse at Court .
BALTHAZAR. Led by the loadstar of her heavenly looks,
Wends poor, oppressed *Balthazar,*
As ore the mountains walks the wanderer,
Incertain to effect his Pilgrimage.

 [*Exeunt.*]

     SCENE XI.

[*Enter two* PORTUGALS, *and* HIERONIMO *meets them.*]

FIRST PORTUGAL. By your leave, Sir.

   THIRD PASSAGE OF ADDITIONS.

HIERONIMO. 'tis neither as you think, nor as you think,
Nor as you think; you 'r wide all:
These slippers are not mine, they were my son *Horatios.*
My son—and what's a son? A thing begot
Within a pair of minutes, thereabout,
A lump bred up in darkness, and doth serve
To ballace these light creatures we call Women;
And at nine months end, creeps forth to light.
What is there yet in a son,

To make a father dote, rave, or run mad?
Being borne, it pouts, cries, and breeds teeth.
What is there yet in a son? He must be fed,
Be taught to go, and speak. I, or yet?
Why might not a man love a Calf as well?
Or melt in passion ore a frisking Kid,
As for a Son? methinks, a young Bacon,
Or a fine little smooth Horse-colt
Should move a man, as much as doth a son.
For one of these, in very little time,
Will grow to some good use; where as a son,
The more he grows in stature and in years,
The more unsquared, unbeveled he appears;
Reckons his parents among the rank of fools;
Strikes care upon their heads with his mad riots;
Makes them look old, before they meet with age.
This is a son:—
And what a loss were this, considered truly?—
Oh, but my *Horatio*
Grew out of reach of these insatiate humours:
He loved his loving parents;
He was my comfort, and his mothers joy,
The very arm that did hold up our house:
Our hopes were stored up in him.
None but a damned murderer could hate him.
He had not seen the back of nineteen year,
When his strong arm unhorsed the proud Prince *Balthazar*,
And his great mind, too full of Honor,
Tooke him unto mercy,
That valiant, but ignoble *Portugal*.
Well, heaven is heaven still,
And there is *Nemesis*, and Furies,
And things called whips,
And they sometimes do meet with murderers:
They do not always scape, that is some comfort.
I, I, I; and then time steals on,
And steals, and steals,
Till violence leaps forth like thunder
Wrapt in a ball of fire,
And so doth bring confusion to them all.

END OF ADDITIONS

HIERONIMO. Good leave have you: nay, I pray you go,
    For I'll leave you, if you can leave me so.
SECOND PORTUGAL. Pray you, which is the next way to my Lord the Dukes?
HIERONIMO. The next way from me.
FIRST PORTUGAL. To his house, we mean.

HIERONIMO. Oh, hard by: 'tis yon house that you see.
SECOND PORTUGAL. You could not tell us, if his Son were there?
HIERONIMO. Who, my Lord *Lorenzo*?
FIRST PORTUGAL. I, Sir.

[*He goeth in at one door and comes out at another.*]

HIERONIMO. Oh, forbear,
    For other talk for us far fitter were.
    But if you be importunate to know
    The way to him, and where to find him out,
    Then list to me, and He resolve your doubt.
    There is a path upon your left hand side,
    That leadeth from a guilty Conscience
    Unto a forest of distrust and fear,
    A darksome place and dangerous to pass:
    There shall you meet with melancholy thoughts,
    Whose baleful humours if you but uphold,
    It will conduct you to despair and death:
    Whose rocky cliffs when you have once beheld,
    Within a huge dale of lasting night,
    That, kindled with the worlds iniquities,
    Dost cast up filthy and detested fumes: —
    Not far from thence, where murderers have built
    A habitation for their cursed souls,
    There, in a brazen Caldron fixed by *Jove*,
    In his fell wrath, upon a sulfur flame,
    Your selves shall find *Lorenzo* bathing him
    In boiling lead and blood of innocents.
FIRST PORTUGAL. Ha, ha, ha.
HIERONIMO. Ha, ha, ha.
    Why, ha, ha, ha. Farewell, good ha, ha, ha. [*Exit.*]
    Doubtless this man is passing lunatic,
    Or imperfection of his age doth make him dote.
    Come, lets away to seek my Lord the Duke.

[*Exeunt.*]

SCENE XII.

[*Enter* HIERONIMO *with a Poniard in one hand, and a Rope in the other.*]

HIERONIMO. Now, Sir, perhaps I come and see the King;
    The King sees me, and fain would hear my suit:
    Why, is not this a strange, and seld-seen thing,
    That standers by with toys should strike me mute?
    Go too, I see their shifts, and say no more.
    Hieronimo, 'tis time for thee to trudge:

Down by the dale that flows with purple gore,
Standeth a fiery Tower; there sits a judge
Upon a seat of steel and molten brass,
And twixt his teeth he holds a fire-brand,
That leads unto the lake where hell doth stand.
Away, *Hieronimo*; to him be gone:
He'll do thee justice for *Horatios* death.
Turn down this path: thou shalt be with him straight;
Or this, and then thou needest not take thy breath:
This way, or that way:—soft and fair, not so:
For if I hang or kill myself, lets know
Who will revenge *Horatios* murder then?
No, no; fie, no: pardon me, I'll none of that.

[*He flings away the dagger and halter.*]

This way I'll take, and this way comes the King,

[*He takes them up again.*]

And here He have a fling at him, that's flat.
And *Balthazar*, He be with thee to bring,
And thee, *Lorenzo*. Here's the King—nay, stay,
And here, I here—there goes the hare away.

[*Enter* KING, AMBASSADOR, CASTILE, *and* LORENZO.]

KING. Now show, *Ambassador*, what our *Viceroy* saith:
     Hath he received the articles we sent?
HIERONIMO. Justice, Oh, justice to *Hieronimo*.
LORENZO. Back, seest thou not the King is busy?
HIERONIMO. Oh, is he so?
KING. Who is he that interrupts our business?
HIERONIMO. Not I. *Hieronimo* beware; go by, go by.
AMBASSADOR. Renowned King, he hath received and read
    Thy kingly proffers, and thy promised league;
    And as a man extremely overjoyed
    To hear his Son so princely entertained,
    Whose death he had so solemnly bewailed,
    This for thy further satisfaction,
    And kingly love, he kindly lets thee know:
    First, for the marriage of his Princely Son
    With *Bel-imperia*, thy beloved Niece,
    The. news are more delightful to his soul,
    Then myrrh or incense to the offended heavens.
    In person, therefore, will he come himself,
    To see the marriage rites solemnized,
    And in the presence of the Court of *Spain*,

To knit a sure inextricable band
Of kingly love and everlasting league
Betwixt the Crowns of *Spain* and *Portugal*.
There will he give his Crown to *Balthazar*,
    And make a Queen of *Bel-imperia*.
KING. Brother, how like you this our Viceroys love?
CASTILE. No doubt, my Lord, it is an argument
    Of honorable care to keep his Friend,
    And wondrous zeal to *Balthazar* his son;
    Nor am I least indebted to his grace,
    That bends his liking to my daughter thus.
AMBASSADOR. Now last (dread Lord) here hath his Highness sent,
    Although he send not that his Son return,
    His ransom due to *Don Horatio*.
HIERONIMO. *Horatio*, who calls *Horatio*?
KING. And well remembered: thank his Majesty.
    Here, see it given to *Horatio*.
HIERONIMO. Justice, Oh, justice, justice, gentle King.
KING. Who is that? *Hieronimo*?
HIERONIMO. Justice, Oh justice: Oh my son, my son,
    My Son, whom naught can ransom or redeem.
LORENZO. *Hieronimo*, you are not well advised.
HIERONIMO. Away, *Lorenzo*, hinder me no more;
    For thou hast made me bankrupt of my bliss.
    Give me my son; you shall not ransom him.
    Away, He rip the bowels of the earth,

[*He diggeth with his dagger.*]

And Ferry over to th' *Elisian* plains,
And bring my Son to show his deadly wounds.
Stand from about me;
He make a pickaxe of my poniard,
And here surrender up my Marshalship;
For He go marshal up the fiends in hell,
To be avenged on you all for this.
KING. What means this outrage?
    Will none of you restrain his fury?
HIERONIMO. Nay, soft and fair; you shall not need to strive:
    Needs must he go that the devils drive. [*Exit.*]
KING. What accident hath hapt Hieronimo?
    I have not seen him to demean him so.
LORENZO. My gracious Lord, he is with extreme pride
    Conceived of Young *Horatio* his Son,
    And covetous of having to himself
    The ransom of the Young Prince *Balthazar*,
    Distract, and in a manner lunatic.
KING. Believe me, Nephew, we are sorry fort:

This is the love that Fathers bear their Sons.
But gentle brother, go give to him this gold,
The Princes ransom; let him have his due.
For what he hath, *Horatio* shall not want;
Happily *Hieronimo* hath need thereof.
LORENZO. But if he be thus helplessly distract,
   'Tis requisite his office be resigned,
   And given to one of more discretion.
KING. We shall increase his melancholy so.
   'Tis best that we see further in it first:
   Till when, our self will exempt (him) the place.
   And, Brother, now bring in the *Ambassador*,
   That he may be a witness of the match
   Twixt *Balthazar* and *Bel-imperia*,
   And that we may prefix a certain time,
   Wherein the marriage shall be solemnized,
   That we may have thy Lord the *Viceroy* here.
AMBASSADOR. Therein your Highness highly shall content
   His Majesty, that longs to hear from hence.
KING. On then, and hear you, Lord Ambassador.

   [*Exeunt.*]

FOURTH PASSAGE OF ADDITIONS.

SCENE XII A.

[*Enter* JAQUES *and* PEDRO.]

JAQUES. I wonder, Pedro, why our Master thus
   At midnight sends us with our Torches light,
   When man and bird and beast are all at rest,
   Save those that watch for rape and bloody murder.
PEDRO. Oh *Jaques*, know thou that our Masters mind
   Is much distraught, since his *Horatio* dyed,
   And—now his aged years should sleep in rest,
   His heart in quiet—like a desperate man,
   Grows lunatic and childish for his Son.
   Sometimes, as he doth at his table sit,
   He speaks as if *Horatio* stood by him;
   Then starting in a rage, falls on the earth,
   Cries out: *Horatio*, Where is my *Horatio*?
   So that with extreme grief and cutting sorrow,
   There is not left in him one inch of man:
   See where he comes.

[*Enter* HIERONIMO.]

HIERONIMO. I pry through every crevice of each wall,
    Look on each tree, and search through every brake,
    Beat at the bushes, stamp our grandam earth,
    Dive in the water, and stare up to heaven,
    Yet cannot I behold my son *Horatio*.
    How now, Who's there, sprits, sprits?
PEDRO. We are your Servants that attend you, sir.
HIERONIMO. What make you with your torches in the dark?
PEDRO. You bid us light them, and attend you here.
HIERONIMO. No, no, you are deceived—not I, you are deceived.
    Was I so mad to bid you light your .torches now?
    Light me your torches at the mid of no one,
    When as the Sun-God rides in all his glory:
    Light me your torches then.
PEDRO. Then we burn day light.
HIERONIMO. Let it be burnt; night is a murderous slut,
    That would not have her treasons to be seen,
    And yonder pale faced He-cat there, the Moon,
    Doth give consent to that is done in darkness;
    And all those Stars that gaze upon her face,
    Are aglets on her sleeve, pins on her train;
    And those that should be powerful and divine,
    Do sleep in darkness when they most should shine.
PEDRO. Provoke them not, fair sir, with tempting words;
    The heavens are gracious, and your miseries
    And sorrow makes you speak, you know not what.
HIERONIMO. Villain, thou liest, and thou doest nought
    But tell me I am mad: thou liest, I am not mad.
    I know thee to be *Pedro*, and he *Jaques*.
    He prove it to thee; and were I mad, how could I?
    Where was she that same night when my *Horatio*
    Was murdered? She should have shone: Search thou the book.
    Had the Moon shone, in my boys face there was a kind of grace,
    That I know—nay, I do know—bad the murderer seen him,
    His weapon would have fallen and cut the earth,
    Had he been framed of naught but blood and death.
    Alack, when mischief doth it knows not what,
    What shall we say to mischief?

[*Enter* ISABELLA.]

ISABELLA. Dear *Hieronimo*, come in a doors;
    Oh, seek not means so to increase thy sorrow.
HIERONIMO. Indeed, *Isabella*, we do nothing here;
    I do not cry: ask *Pedro*, and ask *Jaques*;
      Not I, indeed; we are very merry, very merry.
ISABELLA. How? be merry here, be merry here?
    Is not this the place, and this the very tree,

Where my *Horatio* dyed, where he was murdered?
HIERONIMO. Was—do not say what: let her weep it out.
    This was the tree; I set it of a kernel:
    And when our hot *Spain* could not let it grow,
    But that the infant and the humane sap
    Began to wither, duly twice a morning
    Would I be sprinkling it with fountain water.
    At last it grew, and grew, and bore, and bore,
    Till at the length
    It grew a gallows, and did bear our son,
    It bore thy fruit and mine: Oh wicked, wicked plant.
    One knocks within at the door.
    See who knocks there.
PEDRO. It is a painter, sir.
HIERONIMO. Bid him come in, and paint some comfort,
    For surely there's none lives but painted comfort.
    Let him come in. One knows not what may chance:
    Gods will that I should set this tree—but even so
    Masters ungrateful Servants rear from nought,
    And then they hate them that did bring them up.

    [*Enter the* PAINTER.]

PAINTER. God bless you, sir.
HIERONIMO. Wherefore, why, thou scornful Villain?
    How, where, or by what means should I be blest?
ISABELLA. What wouldst thou have, good fellow?
PAINTER. Justice, Madame.
HIERONIMO. Oh ambitious beggar, wouldest thou have that
    That lives not in the world?
    Why, all the undelved mines cannot buy
    An ounce of justice; 'tis a jewel so inestimable.
    I tell thee, God hath engrossed all justice in his hands,
    And there is none but what comes from him.
PAINTER. Oh then I see
    That God must right me for my murdered son.
HIERONIMO. How, was thy son murdered?
PAINTER. I, sir; no man did hold a son so dear.
HIERONIMO. What, not as thine.' that's a lie
    As massy as the earth: I had a son,
    Whose least unvalued hair did weigh
    A thousand of thy sons: and he was murdered.
PAINTER. Alas, sir, I had no more but he.
HIERONIMO. Nor I, nor I: but this same one of mine
    Was worth a legion. But all is one.
    Pedro, Jaques, go in a doors; *Isabella*, go,
    And this good fellow here and I
    Will range this hideous orchard up and down,

Like to two Lions reaved of their Young.
Go in a doors, I say.

[*Exeunt.*]

[*The* PAINTER *and he sits down.*]

Come, let's talk wisely now. Was thy Son murdered?

PAINTER. I, sir.

HIERONIMO. So was mine. How do'st take it? art thou not sometimes mad? Is there no tricks that comes before thine eyes?

PAINTER. Oh Lord, yes, Sir.

HIERONIMO. Art a Painter? canst paint me a tear, or a wound, a groan or a sigh? canst paint me such a tree as this?

PAINTER. Sir, I am sure you have heard of my painting: my name's *Basardo*.

HIERONIMO. Basardo, afore-god, an excellent fellow. Look you, sir, do you see? I'd have you paint me (for) my Gallery in your oil colours matted, and draw me five years Younger then I am—do ye see, sir, let five years go, let them go like the Marshall of *Spain*—my wife *Isabella* standing by me, with a speaking look to my son *Horatio*, which should intend to this, or some such like purpose: God bless thee, my sweet son,' and my hand leaning upon his head, thus, sir. Do you see? may it be done?

PAINTER. Very well, sir.

HIERONIMO. Nay, I pray mark me, sir: then, sir, would I have you paint me this tree, this very tree. Canst paint a doleful cry?

PAINTER. Seemingly, sir.

HIERONIMO. Nay, it should cry; but all is one. Well, sir, paint me a youth run through and through with villains swords, hanging upon this tree. Canst thou draw a murderer?

PAINTER. He warrant you, sir; I have the pattern of the most notorious villains that ever lived in all *Spain*.

HIERONIMO. Oh let them be worse, worse: stretch thine Arte, and let their beards be of *Judas* his own color, and let their eyebrows jutty over: in any case observe that. Then, sir, after some violent noise, bring me forth in my shirt, and my gown under mine arm, with my torch in my hand, and my sword reared up thus: and with these words:

'*What noise is this? Who calls Hieronimo?*'

May it be done?

PAINTER. Yea, sir.

HIERONIMO. Well, sir, then bring me forth, bring me through alley and alley, still with a distracted countenance going a long, and let my hair heave up my night-cap. Let the Clouds scowl, make the Moon dark, the Stars extinct, the Winds blowing, the Belles tolling, the Owl shrieking, the Toads croaking, the Minutes jarring, and the Clock striking twelve. And then at last, sir, starting, behold a man hanging, and tottering, and tottering, as you know the wind will wave a man, and I with a trice to cut him down. And looking upon him by the advantage of my torch, find it to be my son *Horatio*. There you may (show) a passion, there you may show a passion. Draw me like old *Priam* of *Troy*, crying: 'the house is a fire, the house is a fire, as the torch over my head.' Make me curse, make me rave, make me cry, make me mad, make me well again, make me curse hell, invocate heaven, and in the end leave me in a trance—and so forth.

PAINTER. And is this the end?

HIERONIMO. Oh no, there is no end: the end is death and madness. As I am never better then when I am mad: then methinks I am a brave fellow; then I do wonders: but reason abuseth me, and there's the torment, there's the hell. At the last, sir, bring me to one of the murderers; were he as strong as Hector, thus would I tear and drag him up and down.

[*He beats the* PAINTER *in, then comes out again, with a Book in his hand.*]

END OF ADDITIONS.

SCENE XIII.

[*Enter* HIERONIMO, *with a book in his hand.*]

    Vindicta mihi.
Ay, heaven will be revenged of every ill;
Nor will they suffer murder unrepaid.
Then stay, *Hieronimo*, attend their will:
For mortal men may not appoint their time.
    Per scelus semper tutum est sceleribus iter.
Strike, and strike home, where wrong is offered thee;
For evils unto ills conductors be,
And death's the worst of resolution.
For he that thinks with patience to contend
To quiet life, his life shall easily end.
    Fata si miseros iuuant, habes salutem:
    Fata si vitam negant, habes sepulchrum.
If destiny thy miseries do ease,
Then hast thou health, and happy shalt thou be:
If destiny deny thee life, *Hieronimo*,
Yet shalt thou be assured of a tomb:
If neither, yet let this thy comfort be,
Heaven covereth him that hath no burial!
And to conclude, I will revenge his death,
But how? not as the vulgar wits of men,
With open, but inevitable ills,
As by a secret, yet a certain mean,
Which under kind-ship will be cloaked best.
Wise men will take their opportunity,
Closely and safely fitting things to time.
But in extremes advantage hath no time;
And therefore all times fit not for revenge

Thus therefore will I rest me in unrest,
Dissembling quiet in unquietness,
Not seeming that I know their villainies,
That my simplicity may make them think
That ignorantly I will let all slip:
For ignorance, I wot, and well they know,
   Remedium malorum iners est.
Nor ought avails it me to menace them
Who, as a wintry storm upon a plain,
Will bear me down with their nobility.
No, no, *Hieronimo*, thou must enjoin
Thine eyes to observation, and thy tongue
To milder speeches then thy spirit affords;
Thy heart to patience, and thy hands to rest,
Thy Cap to curtsy, and thy knee to bow,
Till to revenge thou know when, where, and how.

[*A noise within.*]

How now, what noise? what coil is that you keep?

[*Enter a* SERVANT.]

SERBERINE. Here are a sort of poor Petitioners,
   That are importunate, and it shall please you, sir,
   That you should plead their cases to the King.
HIERONIMO. That I should plead their several actions?
   Why, let them enter, and let me see them.

[*Enter three* CITIZENS, *and an old Man.*]

FIRST CITIZEN. So, I tell you this: for learning and for law,
   There is not any Advocate in *Spain*
   That can prevail, or will take half the pain
   That he will in pursuit of equity.
HIERONIMO. Come near, you men, that thus importune me.—
   Now must I bear a face of gratuity,
   For thus I used, before my Marshalship,
   To plead in causes as Corregidor.—
   Come on, sirs, what's the matter?
SECOND CITIZEN. Sir, an Action.
HIERONIMO. Of Battery?
FIRST CITIZEN. Mine of Debt.
HIERONIMO. Give place.
SECOND CITIZEN. No, sir, mine is an action of the Case.
THIRD CITIZEN. Mine an *Eiectione firmae* by a Lease.
HIERONIMO. Content you, sirs; are you determined
   That I should plead your several actions?

FIRST CITIZEN. I, sir, and here's my declaration.
SECOND CITIZEN. And here is my band.
THIRD CITIZEN. And here is my lease.

[*They give him papers.*]

HIERONIMO. But wherefore stands yon silly man so mute,
    With mournful eyes and hands to heaven upreared?
    Come hither, father, let me know thy cause.
SENEX. Oh worthy sir, my cause, but slightly known,
    May move the hearts of warlike Myrmidons,
    And melt the Corsic rocks with ruthful tears.
HIERONIMO. Say, Father, tell me what's thy suit?
SENEX. No, sir; could my woes
    Give way unto my most distressful words,
    Then should I not in paper, as you see,
    With ink bewray what blood began in me.
HIERONIMO. What's here? 'The humble supplication
    Of *Don Bazulto* for his murdered Son.'
SENEX. I, sir.
HIERONIMO. No, sir, it was my murdered Son,
    Oh my Son, my Son, oh my Son *Horatio*.
    But mine, or thine, *Bazulto*, be content.
    Here, take my handkerchief, and wipe thine eyes,
    Whiles wretched I in thy mishaps may see
    The lively portrait of my dying self.

[*He draweth out a bloody Napkin.*]

    Oh no, not this; *Horatio*, this was thine;
    And when I dyed it in thy dearest blood,
    This was a token twixt thy soul and me,
    That of thy death revenged I should be.
    But here, take this, and this—what, my purse?—
    I, this, and that, and all of them are thine;
    For all as one are our extremities.
FIRST CITIZEN. Oh, see the kindness of *Hieronimo*.
SECOND CITIZEN. This gentleness shows him a Gentleman.
HIERONIMO. See, see, oh see thy shame, *Hieronimo*;
    See here a loving Father to his Son:
    Behold the sorrows and the sad laments
    That he delivereth for his Sons decease.
    If loves effects so strives in lesser things,
    If love enforce such moods in meaner wits,
    If love express such power in poor estates:
    Hieronimo, when, as a raging Sea,
    Tossed with the wind and tide, ore turnest then
    The upper billows course of waves to keep,

Whilest lesser waters labour in the deep:
Then shamest thou not, *Hieronimo*, to neglect
The sweet revenge of thy *Horatio*?
Though on this earth justice will not be found,
He down to hell, and in this passion
Knock at the dismal gates of *Plutos* Court, no
Getting by force, as once *Alcides* did,
A troupe of furies and tormenting hags,
To torture *Don Lorenzo* and the rest.
Yet least the triple headed porter should
Deny my passage to the slimy strand,
The Thracian Poet thou shalt counterfeit.
Come on, old Father, be my Orpheus,
And if thou canst no notes upon the Harp,
Then sound the burden of thy sore hearts grief,
Till we do gain that *Proserpine* may grant
Revenge on them that murdered my Son.
Then will I rent and tear them, thus, and thus,
Shivering their limbs in pieces with my teeth.

[*Tears the Papers.*]

FIRST CITIZEN. Oh, sir, my declaration.

[*Exit* HIERONIMO, *and they after.*]

SECOND CITIZEN. Save my bond.

[*Enter* HIERONIMO.]

SECOND CITIZEN. Save my bond.
THIRD CITIZEN. Alas, my lease, it cost me ten pound, and you, my Lord, have torn the
    same.
HIERONIMO. That cannot be, I gave it never a wound;
    Show me one drop of blood fall from the same:
    How is it possible I should slay it then?
    Tush, no; run after, catch me if you can.

[*Exeunt all but the old man.*]

[*Bazulto remains till Hieronimo enters again, who, staring him in the face, speaks.*]

HIERONIMO. And art thou come, *Horatio*, from the depth,
    To ask for justice in this upper earth,
    To tell thy father thou art unrevenged,
    To wring more tears from *Isabellas* eyes,
    Whose lights are dimmed with over-long laments?
    Go back, my son, complain to *Eacus*,

For here's no justice; gentle boy, be gone,
For justice is exiled from the earth:
Hieronimo will bear thee company.
Thy mother cries on righteous *Radamant*
For just revenge against the murderers.
SENEX. Alas, my Lord, whence springs this troubled speech?
HIERONIMO. But let me look on my *Horatio*:
Sweet boy, how art thou changed in deaths black shade.
Had Prospering no pity on thy youth,
But suffered thy fair crimson coloured spring
With withered winter to be blasted thus?
Horatio, thou art older then thy Father:
Ah, ruthless fate, that favor thus transforms.
BAZULTO. Ah, my good Lord, I am not your Young Son.
HIERONIMO. What, not my Son? thou then a Curie art,
Sent from the empty Kingdome of black night,
To summon me to make appearance
Before grim Mynos and just Radamant,
To plague *Hieronimo* that is remiss,
And seeks not vengeance for Horatioes death.
BAZULTO. I am a grieved man, and not a Ghost,
That came for justice for my murdered Son.
HIERONIMO. I, now I know thee, now thou namest thy Son:
Thou art the lively image of my grief;
Within thy face my sorrows I may see.
Thy eyes are gummed with tears, thy cheeks are wan,
Thy forehead troubled, and thy muttering lips
Murmur sad words abruptly broken off
By force of windy sighs thy spirit breathes;
And all this sorrow riseth for thy Son:
And self same sorrow feel I for my Son.
Come in, old man, thou shalt to Izabell;
Lean on my arm: I thee, thou me shalt stay,
And thou, and I, and she will sing a song,
Three parts in one, but all of discords framed:—
Talk not of cords, but let us now be gone,
For with a cord *Horatio* was slain.

[*Exeunt.*]

SCENE XIV.

[*Enter* KING *of Spain, the* DUKE, VICEROY, *and* LORENZO, BALTHAZAR, *Don* PEDRO, *and* BEL-IMPERIA.]

KING. Go, Brother, it is the Duke of *Castiles* cause;
Salute the *Viceroy* in our name.
CASTILE. I go.

VICEROY. Go forth, *Don Pedro*, for thy Nephews sake,
    And greet the Duke of Castile.
PEDRO. It shall be so.
KING. And now to meet these Portuguese:
    For, as we now are, so sometimes were these,
    Kings and commanders of the western Indies.
    Welcome, brave *Viceroy*, to the Court of *Spain*,
    And welcome all his honorable train:
    'Tis not unknown to us, for why you come,
    Or have so kingly crossed the seas.
    Sufficeth it, in this we note the troth
    And more then common love you lend to us.
    So is it that mine honorable Niece
    (For it beseems us now that it be known)
    Already is betrothed to *Balthazar*:
    And by appointment and our condescent
    Tomorrow are they to be married.
    To this intent we entertain thy self,
    Thy followers, their pleasure, and our peace:
    Speak, men of *Portugal*, shall it be so?
    If I, say so; if not, say flatly no.
VICEROY. Renowned King, I come not as thou thinkest,
    With doubtful followers, unresolved men,
    But such as have upon thine articles
    Confirmed thy motion, and contented me.
    Know, Sovereign, I come to solemnize
    The marriage of thy beloved Niece,
    Fair *Bel-imperia*, with my *Balthazar*—
    With thee, my Son; whom sith I live to see,
    Here take my Crown, I give it her and thee;
    And let me live a solitary life,
    In ceaseless prayers,
    To think how strangely heaven hath thee preserved.
KING. See, brother, see, how nature strives in him.
    Come, worthy *Viceroy*, and accompany
    Thy friend with thine extremities:
    A place more private fits this princely mood.
VICEROY. Or here, or where your Highness thinks it good.

[*Exeunt all but* CASTILE *and* LORENZO.]

CASTILE. Nay, stay, *Lorenzo*, let me talk with you.
    Seest thou this entertainment of these Kings?
LORENZO. I do, my Lord, and joy to see the same.
CASTILE. And knowest thou why this meeting is?
LORENZO. For her, my Lord, whom *Balthazar* doth love,
    And to confirm their promised marriage.
CASTILE. She is thy Sister?

LORENZO. Who, *Bel-imperial* I, My gracious Lord, and this is the day
 That I have longed so happily to see.
CASTILE. Thou wouldst be loath that any fault of thine
 Should intercept her in her happiness?
LORENZO. Heavens will not let *Lorenzo* err so much.
CASTILE. Why then, *Lorenzo*, listen to my words:
 It is suspected, and reported too,
 That thou, *Lorenzo*, wrongest *Hieronimo*,
 And in his sutes towards his Majesty
 Still keepest him back, and seeks to cross his suit.
LORENZO. That I, my Lord?
CASTILE. I tell thee, Son, myself have heard it said,
 When, to my sorrow, I have been ashamed
 To answer for thee, though thou art my Son.
 Lorenzo, knowest thou not the common love
 And kindness that *Hieronimo* hath won
 By his deserts within the Court of *Spain*?
 Or seest thou not the King my brothers care
 In his behalf, and to procure his health?
 Lorenzo, shouldst thou thwart his passions,
 And he exclaim against thee to the King,
 What honor wert in this assembly,
 Or what a scandal wert among the Kings,
 To hear *Hieronimo* exclaim on thee?
 Tell me, and look thou tell me truly too,
 Whence grows the ground of this report in Court?
LORENZO. My Lord, it lies not in Lorenzos power
 To stop the vulgar, liberal of their tongues:
 A small advantage makes a water breach,
 And no man lives that long contenteth all.
CASTILE. Myself have seen thee busy to keep back
 Him and his supplications from the King.
LORENZO. Yourself, my Lord, hath seen his passions
 That ill beseemed the presence of a King;
 And, for I pitied him in his distress,
 I held him thence with kind and courteous words,
 As free from malice to *Hieronimo*
 As to my soul, my Lord.
CASTILE. *Hieronimo*, my son, mistakes thee then.
LORENZO. My gracious father, believe me, so he doth.
 But what's a silly man, distract in mind
 To think upon the murder of his son?
 Alas, how easy is it for him to err.
 But for his satisfaction and the worlds,
 Twere good, my Lord, that *Hieronimo* and I
 Were reconciled, if he misconster me.
CASTILE. *Lorenzo*, thou hast said; it shall be so.
 Go one of you, and call *Hieronimo*.

[*Enter* BALTHAZAR *and* BEL-IMPERIA.]

BALTHAZAR. Come, *Bel-imperia*, *Balthazars* content,
 My sorrows ease and Sovereign of my bliss,
 Sith heaven hath ordained thee to be mine:
 Disperse those clouds and melancholy looks,
 And clear them up with those thy Sun bright eyes,
 Wherein my hope and heavens fair beauty lies.
BEL-IMPERIA. My looks, my Lord, are fitting for my love,
 Which, new begun, can show no brighter yet.
BALTHAZAR. New kindled flames should burn as morning sun.
BEL-IMPERIA. But not too fast, least heat and all be done.
 I see my Lord, my father.
BALTHAZAR. Truce, my love;
 I will go salute him.
CASTILE. Welcome, *Balthazar*,
 Welcome, brave Prince, the pledge of *Castiles* peace;
 And welcome, *Bel-imperia*. How now, girl?
 Why comest thou sadly to salute us thus?
 Content thy self, for I am satisfied: no
 It is not now as when *Andrea* lived;
 We have forgotten and forgiven that,
 And thou art graced with a happier Love.
 But, *Balthazar*, here comes *Hieronimo*;
 He have a word with him.

[*Enter* HIERONIMO *and a* SERVANT.]

HIERONIMO. And where's the Duke?
SERBERINE. Yonder.
HIERONIMO. Even so:—
 What new device have they devised, tro?
 Pocas Palabras, mild as the Lamb:
 1st I will be revenged? no, I am not the man.
CASTILE. Welcome, *Hieronimo*.
LORENZO. Welcome, *Hieronimo*.
BALTHAZAR. Welcome, *Hieronimo*.
HIERONIMO. My Lords, I thank you for *Horatio*.
CASTILE. *Hieronimo*, the reason that I sent
 To speak with you, is this.
HIERONIMO. What, so short?
 Then He be gone, I thank you forth.
CASTILE. Nay, stay, *Hieronimo*—go, call him, son.
LORENZO. *Hieronimo*, my father craves a word with you.
HIERONIMO. With me, sir? why, my Lord, I thought you had done.
LORENZO. No; would he had.
CASTILE. *Hieronimo*, I hear

You find yourself aggrieved at my Son,
Because you have not access unto the King;
And say 'tis he that intercepts your sutes.
HIERONIMO. Why, is not this a miserable thing, my Lord?
CASTILE. *Hieronimo*, I hope you have no cause,
And would be loth that one of your deserts
Should once have reason to suspect my son,
Considering how I think of you myself.
HIERONIMO. Your son *Lorenzo*? whom, my noble Lord?
The hope of *Spain*, mine honorable Friend?
Grant me the combat of them, if they dare.

[*Draws out his sword.*]

He meet him face to face, to tell me so.
These be the scandalous reports of such
As love not me, and hate my Lord too much.
Should I suspect *Lorenzo* would prevent
Or cross my suit, that loved my Son so well?
My Lord, I am ashamed it should be said.
LORENZO. *Hieronimo*, I never gave you cause.
HIERONIMO. My good Lord, I know you did not.
CASTILE. There then pause;
And for the satisfaction of the world,
Hieronimo, frequent my homely house,
The Duke of Castile, *Ciprians* ancient seat;
And when thou wilt, use me, my son, and it:
But here, before Prince *Balthazar* and me,
Embrace each other, and be perfect Friends.
HIERONIMO. I marry, my Lord, and shall.
Friends, quoth he? see, He be Friends with you all:
Specially with you, my lovely Lord;
For divers causes it is fit for us
That we be Friends: the world is suspicious,
And men may think what we imagine not.
BALTHAZAR. Why, this is friendly done, *Hieronimo*.
LORENZO. And that, I hope, old grudges are forgot.
HIERONIMO. What else? it were a shame it should not be so.
CASTILE. Come on, *Hieronimo*, at my request;
Let us entreat your company today.

[*Exeunt.*]

HIERONIMO. Your Lordships to command. Pah: keep your way.
Chi mi fa più carezze che non suole,
Tradito mi ha, o tradir mi vuole. [*Exit.*]

SCENE XV.

[*Enter* GHOST *and* REVENGE.]

GHOST. Awake, *Erichtho*; Cerberus, awake.
    Solicit Pluto, gentle Proserpine,
    To combat, *Acheron* and *Erebus*.
    For near, by *Styx* and *Phlegeton* in hell,
    Oh'er-ferried *Caron* to the fiery lakes
    Such fearful sights, as poor *Andrea* sees.
    Revenge, awake.
REVENGE. Awake? for why?
GHOST. Awake, *Revenge*; for thou art ill advised
    To sleep away what thou art warned to watch.
REVENGE. Content thy self, and do not trouble me.
GHOST. Awake, *Revenge*, if love, as love hath had,
    Have yet the power or prevalence in hell.
    Hieronimo with *Lorenzo* is joined in league,
    And intercepts our passage to revenge:
    Awake, *Revenge*, or we are woe begone.
REVENGE. Thus worldlings ground, what they have dreamed, upon.
    Content thy self, *Andrea*; though I sleep,
    Yet is my mood soliciting their souls.
    Sufficeth thee that poor *Hieronimo*
    Cannot forget his son *Horatio*.
    Nor dies *Revenge*, although he sleep awhile;
    For in unquiet quietness is feigned,
    And slumbering is a common worldly wile.
    Behold, *Andrea*, for an instance, how
    Revenge hath slept, and then imagine thou
    What 'tis to be subject to destiny.

[*Enter a Dumb Show.*]

GHOST. Awake, *Revenge*; reveal this mystery.
REVENGE. The two first the nuptial torches boar
    As brightly burning as the mid-days Sun:
    But after them doth *Hymen* hie as fast,
    Clothed in Sable and a Saffron robe,
    And blows them out, and quencheth them with blood,
    As discontent that things continue so.
GHOST. Sufficeth me; thy meanings understood,
    And thanks to thee and those infernal powers
    That will not tolerate a Lovers woe.
    Rest thee, for I will sit to see the rest.
REVENGE. Then argue not, for thou hast thy request.

[*Exeunt.*]

ACT IV.

SCENE I.

[*Enter* BEL-IMPERIA *and* HIERONIMO.]

BEL-IMPERIA. Is this the love thou bear'st *Horatio*?
    Is this the kindness that thou counterfeits?
    Are these the fruits of thine incessant tears?
    Hieronimo, are these thy passions,
    Thy protestations, and thy deep laments,
    That thou wert wont to weary men withal.
    Oh unkind father, Oh deceitful world,
    With what excuses canst thou show thy self,
    With what dishonor and the hate of men,
    From this dishonor and the hate of men?
    Thus to neglect the lose and life of him,
    Whom both my letters and thine own belief
    Assures thee to be causeless slaughtered.
    Hieronimo, for shame, *Hieronimo*,
    Be not a history to after times
    Of such ingratitude unto thy Son:
    Unhappy Mothers of such children then,
    But monstrous Fathers to forget so soon
    The death of those, whom they with care and cost
    Have tendered so, thus careless should be lost.
    Myself, a stranger in respect of thee,
    So loved his life, as still I wish their deaths.
    Nor shall his death be unrevenged by me,
    Although I bear it out for fashions sake:
    For here I swear, in sight of heaven and earth,
    Shouldst thou neglect the love thou should'st retain,
    And give it over, and devise no more,
    Myself should send their hateful souls to hell,
    That wrought his downfall with extremest death.
HIERONIMO. But may it be that *Bel-imperia*,
    Vows such revenge as she hath deigned to say?
    Why then I see that heaven applies our drift';
    And all the Saints do sit soliciting
    For vengeance on those cursed murderers.
    Madame, 'tis true, and now I find it so,
    I found a letter, written in your name,
    And in that Letter how *Horatio* died.
    Pardon, Oh pardon, *Bel-imperia*,
    My fear and care in not believing it;
    Nor think I thoughtless think upon a mean

To let his death be unrevenged at full:
And here I vow—so you but give consent,
And will conceal my resolution—
I will ere long determine of their deaths
That causeless thus have murdered my son.
BEL-IMPERIA. *Hieronimo*, I will consent, conceal,
And ought that may effect for thine avail,
Join with thee to revenge *Horatioes* death.
HIERONIMO. On then; whatsoever I devise,
Let me entreat you, grace my practices:
For why the plots already in mine head.
Here they are.

[*Enter* BALTHAZAR *and* LORENZO.]

BALTHAZAR. How now, *Hieronimo*? what, courting *Bel-imperia*?
HIERONIMO. I, my Lord; such courting as, I promise you,
She hath my heart, but you, my Lord, have hers.
LORENZO. But now, *Hieronimo*, or never, wee
Are to entreat your help.
HIERONIMO. My help? Why, my good Lords, assure your selves of me;
For you have given me cause; I, by my faith, have you.
BALTHAZAR. It pleased you, at the entertainment of the Ambassador,
To grace the King so much as with a show:
Now, were your study so well furnished,
As for the passing of the first nights sport
To entertain my father with the like,
Or any such like pleasing motion,
Assure yourself, it would content them well.
HIERONIMO. Is this all?
BALTHAZAR. I, this is all.
HIERONIMO. Why then, I'll fit you; say no more.
When I was Young, I gave my mind
And plied myself to fruitless Poetry;
Which though it profit the professor naught,
Yet is it passing pleasing to the world.
LORENZO. And how for that?
HIERONIMO. Marry, my good Lord, thus:
(And yet me thinks you are too quick with us):—
When in *Tolledo* there I studied
It was my chance to write a Tragedy,
See here, my Lords.—

[*He shows them a book.*]

Which, long forgot, I found this other day.
Now would your Lordships favor me so much
As but to grace me with your acting it—

I mean, each one of you to play a part—
Assure you it will prove most passing strange,
And wondrous plausible to that assembly.
BALTHAZAR. What? would you have us play a Tragedy?
HIERONIMO. Why, Nero thought it no disparagement,
　　And Kings and Emperors have ta'en delight
　　To make experience of their wits in plays.
LORENZO. Nay, be not angry, good *Hieronimo*;
　　The Prince but asked a question.
BALTHAZAR. In faith, *Hieronimo*, and you be in earnest,
　　He make one.
LORENZO. And I, another.
HIERONIMO. Now, my good Lord, could you entreat
　　Your sister *Bel-imperia* to make one?
　　For what's a play without a woman in it?
BEL-IMPERIA. Little entreaty shall serve me, *Hieronimo*;
　　For I must needs be employed in your play.
HIERONIMO. Why this is well; I tell you, Lordings,
　　It was determined to have been acted
　　By Gentlemen and scholars too,
　　Such as could tell what to speak.
BALTHAZAR. And now it shall be played by Princes and Courtiers,
　　Such as can tell how to speak:
　　If, as it is our Country manner,
　　You will but let us know the Argument.
HIERONIMO. That shall I roundly. The Chronicles of *Spain*
　　Record this written of a Knight of Rhodes:
　　He was betrothed, and wedded at the length,
　　To one *Perseda*, an Italian Dame, no
　　Whose beauty ravished all that her beheld,
　　Especially the soul of *Soliman*,
　　Who at the marriage was the chiefest guest.
　　By sundry means sought *Soliman* to win
　　Persedas love, and could not gain the same.
　　Then again he break his passions to a Friend,
　　One of his Bashawes whom he held full dear;
　　Her had this Bashaw long solicited,
　　And saw she was not otherwise to be won,
　　But by her husband's death, this Knight of Rhodes,
　　Whom presently by treachery he slew.
　　She, stirred with an exceeding hate therefore,
　　As cause of this, slew *Soliman*,
　　And, to escape the Bashawes tyranny,
　　Did stab herself, and this the Tragedy.
LORENZO. Oh, excellent!
BEL-IMPERIA. But say, *Hieronimo*,
　　What then became of him that was the Bashaw?
HIERONIMO. Marry, thus: roooued with remorse of his misdeeds,

Ran to a mountain top and hung himself.
BALTHAZAR. But which of us is to perform that part?
HIERONIMO. Oh, that will I, my Lords, make no doubt of it:
    I'll play the murderer, I warrant you,
    For I already have conceited that.
BALTHAZAR. And what shall I?
HIERONIMO. Great *Soliman*, the Turkish Emperor.
LORENZO. And I?
HIERONIMO. *Erastus*, the Knight of Rhodes.
BEL-IMPERIA. And I?
HIERONIMO. *Perseda*, chaste and resolute.
    And here, my Lords, are several abstracts drawn,
    For each of you to note your parts,
    And act it as occasion's offered you.
    You must provide a Turkish cap,
    A black mustachio, and a Fauchion.

[*Gives a paper to* BALTHAZAR.]

You, with a Crosse, like to a Knight of Rhodes.

[*Gives another to* LORENZO.]

And, Madame, you must attire yourself

[*He gives* BEL-IMPERIA *another*.]

Like *Phoebe*, *Flora*, or the huntress,
    Which to your discretion shall seem best.
    And as for me, my Lords, He look to one,
    And with the ransom that the *Viceroy* sent,
    So furnish and perform this Tragedy,
    As all the world shall say, *Hieronimo*
    Was liberal in gracing of it so.
BALTHAZAR. *Hieronimo*, methinks a Comedy were better.
HIERONIMO. A Comedy?
    Fie, Comedies are fit for common wits:
    But to present a Kingly troupe withal,
    Give me a stately written Tragedy;
    Tragedia cothurnata, fitting Kings,
    Containing matter, and not common things.
    My Lords, all this must be performed,
    As fitting for the first nights reveling.
    The Italian Tragedians were so sharp of wit
    That in one hours meditation
    They would perform any thing in action.
LORENZO. And well it may; for I have seen the like
    In *Paris*, mongst the French Tragedians.

HIERONIMO. In *Paris*? mas, and well remembered.
    There's one thing more that rests for us to do.
BALTHAZAR. What's that, *Hieronimo*? forget not any thing.
HIERONIMO. Each one of us must act his part
    In unknown languages,
    That it may breed the more variety:
    As you, my Lord, in Latin; I in Greek;
    You in Italian; and, for because I know
    That *Bel-imperia* hath practiced the French,
    In courtly French shall all her phrases be.
BEL-IMPERIA. You mean to try my cunning then, *Hieronimo*?
BALTHAZAR. But this will be a mere confusion,
    And hardly shall we all be understood.
HIERONIMO. It must be so; for the conclusion
    Shall prove the intention, and all was good:
    And I myself in an Oration,
    And with a strange and wondrous show besides,
    That I will have there behind a curtain,
    Assure yourself, shall make the matter known:
    And all shall be concluded in one Scene,
    For there's no pleasure ta'en in tediousness.
BALTHAZAR. How like you this?
LORENZO. Why thus, my Lord, we must resolve
    To soothe his humors up.
BALTHAZAR. On, then, *Hieronimo*; farewell till soon.
HIERONIMO. You'll ply this gear?
LORENZO. I warrant you.

    [*Exeunt all but* HIERONIMO.]

HIERONIMO. Why so:
    Now shall I see the fall of Babylon,
    Wrought by the heavens in this confusion.
    And if the world like not this Tragedy,
    Hard is the hap of old *Hieronimo*. [*Exit.*]

SCENE II.

    [*Enter* ISABELLA *with a weapon.*]

ISABELLA. Tell me no more:—Oh monstrous homicides.
    Since neither piety nor pity moves
    The King to justice or compassion,
    I will revenge myself upon this place,
    Where thus they murdered my beloved son.

    [*She cuts down the Arbor.*]

Down with these branches and these loathsome bows
Of this unfortunate and fatal Pine:
Down with them, *Isabella*; rent them up,
And burn the roots from whence the rest is sprung.
I will not leave a root, a stalk, a tree,
A bough, a branch, a blossom, nor a leaf,
No, not an herb within this garden Plot—
Accursed complot of my misery.
Fruitless for ever may this garden be,
Barren the earth, and blissless whosoever
Imagines not to keep it unmannered.
An Eastern wind, commix'd with noisome airs,
Shall blast the plants and the Young saplings;
The earth with Serpents shall be pestered,
And passengers, for fear to be infect,
Shall stand aloof and looking at it, tell:
'There, murdered, did the son of *Isabel*.'
I, here he died, and here I him embrace:
See, where his Ghost solicits with his wounds
Revenge on her that should revenge his death.
Hieronimo, make haste to see thy son;
For sorrow and despair hath cited me
To hear *Horatio* plead with *Rhadamanth*:
Make haste, *Hieronimo*, to hold excused
Thy negligence in pursuit of their deaths
Whose hateful wrath bereaved him of his breath.
Ah nay, thou doest delay their deaths,
Forgives the murderers of thy noble son,
And none but I bestir me—to no end.
And as I curse this tree from further fruit,
So shall my womb be cursed for his sake;
And with this weapon will I wound the breast,
The hapless breast, that gave *Horatio* suck.

[*She stabs herself.*]

SCENE III.

[*Enter* HIERONIMO; *he knocks up the curtain.*]

[*Enter the Duke of* CASTILE.]

CASTILE. How now, *Hieronimo*, where's your fellows,
    That you take all this pain?
HIERONIMO. Oh sir, it is for the authors credit
    To look that all things may go well.
    But, good my Lord, let me entreat your grace
    To give the King the copy of the play:

This is the argument of what we show.
CASTILE. I will, *Hieronimo*.
HIERONIMO. One thing more, my good Lord.
CASTILE. What's that?
HIERONIMO. Let me entreat your grace
    That, when the train are past into the gallery,
    You would vouchsafe to throw me down the key.
CASTILE. I will, *Hieronimo*.

    [*Exit* CASTILE.]

HIERONIMO. What, are you ready, *Balthazar*?
    Bring a chair and a cushion for the King.

    [*Enter* BALTHAZAR, *with a Chair.*]

    Well done, *Balthazar*, hang up the Title:
    Our scene is Rhodes:—what, is your beard on?
BALTHAZAR. Half on; the other is in my hand.
HIERONIMO. Dispatch, for shame; are you so long?

    [*Exit* BALTHAZAR.]

    Bethink thy self, *Hieronimo*,
    Recall thy wits, recount thy former wrongs
    Thou hast received by murder of thy son.
    And lastly, not least, how *Isabel*,
    Once his mother and thy dearest wife,
    All woe begone for him, hath slain herself.
    Behooves thee then, *Hieronimo*, to be revenged.
    The plot is laid of dire revenge:
    On, then, *Hieronimo*, pursue revenge,
    For nothing wants but acting of revenge.

    [*Exit* HIERONIMO.]

SCENE IV.

    [*Enter Spanish* KING, VICEROY, *Duke of* CASTILE, *and their train.*]

KING. Now, *Viceroy*, shall we see the Tragedy
    Of *Soliman*, the Turkish Emperor,
    Performed of pleasure by your Son the Prince,
    My Nephew *Don Lorenzo*, and my Niece?
VICEROY. Who? *Bel-imperia*?
KING. I, and *Hieronimo* our Marshall,
    At whose request they deine to doo't themselves.
    These be our pastimes in the Court of *Spain*:

Here, brother, you shall be the book-keeper:
This is the argument of that they show.

[*He gives him a book.*]

[*Gentlemen, this Play of Hieronimo, in sundry languages, was thought good to be set down in English, more largely, for the easier understanding to every public Reader.*]

[*Enter* BALTHAZAR, BEL-IMPERIA, *and* HIERONIMO.]

BALTHAZAR. *Bashaw, that Rhodes is ours, yield heavens the honor,*
  And holy Mahomet, our sacred Prophet:
  And be thou graced with every excellence
  That Soliman can give, or thou desire.
  But thy desert in conquering Rhodes is less
  Then in reserving this fair Christian Nymph,
  Perseda, blissful lamp of Excellence,
  Whose eyes compel, like powerful Adamant,
  The warlike heart of Soliman to wait.
KING. See, *Viceroy*, that is *Balthazar*, your son,
  That represents the Emperor *Soliman*:
  How well he acts his amorous passion.
VICEROY. I, *Bel-imperia* hath taught him that.
CASTILE. That's because his mind runs all on *Bel-imperia*.
HIERONIMO. *Whatever joy earth yields, betide your Majesty.*
BALTHAZAR. *Earth yields no joy without Persedaes love,*
HIERONIMO. *Let then Perseda on your grace attend.*
BALTHAZAR. *She shall not wait on me, but I on her:*
  Drawn by the influence of her lights, I yield.
  But let my friend, the Rhodian Knight, come forth,
  Erasto, dearer than my life to me,
  That he may see Perseda my beloved.

[*Enter* ERASTO.]

KING. Here comes *Lorenzo*: look upon the plot,
  And tell me, brother, what part plays he?
BEL-IMPERIA. *Ah, my Erasto, welcome to Perseda.*
ERASTO. *Thrice happy is Erasto, that thou livest;*
  Rhodes loss is nothing to Erastoes joy:
  Sith his Perseda lives, his life survives.
BALTHAZAR. *Ah, Bashaw, here is love betwixt Erasto*
  And fair Perseda, Sovereign of my soul.
HIERONIMO. *Remove Erasto, mighty Soliman,*
  And then Perseda will be quickly won.
BALTHAZAR. *Erasto is my friend; and while he lives,*
  Perseda never will remove her love.

HIERONIMO. *Let not Erasto live to grieve great Soliman.*
BALTHAZAR. *Dear is Erasto in our princely eye.*
HIERONIMO. *But if he be your rival, let him die.*
BALTHAZAR. *Why, let him die; so love commaundeth me,*
    Yet grieve I that Erasto should so die.
HIERONIMO. *Erasto, Soliman saluteth thee,*
    And lets thee wit by me his Highness will,
    Which is, thou shouldst be thus employed.

    [*Stab him.*]

BEL-IMPERIA. *Ay me, Erasto; see, Soliman, Erastoes slain.*
BALTHAZAR. *Yet liveth Soliman to comfort thee.*
    Fair Queen of beauty, let not favor die,
    But with a gracious eye behold his grief,
    That with Persedaes beauty is increased,
    If by Perseda his grief be not released.
BEL-IMPERIA. *Tyrant, desist soliciting vain suits;*
    Relentless are mine ears to thy laments,
    As thy butcher is pitiless and base,
    Which seized on my Erasto, harmless Knight.
    Yet by thy power thou thinkest to command,
    And to thy power Perseda doth obey:
    But, were she able, thus she would revenge
    Thy treacheries on thee, ignoble Prince:

    [*Stab him.*]

    And on herself she would be thus revenged.

    [*Stab herself.*]

KING. Well said.—Old Marshall, this was bravely done.
HIERONIMO. But *Bel-imperia* plays *Perseda* well.
VICEROY. Were this in earnest, *Bel-imperia*,
    You would be better to my Son then so.
KING. But now what follows for *Hieronimo*?
HIERONIMO. Marry, this follows for *Hieronimo*:
    Here break we off our sundry languages,
    And thus conclude I in our vulgar tongue.
    Happily you think (but bootless are your thoughts)
    That this is fabulously counterfeit,
    And that we do as all Tragedians doo:
    To die today for fashioning our Scene—
    The death of *Ajax* or some Romaine peer—
    And in a minute starting up again,
    Revive to please too morrows audience.
    No, Princes; know I am *Hieronimo*,

The hopeless father of a hapless Son,
Whose tongue is tuned to tell his latest tale,
Not to excuse gross errors in the play.
I see your looks urge instance of these words;
Behold the reason urging me to this:

[*Shows his dead Son.*]

See here my show, look on this spectacle:
Here lay my hope, and here my hope hath end:
Here lay my heart, and here my heart was slain:
Here lay my treasure, here my treasure lost:
Here lay my bliss, and here my bliss bereft:
But hope, heart, treasure, joy, and bliss,
All fled, failed, died, yea, all decayed with this.
From forth these wounds came breath that gave me life;
They murdered me that made these fatal marks.
The cause was love, whence grew this mortal hate;
The hate: *Lorenzo*, and Young *Balthazar*:
The love: my son to *Bel-imperia*.
But night, the coverer of accursed crimes,
With pitchy silence hushed these traitors harms,
And lent them leave, for they had sorted leisure,
To take advantage in my Garden plot
Upon my Son, my dear *Horatio*:
There merciless they butchered up my boy,
In black dark night, to pale dim cruel death.
He shrikes: I heard, and yet, me thinks, I hear
His dismal out-cry echo in the air.
With soonest speed I hasted to the noise, no
Where hanging on a tree I found my son,
Through girt with wounds, and slaughtered as you see.
And grieved I (think you) at this spectacle?
Speak, Portuguese, whose loss resembles mine:
If thou canst weep upon thy *Balthazar*,
'Tis like I wailed for my *Horatio*.
And you, my Lord, whose reconciled son
Marched in a net, and thought himself unseen,
And rated me for brainsick lunacy,
With *God amend that mad Hieronimo*,
How can you brook our plays Catastrophe?
And here behold this bloody handkerchief,
Which at *Horatios* death I weeping dipped
Within the river of his bleeding wounds:
It as propitious, see, I have reserved,
And never hath it left my bloody heart,
Soliciting remembrance of my vow
With these, Oh, these accursed murderers:

Which now performed, my heart is satisfied.
And to this end the *Bashaw* I became,
That might revenge me on *Lorenzos* life.
Who therefore was appointed to the part,
And was to represent the Knight of Rhodes,
That I might kill him more conveniently.
So, *Viceroy*, was this *Balthazar*, thy Son,
That *Soliman* which *Bel-imperia*,
In person of *Perseda*, murdered:
Solely appointed to that tragic part
That she might slay him that offended her.
Poor *Bel-imperia* mist her part in this,
For though the story saith she should have died,
Yet I of kindness, and of care to her,
Did otherwise determine of her end;
But love of him, whom they did hate too much,
Did urge her resolution to be such.
And, Princes, now behold *Hieronimo*,
Author and actor in this Tragedy,
Bearing his latest fortune in his fist;
And will as resolute conclude his part
As any of the Actors gone before.
And, Gentles, thus I end my play;
Urge no more words: I have no more to say.

[*He runs to hang himself.*]

KING. Oh hearken, *Viceroy*—hold, *Hieronimo*.
    Brother, my Nephew and thy son are slain.
VICEROY. We are betrayed; my *Balthazar* is slain.
    Break open the doors; run, save *Hieronimo*.

[*They break in, and hold* HIERONIMO.]

Hieronimo, do but inform the King of these events;
    Upon mine honor, thou shalt have no harm.
HIERONIMO. *Viceroy*, I will not trust thee with my life,
    Which I this day have offered to my Son.
    Accursed wretch,
    Why stayest thou him that was resolved to die?
KING. Speak, traitor; damned, bloody murderer, speak.
    For now I have thee, I will make thee speak.
    Why hast thou done this undeserving deed?
VICEROY. Why hast thou murdered my *Balthazar*?
CASTILE. Why hast thou butchered both my children thus?
HIERONIMO. Oh, good words: as dear to me was my *Horatio*,
    As yours, or yours, or yours, my Lord, to you.
    My guiltless Son was by *Lorenzo* slain,

And by *Lorenzo* and that *Balthazar*
Am I at last revenged thoroughly,
Upon whose souls may heavens be yet avenged
With greater far than these afflictions.
CASTILE. But who were thy confederates in this?
VICEROY. That was thy daughter *Bel-imperia*;
    For by her hand my *Balthazar* was slain:
    I saw her stab him.
KING. Why speakest thou not?
HIERONIMO. What lesser liberty can Kings afford
    Then harmless silence? then afford it me.
      Sufficeth, I may not, nor I will not tell thee.
KING. Fetch forth the tortures.
    Traitor as thou art, I'll make thee tell.
HIERONIMO. Indeed thou mayest torment me, as his wretched Son
    Hath done in murdering my *Horatio*:
    But never shalt thou force me to reveal
    The thing which I have vowed inviolate.
    And therefore in despite of all thy threats,
    Pleased with their deaths, and eased with their revenge,
    First take my tongue, and afterwards my heart.

FIFTH PASSAGE OF ADDITIONS.

HIERONIMO. But are you sure they are dead?
CASTILE. I, slave, too sure.
HIERONIMO. What, and yours too?
VICEROY. I, all are dead; not one of them survive.
HIERONIMO. Nay, then I care not; come, and we shall be friends;
    Let us lay our heads together:
    See, here's a goodly noise will hold them all.
VICEROY. Oh damned Devil, how secure he is.
HIERONIMO. Secure? why doest thou wonder at it?
    I tell thee, *Viceroy*, this day I have seen revenge,
    And in that sight am grown a prouder Monarch
    Than ever sate under the Crown of *Spain*.
    Had I as many lives as there be Stars,
    As many Heavens to go to, as those lives,
    I'd give them all, I, and my soul to boot,
    But I would see thee ride in this red pool.
CASTILE. Speak, who were thy confederates in this?
VICEROY. That was thy daughter *Bel-imperia*;
    For by her hand my *Balthazar* was slain:
    I saw her stab him.
HIERONIMO. Oh, good words: as dear to me was my *Horatio*,
    As yours, or yours, or yours, my Lord, to you.
    My guiltless Son was by *Lorenzo* slain,
    And by *Lorenzo* and that *Balthazar*

Am I at last revenged thoroughly,
Upon whose souls may heavens be yet revenged
With greater far then these afflictions.

END OF ADDITIONS.

Me thinks, since I grew inward with *Revenge*,
I cannot look with scorn enough on Death.
KING. What, dost thou mock us, slave? bring tortures forth.
HIERONIMO. Do, do, do; and mean time He torture you.
You had a Son (as I take it), and your Son
Should have been married to your daughter: ha, was not so.'
You had a Son too, he was my Liege's Nephew;
He was proud and politic. Had he lived,
He might a come to wear the crown of *Spain*—
I think 'twas so: 'twas I that killed him;
Look you, this same hand 'twas it that stabbed
His heart—do ye see? this hand—
For one *Horatio*, if you ever knew him:
A youth, one that they hanged up in his father's garden,
One that did force your valiant Son to yield,
While you're more valiant Son did take him prisoner.
VICEROY. Be deaf, my senses, I can hear no more.
KING. Fall, heaven, and cover us with thy sad mines.
CASTILE. Roll all the world within thy pitchy cloud.
HIERONIMO. Now do I applaud what I have acted.
　　Nunc iners cad at manus.
Now to express the rupture of my part,
First take my tongue, and afterward my heart.

[*He bites out his tongue.*]

KING. Oh monstrous resolution of a wretch.
See, *Viceroy*, he hath bitten forth his tongue
Rather then to reveal what we required.
CASTILE. Yet can he write.
KING. And if in this he satisfy us not,
We will devise the extremest kind of death
That ever was invented for a wretch.

[*Then he makes signs for a knife to mend his pen.*]

CASTILE. Oh, he would have a knife to mend his pen.
VICEROY. Here, and advise thee that thou write the troth.
KING. Look to my brother, save *Hieronimo*.

[*He with a knife stabs the* DUKE *and himself.*]

What age hath ever heard such monstrous deeds?
My brother, and the whole succeeding hope
That *Spain* expected after my disease.
Go, bear his body hence, that we may mourn
The loss of our beloved brothers death;
That he may be entombed, what ere befall.
I am the next, the nearest, last of all.
VICEROY. And thou, *Don Pedro*, do the like for us:
    Take up our hapless son, untimely slain:
    Set me with him, and he with woeful me,
    Upon the main mast of a ship unmanned,
    And let the wind and tide hall me along
    To *Silla's* barking and untamed gulf,
    Or to the loathsome pool of *Acheron*,
    To weep my want for my sweet *Balthazar*:
    Spain hath no refuge for a *Portugal*.

[*The Trumpets sound a dead march, the* KING *of Spain mourning after his brothers body, and the* KING *of Portugal bearing the body of his son.*]

SCENE V.

[*Enter* GHOST *and* REVENGE.]

GHOST. I, now my hopes have end in their effects,
    When blood and sorrow furnish my desires:
    Horatio murdered in his Fathers bower;
    Wild *Serberine* by *Pedringano* slain;
    False *Pedringano* hanged by quaint device;
    Fair *Isabella* by herself misdone;
    Prince *Balthazar* by *Bel-imperia* stabbed;
    The Duke of Castile and his wicked Son
    Both done to death by old *Hieronimo*;
    My *Bel-imperia* fallen as Dido fell,
    And good *Hieronimo* slain by himself;
    I, these were spectacles to please my soul.
    Now will I beg at lovely *Proserpine*,
    That, by the virtue of her Princely doom,
    I may consort my Friends in pleasing sort,
    And on my foes work just and sharp revenge.
    He lead my Friend *Horatio* through those fields.
    Where never dying wars are still inured;
    He lead fair *Isabella* to that train,
    Where pity weeps, but never feeleth pain;
    He lead my *Bel-imperia* to those joys
    That vestal Virgins and fair Queens possess;
    He lead *Hieronimo* where Orpheus plays,
    Adding sweet pleasure to eternal days.

But say, *Revenge*, for thou must help or none,
Against the rest how shall my hate be shown?
REVENGE. This hand shall hale them down to deepest hell,
Where none but furies, bugs, and tortures dwell.
GHOST. Then, sweet *Revenge*, do this at my request:
Let me be judge, and doom them to unrest.
Let loose poor *Titius* from the Vultures gripe,
And let *Don Ciprian* supply his room;
Place *Don Lorenzo* on *Ixions* Wheel,
And let the lovers endless pains surcease
(Juno forgets old wrath, and grants him ease);
Hang *Balthazar* about *Chimeras* neck,
And let him there bewail his bloody love,
Repining at our joys that are above;
Let *Serberine* go roll the fatal stone,
And take from *Siciphus* his endless money;
False *Pedringano*, for his treachery,
Let him be dragged through boiling *Acheron*,
And there live, dying still in endless flames,
Blaspheming Gods and all their holy names.
REVENGE. Then haste we down to meet thy Friends and foes:
To place thy Friends in ease, the rest in woes;
For here, though death hath end their misery,
He there begin their endless Tragedy.

[*Exeunt.*]

FINIS.

THE REVENGER'S TRAGEDY

By THOMAS MIDDLETON

DRAMATIS PERSONAE IN ORDER OF APPEARANCE

VINDICI, *the revenger, sometimes disguised as Piato*
HIPPOLITO, *his brother*
GRATIANA, *his mother*
CASTIZA, *his sister*
DUKE
TWO JUDGES
DUCHESS
LUSSURIOSO, *the Duke's son by a previous marriage*
AMBITIOSO, *the eldest of the Duchess's three sons by a previous marriage*
SPURIO, *the Duke's bastard son*
JUNIOR, *the Duchess's youngest son*
SUPERVACUO, *the Duchess's middle son*
ANTONIO, *a virtuous old lord*
PIERO, *a virtuous lord*
DONDOLO, *Castiza's servant*
LORDS
TWO SERVANTS *of Spurio*
NOBLES
FOUR PRISON OFFICERS
A PRISON KEEPER
GENTLEMEN
NENCIO, *Lussurioso's attendant*
SORDIDO, *Lussurioso's attendant*
A FOURTH MAN *in the final masque*, AMBITIOSO'S *henchman*
GUARDS

ACT I.

SCENE I. *Outside* VINDICI's *house.*

[*Enter* VINDICI (*with a skull*); *the* DUKE, DUCHESS, LUSSURIOSO *his son,*
SPURIO *the bastard, with a train pass over the stage with torchlight.*]

VINDICI. Duke, royal lecher, go, gray-hair'd adultery;
    And thou his son, as impious steep'd as he;
    And thou his bastard, true-begot in evil;
    And thou his duchess that will do with the devil:
    Four ex'lent characters. Oh, that marrowless age
    Would stuff the hollow bones with damn'd desires,
    And stead of heat kindle infernal fires
    Within the spendthrift veins of a dry duke,
    A parch'd and juiceless luxur! Oh God, one
    That has scarce blood enough to live upon!
    And he to riot it like a son and heir?
    Oh, the thought of that
    Turns my abused heartstrings into fret!
    Thou sallow picture of my poisoned love,
    My study's ornament, thou shell of death,
    Once the bright face of my betrothed lady,
    When life and beauty naturally fill'd out
    These ragged imperfections,
    When two heaven-pointed diamonds were set
    In those unsightly rings: then 'twas a face
    So far beyond the artificial shine
    Of any woman's bought complexion
    That the uprightest man, if such there be,
    That sin but seven times a day, broke custom
    And made up eight with looking after her.
    Oh, she was able to ha' made a usurer's son
    Melt all his patrimony in a kiss,
    And what his father fifty years told
    To have consum'd, and yet his suit been cold!
    But oh, accursed palace!
    Thee, when thou wert apparel'd in thy flesh,
    The old duke poison'd,
    Because thy purer part would not consent
    Unto his palsy-lust, for old men lustful
    Do show like young men angry, eager-violent,
    Outbid like their limited performances.
    Oh, 'ware an old man hot and vicious!
    "Age, as in gold, in lust is covetous."
    Vengeance, thou murder's quit-rent, and whereby
    Thou shouldst thyself tenant to tragedy,

Oh, keep thy day, hour, minute, I beseech,
For those thou hast determin'd! Hum: whoe'er knew
Murder unpaid? Faith, give revenge her due:
Sh'as kept touch hitherto. Be merry, merry;
Advance thee, O thou terror to fat folks,
To have their costly three-pil'd flesh worn of
As bare as this: for banquets, ease, and laughter
Can make great men, as greatness goes by clay,
But wise men little are more great than they.

[*Enter his brother* HIPPOLITO.]

HIPPOLITO. Still sighing o'er death's vizard?
VINDICI. Brother, welcome;
    What comfort bringst thou? How go things at court?
HIPPOLITO. In silk and silver, brother; never braver.
VINDICI. Puh,
    Thou play'st upon my meaning. Prithee say,
    Has that bald madam, opportunity,
    Yet thought upon's? Speak, are we happy yet?
    Thy wrongs and mine are for one scabbard fit.
HIPPOLITO. It may prove happiness.
VINDICI. What is't may prove?
    Give me to taste.
HIPPOLITO. Give me your hearing then.
    You know my place at court.
VINDICI. Ay, the duke's chamber.
    But 'tis a marvel thou'rt not turn'd out yet!
HIPPOLITO. Faith, I have been shov'd at, but 'twas still my hap
    To hold by th' duchess' skirt. You guess at that;
    Whom such a coat keeps up can ne'er fall flat.
    But to the purpose.
    Last evening predecessor unto this,
    The duke's son warily enquir'd for me,
    Whose pleasure I attended: he began
    By policy to open and unhusk me
    About the time and common rumour;
    But I had so much wit to keep my thoughts
    Up in their built houses, yet afforded him
    An idle satisfaction without danger.
    But the whole aim and scope of his intent
    Ended in this: conjuring me in private
    To seek some strange-digested fellow forth
    Of ill-contented nature, either disgrac'd
    In former times, or by new grooms displac'd
    Since his stepmother's nuptials, such a blood
    A man that were for evil only good;
    To give you the true word, some base-coin'd pander.

VINDICI. I reach you, for I know his heat is such:
    Were there as many concubines as ladies
    He would not be contain'd, he must fly out.
    I wonder how ill-featur'd, vild-proportion'd
    That one should be, if she were made for woman,
    Whom at the insurrection of his lust
    He would refuse for once. Heart, I think none,
    Next to a skull, tho' more unsound than one:
    Each face he meets he strongly dotes upon.
HIPPOLITO. Brother, y'ave truly spoke him.
    He knows not you, but I'll swear you know him.
VINDICI. And therefore I'll put on that knave for once,
    And be a right man then, a man a' th' time,
    For to be honest is not to be i' th' world.
    Brother, I'll be that strange-composed fellow.
HIPPOLITO. And I'll prefer you, brother.
VINDICI. Go to then;
    The small'st advantage fattens wronged men,
    It may point out. Occasion, if I meet her,
    I'll hold her by the foretop fast enough,
    Or like the French mole heave up hair and all.
    I have a habit that will fit it quaintly.

    [*Enter* GRATIANA *and* CASTIZA.]

    Here comes our mother.
HIPPOLITO. And sister.
VINDICI. We must coin.
    Women are apt, you know, to take false money,
    But I dare stake my soul for these two creatures,
    Only excuse excepted that they'll swallow
    Because their sex is easy in belief.
GRATIANA. What news from court, son Carlo?
HIPPOLITO. Faith, Mother,
    'Tis whisper'd there the duchess' youngest son
    Has play'd a rape on Lord Antonio's wife.
GRATIANA. On that religious lady!
CASTIZA. Royal blood!
    Monster, he deserves to die,
    If Italy had no more hopes but he.
VINDICI. Sister, y'ave sentenc'd most direct and true:
    The law's a woman, and would she were you.
    Mother, I must take leave of you.
GRATIANA. Leave for what?
VINDICI. I intend speedy travel.
HIPPOLITO. That he does, madam.
GRATIANA. Speedy indeed!
VINDICI. For since my worthy father's funeral,

My life's unnatural to me, e'en compell'd
As if I liv'd now when I should be dead.
GRATIANA. Indeed he was a worthy gentleman,
Had his estate been fellow to his mind.
VINDICI. The duke did much deject him.
GRATIANA. Much?
VINDICI. Too much.
And through disgrace oft smother'd in his spirit
When it would mount, surely I think he died
Of discontent, the nobleman's consumption.
GRATIANA. Most sure he did!
VINDICI. Did he? 'Lack, you know all;
You were his midnight secretary.
GRATIANA. No.
He was too wise to trust me with his thoughts.
VINDICI. I'faith then, father, thou wast wise indeed:
"Wives are but made to go to bed and feed."
Come mother, sister; you'll bring me onward, brother?
HIPPOLITO. I will.
VINDICI. [*aside to him.*] I'll quickly turn into another.

[*Exeunt.*]

SCENE II. *A court of law.*

[*Enter the old* DUKE, LUSSURIOSO *his son, the* DUCHESS, *the* BASTARD, *the*
DUCHESS' *two sons* AMBITIOSO *and* SUPERVACUO, *the third her youngest
brought out with* OFFICERS *for the rape, two* JUDGES.]

DUKE. Duchess, it is your youngest son; we're sorry.
His violent act has e'en drawn blood of honour
And stain'd our honours,
Thrown ink upon the forehead of our state,
Which envious spirits will dip their pens into
After our death and blot us in our tombs,
For that which would seem treason in our lives
Is laughter when we're dead: who dares now whisper
That dares not then speak out, and e'en proclaim,
With loud words and broad pens our closest shame?
FIRST JUDGE. Your grace hath spoke like to your silver years
Full of confirmed gravity, for what is it to have
A flattering false insculption on a tomb,
And in men's hearts' reproach? The bowell'd corpse
May be cer'd in, but with free tongue I speak,
"The faults of great men through their cerecloths break."
DUKE. They do, we're sorry for't; it is our fate:
To live in fear and die to live in hate.
I leave him to your sentence; doom him, lords,

    The fact is great, whilst I sit by and sigh.

DUCHESS. My gracious lord, I pray be merciful.
    Although his trespass far exceed his years,
    Think him to be your own as I am yours;
    Call him not son-in-law. The law I fear
    Will fall too soon upon his name and him;
    Temper his fault with pity.

LUSSURIOSO. Good my lord,
    Then 'twill not taste so bitter and unpleasant
    Upon the judge's palate, for offenses
    Gilt o'er with mercy show like fairest women,
    Good only for their beauties, which wash'd of,
    No sin is uglier.

AMBITIOSO. I beseech your grace,
    Be soft and mild: let not relentless law,
    Look with an iron forehead on our brother.

SPURIO. He yields small comfort yet; hope he shall die,
    And if a bastard's wish might stand in force,
    Would all the court were turn'd into a corse.

DUCHESS. No pity yet? Must I rise fruitless then?
    A wonder in a woman. Are my knees
    Of such low metal that without respect—

FIRST JUDGE. Let the offender stand forth.
    'Tis the duke's pleasure that impartial doom
    Shall take fast hold of his unclean attempt.
    A rape! Why, 'tis the very core of lust,
    Double adultery!

JUNIOR. So, sir.

SECOND JUDGE. And which was worse,
    Committed on the Lord Antonio's wife,
    That general honest lady. Confess, my lord!
    What mov'd you to't?

JUNIOR. Why, flesh and blood, my lord.
    What should move men unto a woman else?

LUSSURIOSO. Oh, do not jest thy doom; trust not an axe
    Or sword too far: the law is a wise serpent
    And quickly can beguile thee of thy life.
    Tho' marriage only has [made.] thee my brother,
    I love thee so far; play not with thy death.

JUNIOR. I thank you, troth; good admonitions, faith,
    If I'd the grace now to make use of them.

FIRST JUDGE. That lady's name has spread such a fair wing
    Over all Italy, that if our tongues
    Were sparing toward the fact, judgment itself
    Would be condemned and suffer in men's thoughts.

JUNIOR. Well then, 'tis done, and it would please me well
    Were it to do again: sure she's a goddess,
    For I'd no power to see her and to live.

It falls out true in this, for I must die:
Her beauty was ordain'd to be my scaffold.
And yet methinks I might be easier cess'd,
My fault being sport, let me but die in jest.
FIRST JUDGE. This be the sentence.
DUCHESS. Oh, keep 't upon your tongue; let it not slip:
Death too soon steals out of a lawyer's lip.
Be not so cruel-wise.
FIRST JUDGE. Your grace must pardon us;
'Tis but the justice of the law.
DUCHESS. The law
Is grown more subtle than a woman should be.
SPURIO. [aside.] Now, now he dies; rid 'em away.
DUCHESS. [aside.] Oh, what it is to have an old, cool duke,
To be as slack in tongue as in performance!
FIRST JUDGE. Confirm'd; this be the doom irrevocable.
DUCHESS. Oh!
FIRST JUDGE. Tomorrow early—
DUCHESS. Pray be a-bed, my lord.
FIRST JUDGE. Your grace much wrongs yourself.
AMBITIOSO. No, 'tis that tongue,
Your too much right, does do us too much wrong.
FIRST JUDGE. Let that offender—
DUCHESS. Live, and be in health.
FIRST JUDGE. Be on a scaffold—
DUKE. Hold, hold, my lord.
SPURIO. [aside.] Pax on't,
What makes my dad speak now?
DUKE. We will defer the judgment till next sitting.
In the meantime let him be kept close prisoner:
Guard, bear him hence.

[AMBITIOSO and SUPERVACUO take Junior aside.]

AMBITIOSO. Brother, this makes for thee;
Fear not, we'll have a trick to set thee free.
JUNIOR. Brother, I will expect it from you both,
And in that hope I rest.
SUPERVACUO. Farewell, be merry.

[Exit JUNIOR with a guard.]

SPURIO. [aside.] Delay'd, deferr'd! Nay, then if judgment have cold blood,
Flattery and bribes will kill it.
DUKE. About it then, my lords, with your best powers;
More serious business calls upon our hours.

[Exeunt omnes. Manet DUCHESS.]

DUCHESS. Wast ever known step-duchess was so mild
    And calm as I? Some now would plot his death
    With easy doctors, those loose-living men,
    And make his wither'd grace fall to his grave
    And keep church better.
    Some second wife would do this, and dispatch
    Her double-loath'd lord at meat and sleep.
    Indeed, 'tis true an old man's twice a child.
    Mine cannot speak; one of his single words
    Would quite have freed my youngest, dearest son
    From death or durance, and have made him walk
    With a bold foot upon the thorny law,
    Whose prickles should bow under him: but 'tis not,
    And therefore wedlock, faith, shall be forgot.
    I'll kill him in his forehead; hate there feed:
    That wound is deepest tho' it never bleed.

    [*Enter* SPURIO.]

    [*aside.*] And here comes he whom my heart points unto,
    His bastard son, but my love's true-begot.
    Many a wealthy letter have I sent him,
    Swell'd up with jewels, and the timorous man
    Is yet but coldly kind;
    That jewel's mine that quivers in his ear,
    Mocking his master's chillness and vain fear.
    H'as spied me now.
SPURIO. Madam? Your grace so private?
    My duty on your hand.

    [*He kisses her hand.*]

DUCHESS. Upon my hand, sir! Troth, I think you'd fear
    To kiss my hand too if my lip stood there.
SPURIO. Witness I would not, madam.
DUCHESS. Tis a wonder,
    For ceremony has made many fools.
    It is as easy way unto a duchess
    As to a hatted dame, if her love answer,
    But that by timorous honours, pale respects,
    Idle degrees of fear, men make their ways
    Hard of themselves. What have you thought of me?
SPURIO. Madam, I ever think of you in duty,
    Regard, and—
DUCHESS. Puh, upon my love, I mean!
SPURIO. I would 'twere love, but 't 'as a fouler name
    Than lust; you are my father's wife: your grace may guess now

    What I could call it.

DUCHESS. Why, th'art his son but falsely;
    'Tis a hard question whether he begot thee.

SPURIO. I'faith, 'tis true too; I'm an uncertain man,
    Of more uncertain woman. Maybe his groom
    A' th' stable begot me; you know I know not.
    He could ride a horse well; a shrewd suspicion, marry!
    He was wondrous tall; he had his length, i'faith,
    For peeping over half shut holy-day windows:
    Men would desire him light! When he was afoot,
    He made a goodly show under a penthouse,
    And when he rid, his hat would check the signs
    And clatter barbers' basins.

DUCHESS. Nay, set you a-horseback once,
    You'll ne'er light off.

SPURIO. Indeed, I am a beggar.

DUCHESS. That's more the sign thou art great. But to our love:
    Let it stand firm both in thought and mind.
    That the duke was thy father, as no doubt then
    He bid fair for't, thy injury is the more,
    For had he cut thee a right diamond,
    Thou hadst been next set in the dukedom's ring
    When his worn self like age's easy slave
    Had dropp'd out of the collet into th' grave.
    What wrong can equal this? Canst thou be tame
    And think upon't?

SPURIO. No, mad and think upon't!

DUCHESS. Who would not be reveng'd of such a father,
    E'en in the worst way? I would thank that sin
    That could most injury him and be in league with it.
    Oh, what a grief 'tis, that a man should live
    But once i' th' world, and then to live a bastard,
    The curse a' the womb, the thief of nature,
    Begot against the seventh commandment,
    Half-damn'd in the conception, by the justice
    Of that unbribed, everlasting law!

SPURIO. Oh, I'd a hot-back'd devil to my father!

DUCHESS. Would not this mad e'en patience, make blood rough?
    Who but an eunuch would not sin, his bed
    By one false minute disinherited?

SPURIO. Ay, there's the vengeance that my birth was wrapp'd in;
    I'll be reveng'd for all. Now hate begin;
    I'll call foul incest but a venial sin.

DUCHESS. Cold still? In vain then must a duchess woo?

SPURIO. Madam, I blush to say what I will do.

DUCHESS. Thence flew sweet comfort, earnest and farewell.

[She kisses him.]

SPURIO. Oh, one incestuous kiss picks open hell!
DUCHESS. [*aside.*] Faith, now, old duke, my vengeance shall reach high;
    I'll arm thy brow with woman's heraldry.

    [*Exit.*]

SPURIO. Duke, thou didst do me wrong, and by thy act
    Adultery is my nature.
    Faith, if the truth were known, I was begot
    After some gluttonous dinner; some stirring dish
    Was my first father. When deep healths went round,
    And ladies' cheeks were painted red with wine,
    Their tongues as short and nimble as their heels,
    Uttering words sweet and thick, and when they rose
    Were merrily dispos'd to fall again:
    In such a whisp'ring and withdrawing hour,
    When base male-bawds kept sentinel at stair-head,
    Was I stol'n softly. Oh, damnation met
    The sin of feasts, drunken adultery!
    I feel it swell me; my revenge is just:
    I was begot in impudent wine and lust.
    Stepmother, I consent to thy desires;
    I love thy mischief well, but I hate thee
    And those three cubs, thy sons, wishing confusion,
    Death, and disgrace may be their epitaphs.
    As for my brother, the duke's only son,
    Whose birth is more beholding to report
    Than mine, and yet perhaps as falsely sown—
    Women must not be trusted with their own—
    I'll loose my days upon him: hate all I.
    Duke, on thy brow I'll draw my bastardy,
    For indeed a bastard by nature should make cuckolds,
    Because he is the son of a cuckold-maker.

    [*Exit.*]

SCENE III. *The palace.*

[*Enter* VINDICI *and* HIPPOLITO, VINDICI *in disguise as* PIATO *to attend* LORD
    LUSSURIOSO, *the duke's son.*]

VINDICI. What, brother? Am I far enough from myself?
HIPPOLITO. As if another man had been sent
    Into the world, and none wist how he came.
VINDICI. It will confirm me bold, the child a' th' court:
    Let blushes dwell i' th' country. Impudence,
    Thou goddess of the palace, mistress of mistresses

To whom the costly-perfum'd people pray,
Strike thou my forehead into dauntless marble,
Mine eyes to steady sapphires: turn my visage,
And if I must needs glow, let me blush inward
That this immodest season may not spy
That scholar in my cheeks, fool-bashfulness,
That maid in the old time, whose flush of grace
Would never suffer her to get good clothes.
Our maids are wiser and are less asham'd;
Save grace the bawd I seldom hear grace nam'd!
HIPPOLITO. Nay, brother, you reach out a' th' verge now.

[*Enter* LUSSURIOSO.]

'Sfoot, the duke's son! Settle your looks.
VINDICI. Pray let me not be doubted.
HIPPOLITO. My lord—
LUSSURIOSO. Hippolito? Be absent; leave us.
HIPPOLITO. My lord, after long search, wary inquiries
And politic siftings, I made choice of yon fellow,
Whom I guess rare for many deep employments;
This our age swims within him: and if Time
Had so much hair, I should take him for Time,
He is so near kin to this present minute.
LUSSURIOSO. 'Tis enough;
We thank thee. Yet words are but great men's blanks:
Gold, tho' it be dumb, does utter the best thanks.

[*He gives* HIPPOLITO *gold.*]

HIPPOLITO. Your plenteous honour; an ex'lent fellow, my lord.
LUSSURIOSO. So, give us leave.

[*Exit* HIPPOLITO.]

Welcome, be not far off, we must be better acquainted. Push, be bold with us, thy
hand!
VINDICI. With all my heart, i'faith. How dost, sweet musk-cat?
When shall we lie together?
LUSSURIOSO. [*aside.*] Wondrous knave!
Gather him into boldness? 'Sfoot, the slave's
Already as familiar as an ague,
And shakes me at his pleasure!—Friend, I can
Forget myself in private, but elsewhere,
I pray do you remember me.
VINDICI. Oh, very well, sir.
I construe myself saucy.
LUSSURIOSO. What hast been?

Of what profession?

VINDICI. A bone-setter.

LUSSURIOSO. A bone-setter!

VINDICI. A bawd, my lord,
One that sets bones together.

LUSSURIOSO. [*aside.*] Notable bluntness!
Fit, fit for me, e'en train'd up to my hand.—
Thou hast been scrivener to much knavery then?

VINDICI. Fool to abundance, sir. I have been witness
To the surrenders of a thousand virgins,
And not so little;
I have seen patrimonies wash'd a' pieces,
Fruit-fields turn'd into bastards,
And in a world of acres,
Not so much dust due to the heir 'twas left to
As would well gravel a petition!

LUSSURIOSO. [*aside.*] Fine villain! Troth, I like him wondrously.
He's e'en shap'd for my purpose.—Then thou know'st
I' th' world strange lust.

VINDICI. Oh, Dutch lust! Fulsome lust!
Drunken procreation, which begets
So many drunkards! Some father dreads not, gone
To bed in wine, to slide from the mother
And cling the daughter-in-law,
Some uncles are adulterous with their nieces,
Brothers with brothers' wives. Oh, hour of incest!
Any kin now next to the rim a' th' sister
Is man's meat in these days, and in the morning
When they are up and dress'd, and their mask on,
Who can perceive this save that eternal eye
That sees through flesh and all well. If anything be damn'd,
It will be twelve a' clock at night; that twelve
Will never 'scape:
It is the Judas of the hours, wherein
Honest salvation is betray'd to sin.

LUSSURIOSO. In troth, it is too; but let this talk glide.
It is our blood to err, tho' hell gap'd loud:
Ladies know Lucifer fell, yet still are proud.
Now, sir. Wert thou as secret as thou'rt subtle,
And deeply fadom'd into all estates,
I would embrace thee for a near employment,
And thou shouldst swell in money, and be able
To make lame beggars crouch to thee.

VINDICI. My lord?
Secret? I ne'er had that disease a' th' mother,
I praise my father: why are men made close,
But to keep thoughts in best? I grant you this,
Tell but some woman a secret overnight,

Your doctor may find it in the urinal i' th' morning.
But, my lord—
LUSSURIOSO. So, thou'rt confirmed in me,
And thus I *enter* thee.
VINDICI. This Indian devil
Will quickly *enter* any man but a usurer;
He prevents that by ent'ring the devil first.
LUSSURIOSO. Attend me: I am past my depth in lust
And I must swim or drown; all my desires
Are level'd at a virgin not far from court,
To whom I have convey'd by messenger
Many wax'd lines, full of my neatest spirit,
And jewels that were able to ravish her
Without the help of man, all which and more
She, foolish-chaste, sent back, the messengers
Receiving frowns for answers.
VINDICI. Possible?
'Tis a rare phoenix, whoe'er she be,
If your desires be such, she so repugnant.
In troth, my lord, I'd be reveng'd and marry her.
LUSSURIOSO. Push, the dowry of her blood and of her fortunes
Are both too mean, good enough to be bad withal.
I'm one of that number can defend
Marriage is good, yet rather keep a friend.
Give me my bed by stealth; there's true delight:
What breeds a loathing in't but night by night?
VINDICI. A very fine religion!
LUSSURIOSO. Therefore thus:
I'll trust thee in the business of my heart
Because I see thee well experienc'd
In this luxurious day wherein we breathe.
Go thou, and with a smooth, enchanting tongue
Bewitch her ears and cozen her of all grace.
Enter upon the portion of her soul,
Her honour, which she calls her chastity,
And bring it into expense, for honesty
Is like a stock of money laid to sleep,
Which ne'er so little broke does never keep.
VINDICI. You have gi'n 't the tang, i'faith, my lord.
Make known the lady to me, and my brain
Shall swell with strange invention: I will move it
Till I expire with speaking, and drop down
Without a word to save me; but I'll work.
LUSSURIOSO. We thank thee, and will raise thee: receive her name;
It is the only daughter to Madam Gratiana,
The late widow.
VINDICI. [*aside.*] Oh, my sister, my sister!
LUSSURIOSO. Why dost walk aside?

VINDICI. My lord, I was thinking how I might begin,
   As thus, "Oh, lady," or twenty hundred devices;
   Her very bodkin will put a man in.
LUSSURIOSO. Ay, or the wagging of her hair.
VINDICI. No, that shall put you in, my lord.
LUSSURIOSO. Shall 't? Why, content. Dost know the daughter then?
VINDICI. Oh, ex'lent well by sight.
LUSSURIOSO. That was her brother
   That did prefer thee to us.
VINDICI. My lord, I think so;
   I knew I had seen him somewhere.
LUSSURIOSO. And therefore, prithee, let thy heart to him
   Be as a virgin, close.
VINDICI. Oh, [my.] good lord!
LUSSURIOSO. We may laugh at that simple age within him.
VINDICI. Ha, ha, ha!
LUSSURIOSO. Himself being made the subtle instrument
   To wind up a good fellow.
VINDICI. That's I, my lord.
LUSSURIOSO. That's thou,
   To entice and work his sister.
VINDICI. A pure novice!
LUSSURIOSO. 'Twas finely manag'd.
VINDICI. Gallantly carried.
   [*aside.*] A pretty, perfum'd villain!
LUSSURIOSO. I've bethought me,
   If she prove chaste still and immoveable,
   Venture upon the mother, and with gifts
   As I will furnish thee, begin with her.
VINDICI. Oh, fie, fie, that's the wrong end, my lord! 'Tis mere impossible that a mother
   by any gifts should become a bawd to her own daughter!
LUSSURIOSO. Nay, then I see thou'rt but a puny in the subtle mystery of a woman.
   Why, 'tis held now no dainty dish: the name
   Is so in league with age that nowadays
   It does eclipse three quarters of a mother.
VINDICI. Dost so, my lord?
   Let me alone then to eclipse the fourth.
LUSSURIOSO. Why, well said; come, I'll furnish thee, but first
   Swear to be true in all.
VINDICI. True?
LUSSURIOSO. Nay, but swear!
VINDICI. Swear?
   I hope your honour little doubts my faith.
LUSSURIOSO. Yet for my humour's sake, 'cause I love swearing.
VINDICI. 'Cause you love swearing, 'slud, I will.
LUSSURIOSO. Why, enough,
   Ere long look to be made of better stuff.
VINDICI. That will do well indeed, my lord.

LUSSURIOSO. Attend me.

[*Exit.*]

VINDICI. Oh,
    Now let me burst: I've eaten noble poison!
    We are made strange fellows, brother, innocent villains.
    Wilt not be angry when thou hear'st on't, think'st thou?
    I'faith, thou shalt; swear me to foul my sister!
    Sword, I durst make a promise of him to thee,
    Thou shalt dis-heir him, it shall be thine honour!
    And yet now angry froth is down in me,
    It would not prove the meanest policy
    In this disguise to try the faith of both;
    Another might have had the selfsame office,
    Some slave that would have wrought effectually,
    Ay, and perhaps o'erwrought 'em. Therefore I,
    Being thought travell'd, will apply myself
    Unto the selfsame form, forget my nature,
    As if no part about me were kin to 'em;
    So touch 'em, tho' I durst almost for good
    Venture my lands in heaven upon their blood.

[*Exit.*]

SCENE IV. ANTONIO's *house.*

[*Enter the discontented* LORD ANTONIO, *whose wife the* DUCHESS' *youngest son ravish'd, he discovering the body of her dead to* PIERO *and other certain Lords and* HIPPOLITO.]

ANTONIO. Draw nearer, lords, and be sad witnesses
    Of a fair, comely building newly fall'n,
    Being falsely undermined: violent rape
    Has play'd a glorious act. Behold, my lords,
    A sight that strikes man out of me.
PIERO. That virtuous lady?
ANTONIO. President for wives!
HIPPOLITO. The blush of many women, whose chaste presence
    Would e'en call shame up to their cheeks,
    And make pale wanton sinners have good colours—
ANTONIO. Dead!
    Her honour first drunk poison, and her life,
    Being fellows in one house, did pledge her honour.
PIERO. Oh, grief of many!
ANTONIO. I mark'd not this before.
    A prayer book the pillow to her cheek,
    This was her rich confection, and another

    Plac'd in her right hand, with a leaf tuck'd up,
    Pointing to these words:
       "Melius virtute mori, quam per dedecus vivere."
    True and effectual it is indeed.
HIPPOLITO. My lord, since you invite us to your sorrows,
    Let's truly taste 'em, that with equal comfort
    As to ourselves we may relieve your wrongs;
    We have grief too that yet walks without tongue:
      Curae leves loquuntur, majores stupent.
ANTONIO. You deal with truth, my lord.
    Lend me but your attentions, and I'll cut
    Long grief into short words: last revelling night,
    When torch-light made an artificial noon
    About the court, some courtiers in the masque,
    Putting on better faces than their own,
    Being full of fraud and flattery, amongst whom
    The duchess' youngest son, that moth to honour,
    Fill'd up a room, and with long lust to eat
    Into my wearing, amongst all the ladies,
    Singled out that dear form, who ever liv'd
    As cold in lust as she is now in death,
    Which that step-duchess' monster knew too well;
    And therefore in the height of all the revels,
    When music was hard loudest, courtiers busiest,
    And ladies great with laughter. Oh, vicious minute!
    Unfit but for relation to be spoke of!
    Then with a face more impudent than his vizard,
    He harried her amidst a throng of panders,
    That live upon damnation of both kinds,
    And fed the ravenous vulture of his lust!
    Oh, death to think on't! She, her honour forc'd,
    Deem'd it a nobler dowry for her name
    To die with poison than to live with shame.
HIPPOLITO. A wondrous lady; of rare fire compact:
    Sh'as made her name an empress by that act.
PIERO. My lord, what judgment follows the offender?
ANTONIO. Faith, none, my lord: it cools and is deferr'd.
PIERO. Delay the doom for rape?
ANTONIO. Oh, you must note who 'tis should die:
    The Duchess' son; she'll look to be a saver.
    "Judgment in this age is ne'er kin to favour."
HIPPOLITO. [*Drawing his sword.*] Nay, then step forth, thou bribeless officer.
    I'll bind you all in steel to bind you surely:
    Here let your oaths meet to be kept and paid,
    Which else will stick like rust and shame the blade.
    Strengthen my vow, that if at the next sitting
    Judgment speak all in gold, and spare the blood
    Of such a serpent, e'en before their seats,

To let his soul out, which long since was found
    Guilty in heaven.
ALL LORDS. We swear it and will act it.
ANTONIO. Kind gentlemen, I thank you in mine ire.
HIPPOLITO. 'Twere pity
    The ruins of so fair a monument
    Should not be dipp'd in the defacer's blood.
PIERO. Her funeral shall be wealthy, for her name
    Merits a tomb of pearl. My Lord Antonio,
    For this time wipe your lady from your eyes;
    No doubt our grief and yours may one day court it,
    When we are more familiar with revenge.
ANTONIO. That is my comfort, gentlemen, and I joy
    In this one happiness above the rest,
    Which will be call'd a miracle at last,
    That being an old man I'd a wife so chaste.

    [*Exeunt.*]

ACT II.

SCENE I. VINDICI'*s house.*

[*Enter* CASTIZA, *the sister.*]

CASTIZA. How hardly shall that maiden be beset
    Whose only fortunes are her constant thoughts,
    That has no other child's part but her honour
    That keeps her low and empty in estate.
    Maids and their honours are like poor beginners:
    Were not sin rich there would be fewer sinners.
    Why had not virtue a revenue? Well,
    I know the cause: 'twould have impoverish'd hell.

[*Enter* DONDOLO.]

    How now, Dondolo?
DONDOLO. Madonna, there is one, as they say, a thing of flesh and blood, a man I take
    him by his beard, that would very desirously mouth to mouth with you.
CASTIZA. What's that?
DONDOLO. Show his teeth in your company.
CASTIZA. I understand thee not.
DONDOLO. Why, speak with you, Madonna!
CASTIZA. Why, say so, madman, and cut of a great deal of dirty way. Had it not been
    better spoke in ordinary words that one would speak with me?
DONDOLO. Ha, ha, that's as ordinary as two shillings! I would strive a little to show
    myself in my place: a gentleman usher scorns to use the phrase and fancy of a
    serving-man.

CASTIZA. Yours be your own, sir; go direct him hither.

[*Exit* DONDOLO.]

I hope some happy tidings from my brother
That lately travell'd, whom my soul affects.

[*Enter* VINDICI *her brother disguised as* PIATO.]

Here he comes.
VINDICI. [*Giving her a jewel.*] Lady, the best of wishes to your sex,
    Fair skins and new gowns.
CASTIZA. Oh, they shall thank you, sir.
    Whence this?
VINDICI. Oh, from a dear and worthy friend, mighty!
CASTIZA. From whom?
VINDICI. The duke's son!
CASTIZA. Receive that!
    [*A box a' th' ear to her brother.*]
    I swore I'd put anger in my hand
    And pass the virgin limits of myself
    To him that next appear'd in that base office
    To be his sin's attorney; bear to him
    That figure of my hate upon thy cheek
    Whilst 'tis yet hot, and I'll reward thee for't.
    Tell him my honour shall have a rich name
    When several harlots shall share his with shame.
    Farewell; commend me to him in my hate!

    [*Exit.*]

VINDICI. It is the sweetest box
    That e'er my nose came nigh,
    The finest drawn-work cuff that e'er was worn.
    I'll love this blow forever, and this cheek
    Shall still hence forward take the wall of this.
    Oh, I'm above my tongue! Most constant sister,
    In this thou hast right honourable shown;
    Many are call'd by their honour that have none.
    Thou art approv'd forever in my thoughts.
    It is not in the power of words to taint thee,
    And yet for the salvation of my oath,
    As my resolve in that point, I will lay
    Hard siege unto my mother, tho' I know
    A siren's tongue could not bewitch her so.

    [*Enter* GRATIANA.]

[*aside.*] Mass, fitly here she comes; thanks, my disguise.—
    Madam, good afternoon.
GRATIANA. Y'are welcome, sir.
VINDICI. The next of Italy commends him to you,
    Our mighty expectation, the duke's son.
GRATIANA. I think myself much honour'd that he pleases
    To rank me in his thoughts.
VINDICI. So may you, lady:
    One that is like to be our sudden duke;
    The crown gapes for him every tide, and then
    Commander o'er us all. Do but think on him;
    How bless'd were they now that could pleasure him
    E'en with anything almost.
GRATIANA. Ay, save their honour.
VINDICI. Tut, one would let a little of that go too
    And ne'er be seen in't: ne'er be seen in't, mark you;
    I'd wink and let it go.
GRATIANA. Marry, but I would not.
VINDICI. Marry, but I would I hope; I know you would too,
    If you'd that blood now which you gave your daughter.
    To her indeed 'tis this wheel comes about:
    That man that must be all this, perhaps ere morning,
    For his white father does but mould away,
    Has long desir'd your daughter.
GRATIANA. Desir'd?
VINDICI. Nay, but hear me:
    He desires now that will command hereafter.
    Therefore be wise; I speak as more a friend
    To you than him. Madam, I know y'are poor
    And 'lack the day, there are too many poor ladies already:
    Why should you vex the number? 'Tis despis'd.
    Live wealthy, rightly understand the world,
    And chide away that foolish country girl
    Keeps company with your daughter, chastity.
GRATIANA. Oh, fie, fie,
    The riches of the world cannot hire
    A mother to such a most unnatural task!
VINDICI. No, but a thousand angels can:
    Men have no power; angels must work you to't.
    The world descends into such base-born evils
    That forty angels can make fourscore devils.
    There will be fools still, I perceive, still fools.
    Would I be poor, dejected, scorn'd of greatness,
    Swept from the palace, and see other daughters
    Spring with the dew a' th' court, having mine own
    So much desir'd and lov'd by the duke's son?
    No, I would raise my state upon her breast
    And call her eyes my tenants; I would count

My yearly maintenance upon her cheeks,
Take coach upon her lip, and all her parts
Should keep men after men, and I would ride
In pleasure upon pleasure.
You took great pains for her, once when it was;
Let her requite it now, tho' it be but some:
You brought her forth; she may well bring you home.

GRATIANA. Oh, heavens! This overcomes me.

VINDICI. [*aside.*] Not, I hope, already?

GRATIANA. It is too strong for me; men know that know us:
We are so weak their words can overthrow us.
He touch'd me nearly, made my virtues bate
When his tongue struck upon my poor estate.

VINDICI. [*aside.*] I e'en quake to proceed; my spirit turns edge.
I fear me she's unmother'd, yet I'll venture:
"That woman is all male whom none can *enter*."—
What think you now, lady? Speak, are you wiser?
What said advancement to you? Thus it said:
The daughter's fall lifts up the mother's head.
Did it not, madam? But I'll swear it does
In many places; tut, this age fears no man:
"'Tis no shame to be bad, because 'tis common."

GRATIANA. Ay, that's the comfort on't.

VINDICI. [*aside.*] The comfort on't!—
[Giving her gold.] I keep the best for last: can these persuade you
To forget heaven and—

GRATIANA. Ay, these are they—

VINDICI. [*aside.*] Oh!

GRATIANA. That enchant our sex; these are the means
That govern our affections. That woman
Will not be troubled with the mother long
That sees the comfortable shine of you;
I blush to think what for your sakes I'll do!

VINDICI. [*aside.*] Oh, suff'ring heaven, with thy invisible finger
E'en at this instant turn the precious side
Of both mine eye-balls inward, not to see myself!

GRATIANA. Look you, sir.

VINDICI. Holla.

GRATIANA. [*Giving him gold.*] Let this thank your pains.

VINDICI. Oh, you're a kind [madam.].

GRATIANA. I'll see how I can move.

VINDICI. Your words will sting.

GRATIANA. If she be still chaste I'll ne'er call her mine.

VINDICI. [*aside.*] Spoke truer than you meant it.

[*Enter* CASTIZA.]

GRATIANA. Daughter Castiza.

CASTIZA. Madam.
VINDICI. Oh, she's yonder.
    Meet her.
    [*aside*.] Troops of celestial soldiers guard her heart;
    Yon dam has devils enough to take her part.
CASTIZA. Madam, what makes yon evil-offic'd man
    In presence of you?
GRATIANA. Why?
CASTIZA. He lately brought
    Immodest writing sent from the duke's son
    To tempt me to dishonourable act.
GRATIANA. Dishonourable act? Good honourable fool,
    That wouldst be honest 'cause thou wouldst be so,
    Producing no one reason but thy will.
    And 't 'as a good report, prettily commended,
    But pray by whom? Mean people, ignorant people;
    The better sort I'm sure cannot abide it.
    And by what rule should we square out our lives
    But by our betters actions? Oh, if thou knew'st
    What 'twere to lose it, thou would never keep it!
    But there's a cold curse laid upon all maids:
    Whilst others clip the sun, they clasp the shades!
    Virginity is paradise, lock'd up.
    You cannot come by yourselves without fee,
    And 'twas decreed that man should keep the key!
    Deny advancement, treasure, the duke's son!
CASTIZA. I cry you mercy. Lady, I mistook you.
    Pray did you see my mother? Which way went you?
    Pray God I have not lost her.
VINDICI. [*aside*.] Prettily put by.
GRATIANA. Are you as proud to me as coy to him?
    Do you not know me now?
CASTIZA. Why, are you she?
    The world's so chang'd, one shape into another:
    It is a wise child now that knows her mother.
VINDICI. [*aside*.] Most right, i'faith.
GRATIANA. I owe your cheek my hand
    For that presumption now, but I'll forget it.
    Come, you shall leave those childish 'haviours
    And understand your time; fortunes flow to you.
    What, will you be a girl?
    If all fear'd drowning that spy waves ashore,
    Gold would grow rich and all the merchants poor.
CASTIZA. It is a pretty saying of a wicked one, but methinks now
    It does not show so well out of your mouth,
    Better in his.
VINDICI. [*aside*.] Faith, bad enough in both,
    Were I in earnest, as I'll seem no less.—

I wonder, lady, your own mother's words
Cannot be taken, nor stand in full force.
'Tis honesty you urge. What's honesty?
'Tis but heavens beggar,
And what woman is so foolish to keep honesty,
And be not able to keep herself? No,
Times are grown wiser and will keep less charge:
A maid that has small portion now intends
To break up house and live upon her friends.
How bless'd are you; you have happiness alone:
Others must fall to thousands, you to one,
Sufficient in himself to make your forehead
Dazzle the world with jewels, and petitionary people
Start at your presence.

GRATIANA. Oh, if I were young,
    I should be ravish'd!

CASTIZA. Ay, to lose your honour.

VINDICI. 'Slid, how can you lose your honour
    To deal with my lord's grace?
    He'll add more honour to it by his title;
    Your mother will tell you how.

GRATIANA. That I will.

VINDICI. Oh, think upon the pleasure of the palace:
    Secured ease and state, the stirring meats,
    Ready to move out of the dishes,
    That e'en now quicken when they're eaten,
    Banquets abroad by torch-light, musics, sports,
    Bare-headed vassals that had ne'er the fortune
    To keep on their own hats but let horns [wear.] 'em,
    Nine coaches waiting. Hurry, hurry, hurry!

CASTIZA. Ay, to the devil.

VINDICI. [aside.] Ay, to the devil!—To th' duke, by my faith.

GRATIANA. Ay, to the duke: daughter, you'd scorn to think
    A' th' devil and you were there once.

VINDICI. True, for most
    There are as proud as he for his heart, i'faith.
    Who'd sit at home in a neglected room,
    Dealing her short-liv'd beauty to the pictures
    That are as useless as old men, when those
    Poorer in face and fortune than herself
    Walk with a hundred acres on their backs,
    Fair meadows cut into green foreparts? Oh,
    It was the greatest blessing ever happened to women
    When farmers' sons agreed, and met again,
    To wash their hands and come up gentlemen;
    The commonwealth has flourish'd ever since.
    Lands that were mete by the rod, that labours spar'd:
    Tailors ride down, and measure 'em by the yard.

Fair trees, those comely foretops of the field,
Are cut to maintain head-tires, much untold.
All thrives but chastity; she lies a-cold.
Nay, shall I come nearer to you? Mark but this:
Why are there so few honest women but
Because 'tis the poorer profession?
That's accounted best that's best followed:
Least in trade, least in fashion,
And that's not honesty. Believe it, and do
But note the low and dejected price of it:
"Lose but a pearl, we search and cannot brook it,
But that once gone, who is so mad to look it?"
GRATIANA. Troth, he says true.
CASTIZA. False! I defy you both!
    I have endur'd you with an ear of fire;
    Your tongues have struck hot irons on my face!
    Mother, come from that poisonous woman there.
GRATIANA. Where?
CASTIZA. Do you not see her? She's too inward then.
    Slave, perish in thy office! You heavens, please
    Henceforth to make the mother a disease,
    Which first begins with me, yet I've outgone you.

    [*Exit.*]

VINDICI. [*aside.*] Oh angels, clap your wings upon the skies,
    And give this virgin crystal plaudities!
GRATIANA. Peevish, coy, foolish! But return this answer:
    My lord shall be most welcome when his pleasure
    Conducts him this way. I will sway mine own;
    Women with women can work best alone.
VINDICI. Indeed, I'll tell him so.

    [*Exit.*]

Oh, more uncivil, more unnatural,
Than those base-titled creatures that look downward!
Why does not heaven turn black, or with a frown
Undo the world? Why does not earth start up
And strike the sins that tread upon't? Oh,
Wert not gold and women, there would be no damnation;
Hell would look like a lord's great kitchen without fire in't!
But 'twas decreed before the world began
That they should be the hooks to catch at man.

    [*Exit.*]

SCENE II. *The palace.*

[*Enter* LUSSURIOSO *with* HIPPOLITO, VINDICI's *brother.*]

LUSSURIOSO. I much applaud thy judgment; thou art well-read in a fellow,
    And 'tis the deepest art to study man.
    I know this, which I never learnt in schools:
    The world's divided into knaves and fools.
HIPPOLITO. [*aside.*] Knave in your face, my lord, behind your back.
LUSSURIOSO. And I much thank thee that thou hast preferr'd
    A fellow of discourse, well-mingled,
    And whose brain time hath season'd.
HIPPOLITO. True, my lord.
    [*aside.*] We shall find season once I hope. Oh, villain,
    To make such an unnatural slave of me! But—

[*Enter* VINDICI, *disguised as* PIATO.]

LUSSURIOSO. Mass, here he comes.
HIPPOLITO. [*aside.*] And now shall I have free leave to depart.
LUSSURIOSO. Your absence; leave us.
HIPPOLITO. [*aside.*] Are not my thoughts true?
    I must remove; but brother, you may stay:
    Heart, we are both made bawds a new-found way!

[*Exit.*]

LUSSURIOSO. Now we're an even number; a third man's dangerous,
    Especially her brother. Say, be free:
    Have I a pleasure toward?
VINDICI. Oh, my lord!
LUSSURIOSO. Ravish me in thine answer. Art thou rare?
    Hast thou beguil'd her of salvation,
    And rubb'd hell o'er with honey? Is she a woman?
VINDICI. In all but in desire.
LUSSURIOSO. Then she's in nothing;
    I bate in courage now.
VINDICI. The words I brought,
    Might well have made indifferent-honest naught.
    A right good woman in these days is chang'd
    Into white money with less labour far:
    Many a maid has turn'd to Mahomet
    With easier working. I durst undertake
    Upon the pawn and forfeit of my life
    With half those words to flat a Puritan's wife,
    But she is close and good. Yet 'tis a doubt
    By this time: oh, the mother, the mother!

LUSSURIOSO. I never thought their sex had been a wonder
    Until this minute. What fruit from the mother?
VINDICI. [*aside.*] Now must I blister my soul, be forsworn,
    Or shame the woman that receiv'd me first.
    I will be true; thou liv'st not to proclaim:
    Spoke to a dying man, shame has no shame.—
    My lord.
LUSSURIOSO. Who's that?
VINDICI. Here's none but I, my lord.
LUSSURIOSO. What would thy haste utter?
VINDICI. Comfort.
LUSSURIOSO. Welcome.
VINDICI. The maid being dull, having no mind to travel
    Into unknown lands, what did me straight
    But set spurs to the mother; golden spurs
    Will put her to a false gallop in a trice.
LUSSURIOSO. Is't possible that in this
    The mother should be damn'd before the daughter?
VINDICI. Oh, that's good manners, my lord; the mother
    For her age must go foremost, you know.
LUSSURIOSO. Thou'st spoke that true! But where comes in this comfort?
VINDICI. In a fine place, my lord. The unnatural mother
    Did with her tongue so hard beset her honour
    That the poor fool was struck to silent wonder,
    Yet still the maid like an unlighted taper
    Was cold and chaste, save that her mothers breath
    Did blow fire on her cheeks; the girl departed,
    But the good, ancient madam half-mad threw me
    These promising words, which I took deeply note of:
    "My lord shall be most welcome"—
LUSSURIOSO. Faith, I thank her.
VINDICI. "When his pleasure conducts him this way"—
LUSSURIOSO. That shall be soon, i'faith.
VINDICI. "I will sway mine own"—
LUSSURIOSO. She does the wiser; I commend her for't.
VINDICI. "Women with women can work best alone."
LUSSURIOSO. By this light, and so they can. Give 'em their due;
    Men are not comparable to 'em.
VINDICI. No,
    That's true, for you shall have one woman knit
    More in a hour than any man can ravel
    Again in seven and twenty year.
LUSSURIOSO. Now my
    Desires are happy, I'll make 'em freemen now.
    Thou art a precious fellow; faith, I love thee.
    Be wise and make it thy revenue: beg, leg!
    What office couldst thou be ambitious for?
VINDICI. Office, my lord? Marry, if I might have my wish

I would have one that was never begg'd yet.
LUSSURIOSO. Nay, then thou canst have none.
VINDICI. Yes, my lord,
    I could pick out another office yet,
    Nay, and keep a horse and drab upon't.
LUSSURIOSO. Prithee, good bluntness, tell me.
VINDICI. Why I would desire but this,
    My lord: to have all the fees behind the arras,
    And all the farthingales that fall plump
    About twelve a' clock at night upon the rushes.
LUSSURIOSO. Thou'rt a mad, apprehensive knave.
    Dost think to make any great purchase of that?
VINDICI. Oh, 'tis an unknown thing,
    My lord; I wonder 't 'as been miss'd so long.
LUSSURIOSO. Well, this night I'll visit her, and 'tis till then
    A year in my desires. Farewell, attend,
    Trust me with thy preferment.
VINDICI. My lov'd lord!

    [*Exit.*]

    Oh, shall I kill him a' th' wrong side now? No.
    Sword, thou wast never a back-biter yet.
    I'll pierce him to his face; he shall die looking upon me.
    Thy veins are swell'd with lust; this shall unfill 'em:
    Great men were gods if beggars could not kill 'em.
    Forgive me, heaven, to call my mother wicked;
    Oh, lessen not my days upon the earth!
    I cannot honour her; by this I fear me
    Her tongue has turn'd my sister into use.
    I was a villain not to be forsworn
    To this our lecherous hope, the duke's son,
    For lawyers, merchants, some divines and all
    Count beneficial perjury a sin small.
    It shall go hard yet, but I'll guard her honour
    And keep the ports sure.

    [*Enter* HIPPOLITO.]

HIPPOLITO. Brother, how goes the world? I would know news of you,
    But I have news to tell you.
VINDICI. What, in the name of knavery?
HIPPOLITO. Knavery? Faith,
    This vicious old duke's worthily abus'd:
    The pen of his bastard writes him cuckold!
VINDICI. His bastard?
HIPPOLITO. Pray, believe it: he and the duchess
    By night meet in their linen; they have been seen

By stair-foot panders!
VINDICI. Oh, sin foul and deep,
    Great faults are wink'd at when the duke's asleep!

[*Enter* SPURIO *and his two* SERVANTS, *one whispering to him.*]

    See, see, here comes the Spurio.
HIPPOLITO. Monstrous luxur!
VINDICI. Unbrac'd, two of his valiant bawds with him.
    Oh, there's a wicked whisper; hell is in his ear!
    Stay, let's observe his passage.

[*They retire.*]

SPURIO. Oh, but are you sure on't?
FIRST SERVANT. My lord, most sure on't, for 'twas spoke by one
    That is most inward with the duke's son's lust,
    That he intends within this hour to steal
    Unto Hippolito's sister, whose chaste life
    The mother has corrupted for his use.
SPURIO. Sweet world, sweet occasion! Faith, then, brother
    I'll disinherit you in as short time,
    As I was when I was begot in haste:
    I'll damn you at your pleasure: precious deed
    After your lust; oh, 'twill be fine to bleed!
    Come, let our passing out be soft and wary.

[*Exeunt* SPURIO *and* SERVANTS.]

VINDICI. Mark, there, there, that step! Now to the duchess:
    This their second meeting writes the duke cuckold
    With new additions, his horns newly reviv'd.
    Night, thou that lookst like funeral heralds' fees
    Torn down betimes i' th' morning, thou hang'st fitly
    To grace those sins that have no grace at all.
    Now 'tis full sea a-bed over the world;
    There's juggling of all sides. Some that were maids
    E'en at sunset are now perhaps i' th' toll-book:
    This woman in immodest, thin apparel
    Lets in her friend by water; here a dame
    Cunning nails leather hinges to a door,
    To avoid proclamation.
    Now cuckolds are a-coining, apace, apace, apace, apace;
    And careful sisters spin that thread i' th' night
    That does maintain them and their bawds i' th' day!
HIPPOLITO. You flow well, brother.
VINDICI. Puh, I'm shallow yet,
    Too sparing and too modest. Shall I tell thee?

If every trick were told that's dealt by night,
There are few here that would not blush outright.
HIPPOLITO. I am of that belief too.

[*Enter* LUSSURIOSO.]

VINDICI. [*aside to* Hippolito.] Who's this comes?
    The duke's son up so late! Brother, fall back,
    And you shall learn some mischief.—My good lord.
LUSSURIOSO. Piato! Why, the man I wish'd for. Come,
    I do embrace this season for the fittest
    To taste of that young lady.
VINDICI. [*aside.*] Heart and hell!
HIPPOLITO. [*aside.*] Damn'd villain!
VINDICI. [*aside.*] I ha' no way now to cross it but to kill him.
LUSSURIOSO. Come, only thou and I.
VINDICI. My lord, my lord.
LUSSURIOSO. Why dost thou start us?
VINDICI. I'd almost forgot: the bastard!
LUSSURIOSO. What of him?
VINDICI. This night, this hour, this minute, now!
LUSSURIOSO. What! What!
VINDICI. Shadows the duchess—
LUSSURIOSO. Horrible word.
VINDICI. And like strong poison eats
    Into the duke your father's forehead.
LUSSURIOSO. Oh!
VINDICI. He makes horn royal.
LUSSURIOSO. Most ignoble slave!
VINDICI. This is the fruit of two beds.
LUSSURIOSO. I am mad!
VINDICI. That passage he trod warily.
LUSSURIOSO. He did!
VINDICI. And hush'd his villains every step he took.
LUSSURIOSO. His villains! I'll confound them!
VINDICI. Take 'em finely, finely now.
LUSSURIOSO. The duchess' chamber-door shall not control me.

[*Exeunt* LUSSURIOSO *and* VINDICI.]

HIPPOLITO. Good, happy, swift; there's gunpowder i' th' court,
    Wildfire at midnight in this heedless fury.
    He may show violence to cross himself;
    I'll follow the event.

[*Exit.*]

SCENE III. *The* DUKE's *bedchamber.*

[*The* DUKE *and* DUCHESS *are discovered in bed.* LUSSURIOSO *and* VINDICI *enter again with* HIPPOLITO *following.*]

LUSSURIOSO. Where is that villain?
VINDICI. Softly, my lord, and you may take 'em twisted.
LUSSURIOSO. I care not how!
VINDICI. Oh, 'twill be glorious
　　To kill 'em doubled, when they're heap'd! Be soft, my lord.
LUSSURIOSO. Away! My spleen is not so lazy; thus and thus
　　I'll shake their eyelids open, and with my sword
　　Shut 'em again forever.

[*He draws his sword and approaches the bed.*]

　　Villain, strumpet!
DUKE. You upper guard defend us!
DUCHESS. Treason, treason!
DUKE. Oh, take me not in sleep; I have great sins: I must have days,
　　Nay, months, dear son, with penitential heaves
　　To lift 'em out and not to die unclear!
　　Oh, thou wilt kill me both in heaven and here!
LUSSURIOSO. I am amaz'd to death.
DUKE. Nay, villain traitor,
　　Worse than the foulest epithet, now I'll gripe thee
　　E'en with the nerves of wrath, and throw thy head
　　Amongst the lawyer's! Guard!

[*Enter* NOBLES *and sons,* AMBITIOSO *and* SUPERVACUO, *with guards.*]

FIRST NOBLE. How comes the quiet of your grace disturb'd?
DUKE. This boy that should be myself after me
　　Would be myself before me, and in heat
　　Of that ambition bloodily rush'd in
　　Intending to depose me in my bed.
SECOND NOBLE. Duty and natural loyalty forfend!
DUCHESS. He call'd his father villain and me strumpet,
　　A word that I abhor to 'file my lips with.
AMBITIOSO. That was not so well done, brother.
LUSSURIOSO. I am abus'd.
　　I know there's no excuse can do me good.
VINDICI. [*aside to* HIPPOLITO.] 'Tis now good policy to be from sight;
　　His vicious purpose to our sister's honour
　　Is cross'd beyond our thought.
HIPPOLITO. [*aside to* VINDICI.] You little dreamt his father slept here.
VINDICI. [*aside to* HIPPOLITO.] Oh, 'twas far beyond me.

But since it fell so—Without frightful word,
Would he had kill'd him, 'twould have eas'd our swords.
DUKE. Be comforted, our duchess: he shall die.

[*The* DUCHESS *exits as the guards seize* LUSSURIOSO. VINDICI *and*
HIPPOLITO *dissemble a flight.*]

LUSSURIOSO. Where's this slave-pander now? Out of mine eye,
Guilty of this abuse.

[*Enter* SPURIO *with his villains to one side.*]

SPURIO. Y'are villains, fablers;
You have knaves' chins and harlots' tongues: you lie,
And I will damn you with one meal a day.
FIRST SERVANT. Oh, good my lord!
SPURIO. 'Sblood, you shall never sup.
SECOND SERVANT. Oh, I beseech you, sir!
SPURIO. To let my sword catch cold so long and miss him!
FIRST SERVANT. Troth, my lord, 'twas his intent to meet there.
SPURIO. Heart, he's yonder!
Ha! What news here? Is the day out a' th' socket
That it is noon at midnight? The court up?
How comes the guard so saucy with his elbows?
LUSSURIOSO. The bastard here?
Nay, then the truth of my intent shall out.
My lord and father, hear me.
DUKE. Bear him hence.
LUSSURIOSO. I can with loyalty excuse.
DUKE. Excuse? To prison with the villain;
Death shall not long lag after him.
SPURIO. [*aside.*] Good, i'faith, then 'tis not much amiss.
LUSSURIOSO. [*To* AMBITIOSO *and* SUPERVACUO *aside.*] Brothers, my best release
lies on your tongues;
I pray persuade for me.
AMBITIOSO. It is our duties: make yourself sure of us.
SUPERVACUO. We'll sweat in pleading.
LUSSURIOSO. And I may live to thank you.

[*Exeunt* LUSSURIOSO *and* guards.]

AMBITIOSO. [*aside.*] No, thy death shall thank me better.
SPURIO. He's gone: I'll after him
And know his trespass, seem to bear a part
In all his ills, but with a puritan heart.

[*Exit with* SERVANTS.]

AMBITIOSO. [*aside to* SUPERVACUO.] Now, brother, let our hate and love be woven
So subtly together, that in speaking one word for his life,
We may make three for his death:
The craftiest pleader gets most gold for breath.
SUPERVACUO. [*aside to* AMBITIOSO.] Set on; I'll not be far behind you, brother.
DUKE. Is't possible a son
Should be disobedient as far as the sword?
It is the highest; he can go no farther.
AMBITIOSO. My gracious lord, take pity—
DUKE. Pity, boys?
AMBITIOSO. Nay, we'd be loath to move your grace too much;
We know the trespass is unpardonable,
Black, wicked, and unnatural.
SUPERVACUO. In a son, oh, monstrous!
AMBITIOSO. Yet, my lord,
A duke's soft hand strokes the rough head of law
And makes it lie smooth.
DUKE. But my hand shall ne'er do't.
AMBITIOSO. That as you please, my lord.
SUPERVACUO. We must needs confess
Some father would have *enter*'d into hate,
So deadly pointed, that before his eyes
He would ha' seen the execution sound
Without corrupted favour.
AMBITIOSO. But, my lord,
Your grace may live the wonder of all times
In pard'ning that offence which never yet
Had face to beg a pardon.
DUKE. Honey? How's this?
AMBITIOSO. Forgive him, good my lord: he's your own son,
And I must needs say 'twas the vildlier done.
SUPERVACUO. He's the next heir, yet this true reason gathers:
None can possess that dispossess their fathers.
Be merciful—
DUKE. [*aside.*] Here's no stepmother's wit:
I'll try 'em both upon their love and hate.
AMBITIOSO. Be merciful, although—
DUKE. You have prevail'd:
My wrath like flaming wax hath spent itself.
I know 'twas but some peevish moon in him:
Go, let him be releas'd.
SUPERVACUO. [*aside to* AMBITIOSO.] 'Sfoot, how now, brother?
AMBITIOSO. Your grace doth please to speak beside your spleen;
I would it were so happy.
DUKE. Why, go, release him.
SUPERVACUO. Oh, my good lord, I know the fault's too weighty
And full of general loathing, too inhuman,
Rather by all men's voices worthy death.

DUKE. 'Tis true too.
    Here then, receive this signet; doom shall pass:
    Direct it to the judges; he shall die
    Ere many days. Make haste.
AMBITIOSO. All speed that may be.
    We could have wish'd his burthen not so sore;
    We knew your grace did but delay before.

    [*Exeunt* AMBITIOSO *and* SUPERVACUO.]

DUKE. Here's envy with a poor, thin cover o'er 't,
    Like scarlet hid in lawn, easily spied through.
    This their ambition by the mother's side
    Is dangerous, and for safety must be purg'd;
    I will prevent their envies. Sure it was
    But some mistaken fury in our son,
    Which these aspiring boys would climb upon:
    He shall be releas'd suddenly.

    [*Enter* Nobles. *They kneel.*]

FIRST NOBLE. Good morning to your grace.
DUKE. Welcome, my lords.
SECOND NOBLE. Our knees shall take away the office of our feet forever,
    Unless your grace bestow a father's eye
    Upon the clouded fortunes of your son,
    And in compassionate virtue grant him that
    Which makes e'en mean men happy: liberty.
DUKE. [*aside.*] How seriously their loves and honours woo
    For that which I am about to pray them do!—
    Rise, my lords, your knees sign his release:
    We freely pardon him.
FIRST NOBLE. We owe your grace much thanks, and he much duty.

    [*Exeunt* Nobles.]

DUKE. It well becomes that judge to nod at crimes
    That does commit greater himself and lives.
    I may forgive a disobedient error
    That expect pardon for adultery,
    And in my old days am a youth in lust:
    Many a beauty have I turn'd to poison
    In the denial, covetous of all.
    Age hot is like a monster to be seen:
    My hairs are white, and yet my sins are green.

    [*Exit.*]

ACT III.

SCENE I. *The palace.*

[*Enter* AMBITIOSO *and* SUPERVACUO.]

SUPERVACUO. Brother, let my opinion sway you once,
    I speak it for the best, to have him die
    Surest and soonest; if the signet come
    Unto the judges' hands, why, then his doom
    Will be deferr'd till sittings and court-days,
    Juries and further. Faiths are bought and sold;
    Oaths in these days are but the skin of gold.
AMBITIOSO. In troth, 'tis true too!
SUPERVACUO. Then let's set by the judges
    And fall to the officers; 'tis but mistaking
    The duke our father's meaning, and where he nam'd
    "Ere many days," 'tis but forgetting that
    And have him die i' th' morning.
AMBITIOSO. Excellent;
    Then am I heir, duke in a minute.
SUPERVACUO. [*aside.*] Nay,
    And he were once puff'd out, here is a pin
    Should quickly prick your bladder.
AMBITIOSO. Bless'd occasion!
    He being pack'd, we'll have some trick and wile
    To wind our younger brother out of prison
    That lies in for the rape; the lady's dead,
    And people's thoughts will soon be buried.
SUPERVACUO. We may with safety do't, and live and feed;
    The duchess' sons are too proud to bleed.
AMBITIOSO. We are, i'faith, to say true. Come, let's not linger.
    I'll to the officers; go you before
    And set an edge upon the executioner.
SUPERVACUO. Let me alone to grind him.
AMBITIOSO. Meet; farewell.

[*Exit* SUPERVACUO.]

I am next now; I rise just in that place
Where thou'rt cut off: upon thy neck, kind brother.
The falling of one head lifts up another.

[*Exit.*]

SCENE II. *Outside the prison.*

[*Enter with the* NOBLES, LUSSURIOSO *from prison.*]

LUSSURIOSO. My lords, I am so much indebted to your loves
    For this, oh, this delivery!
FIRST NOBLE. But our duties,
    My lord, unto the hopes that grow in you.
LUSSURIOSO. If e'er I live to be myself, I'll thank you.
    Oh liberty, thou sweet and heavenly dame!
    But hell for prison is too mild a name.

[*Exeunt.*]

SCENE III. *The prison.*

[*Enter* AMBITIOSO *and* SUPERVACUO, *with* OFFICERS.]

AMBITIOSO. Officers, here's the duke's signet, your firm warrant,
    Brings the command of present death along with it
    Unto our brother, the duke's son; we are sorry
    That we are so unnaturally employ'd
    In such an unkind office, fitter far
    For enemies than brothers.
SUPERVACUO. But you know,
    The duke's command must be obey'd.
FIRST OFFICER. It must and shall my lord; this morning then.
    So suddenly?
AMBITIOSO. Ay, alas, poor good soul,
    He must breakfast betimes; the executioner
    Stands ready to put forth his cowardly valour.
SECOND OFFICER. Already?
SUPERVACUO. Already, i'faith. Oh, sir, destruction hies,
    And that is least impudent soonest dies.
FIRST OFFICER. Troth, you say true, my lord. We take our leaves;
    Our office shall be sound: we'll not delay
    The third part of a minute.
AMBITIOSO. Therein you show
    Yourselves good men and upright officers.
    Pray let him die as private as he may;
    Do him that favour, for the gaping people
    Will but trouble him at his prayers
    And make him curse and swear, and so die black.
    Will you be so far kind?
FIRST OFFICER. It shall be done, my lord.
AMBITIOSO. Why, we do thank you; if we live to be,
    You shall have a better office.

SECOND OFFICER. Your good lordship.
SUPERVACUO. Commend us to the scaffold in our tears.
FIRST OFFICER. We'll weep and do your commendations.

[*Exeunt* OFFICERS.]

AMBITIOSO. Fine fools in office!
SUPERVACUO. Things fall out so fit.
AMBITIOSO. So happily! Come, brother, ere next clock
    His head will be made serve a bigger block.

[*Exeunt.*]

SCEN IV. JUNIOR brother's cell in the prison.

[*Enter in prison* JUNIOR *brother.*]

JUNIOR. Keeper.

[*Enter the* KEEPER.]

KEEPER. My lord.
JUNIOR. No news lately from our brothers?
    Are they unmindful of us?
KEEPER. My lord, a messenger came newly in
    And brought this from 'em.

[*He hands him a letter.*]

JUNIOR. Nothing but paper comforts?
    I look'd for my delivery before this
    Had they been worth their oaths. Prithee be from us.

[*Exit the* KEEPER.]

Now what say you, forsooth? Speak out, I pray.

[*Opens and reads the letter.*]

"Brother be of good cheer."
'Slud, it begins like a whore with good cheer!
"Thou shalt not be long a prisoner."
Not five and thirty year like a bankrout, I think so.
"We have thought upon a device to get thee out by a trick."
By a trick! Pox a' your trick and it be so long a-playing!
"And so rest comforted, be merry and expect it suddenly."
Be merry, hang merry, draw and quarter merry, I'll be mad!
Is't not strange that a man should lie in a whole month for a woman? Well, we shall

120

see how sudden our brothers will be in their promise. I must expect still a trick! I
shall not be long a prisoner!

[*Enter the* KEEPER *with four* OFFICERS.]

How now, what news?
KEEPER. Bad news, my lord; I am discharg'd of you.
JUNIOR. Slave, call'st thou that bad news? I thank you, brothers!
KEEPER. My lord, 'twill prove so; here come the officers
    Into whose hands I must commit you.
JUNIOR. Ha, officers? What, why?
FIRST OFFICER. You must pardon us, my lord;
    Our office must be sound: here is our warrant,
    The signet from the duke; you must straight suffer.
JUNIOR. Suffer? I'll suffer you to be gone, I'll suffer you
    To come no more! What would you have me suffer?
SECOND OFFICER. My lord, those words were better chang'd to prayers;
    The time's but brief with you: prepare to die.
JUNIOR. Sure 'tis not so.
THIRD OFFICER. It is too true, my lord.
JUNIOR. I tell you 'tis not, for the duke my father
    Deferr'd me till next sitting, and I look
    E'en every minute, threescore times an hour,
    For a release, a trick wrought by my brothers.
FIRST OFFICER. A trick, my lord? If you expect such comfort,
    Your hopes as fruitless as a barren woman:
    Your brothers were the unhappy messengers
    That brought this powerful token for your death.
JUNIOR. My brothers? No, no!
SECOND OFFICER. 'Tis most true, my lord.
JUNIOR. My brothers to bring a warrant for my death?
    How strange this shows!
THIRD OFFICER. There's no delaying time.
JUNIOR. Desire 'em hither, call 'em up, my brothers!
    They shall deny it to your faces.
FIRST OFFICER. My lord,
    They're far enough by this, at least at court,
    And this most strict command they left behind 'em,
    When grief swum in their eyes: they show'd like brothers,
    Brimful of heavy sorrow; but the duke
    Must have his pleasure.
JUNIOR. His pleasure?
FIRST OFFICER. These were their last words which my memory bears:
    "Commend us to the scaffold in our tears."
JUNIOR. Pox dry their tears! What should I do with tears?
    I hate 'em worse than any citizen's son
    Can hate salt water. Here came a letter now,
    New-bleeding from their pens, scarce stinted yet;

Would I'd been torn in pieces when I tore it.
  Look, you officious whoresons, words of comfort:
  "Not long a prisoner."
FIRST OFFICER. It says true in that, sir, for you must suffer presently.
JUNIOR. A villainous duns upon the letter! Knavish exposition! Look you then here, sir:
  "we'll get thee out by a trick," says he.
SECOND OFFICER. That may hold too, sir, for you know a trick is commonly four
  cards, which was meant by us four officers.
JUNIOR. Worse and worse dealing!
FIRST OFFICER. The hour beckons us.
  The heads-man waits; lift up your eyes to heaven.
JUNIOR. I thank you, faith; good, pretty, wholesome counsel.
  I should look up to heaven, as you said,
  Whilst he behind me cozens me of my head;
  Ay, that's the trick.
THIRD OFFICER. You delay too long, my lord.
JUNIOR. Stay, good authority's bastards, since I must
  Through brothers' perjury die, oh, let me venom
  Their souls with curses!
FIRST OFFICER. Come, 'tis no time to curse.
JUNIOR. Must I bleed then without respect of sign? Well,
  My fault was sweet sport, which the world approves;
  I die for that which every woman loves.

  [*Exeunt.*]

SCENE V. *A lodge.*

[*Enter* VINDICI *with* HIPPOLITO *his brother.*]

VINDICI. Oh, sweet, delectable, rare, happy, ravishing!
HIPPOLITO. Why, what's the matter, brother?
VINDICI. Oh, 'tis able
  To make a man spring up and knock his forehead
  Against yon silver ceiling!
HIPPOLITO. Prithee tell me.
  Why, may not I partake with you? You vow'd once
  To give me share to every tragic thought.
VINDICI. By th' mass, I think I did too.
  Then I'll divide it to thee: the old duke
  Thinking my outward shape and inward heart
  Are cut out of one piece—for he that prates his secrets,
  His heart stands a' th' outside—hires me by price
  To greet him with a lady
  In some fit place veil'd from the eyes a' th' court,
  Some dark'ned, blushless angle, that is guilty
  Of his forefathers' lusts and great-folks' riots,
  To which I easily, to maintain my shape,

Consented, and did wish his impudent grace
To meet her here in this unsunned lodge,
Wherein 'tis night at noon, and here the rather,
Because unto the torturing of his soul
The bastard and the duchess have appointed
Their meeting too in this luxurious circle,
Which most afflicting sight will kill his eyes
Before we kill the rest of him.
HIPPOLITO. 'Twill, i'faith, most dreadfully digested.
I see not how you could have miss'd me, brother.
VINDICI. True, but the violence of my joy forgot it.
HIPPOLITO. Ay, but where's that lady now?
VINDICI. Oh, at that word
I'm lost again; you cannot find me yet:
I'm in a throng of happy apprehensions!
He's suited for a lady; I have took care
For a delicious lip, a sparkling eye:
You shall be witness brother.
Be ready; stand with your hat off.

[*Exit.*]

HIPPOLITO. Troth, I wonder what lady it should be?
Yet 'tis no wonder, now I think again,
To have a lady stoop to a duke that stoops unto his men.
'Tis common to be common through the world:
And there's more private common shadowing vices
Than those who are known both by their names and prices.
[*Taking off his hat.*] 'Tis part of my allegiance to stand bare
To the duke's concubine, and here she comes.

[*Enter* VINDICI *with the skull of his love dress'd up in tires.*]

VINDICI. Madam, his grace will not be absent long.
Secret? Ne'er doubt us, madam; 'twill be worth
Three velvet gowns to your ladyship. Known?
Few ladies respect that. Disgrace? A poor, thin shell;
'Tis the best grace you have to do it well.
I'll save your hand that labour; I'll unmask you.

[*Draws back the tires.*]

HIPPOLITO. Why, brother, brother!
VINDICI. Art thou beguil'd now? Tut, a lady can
At such, all hid, beguile a wiser man.
Have I not fitted the old surfeiter
With a quaint piece of beauty? Age and bare bone
Are e'er allied in action: here's an eye

Able to tempt a great man to serve God,
A pretty, hanging lip that has forgot now to dissemble;
Methinks this mouth should make a swearer tremble,
A drunkard clasp his teeth and not undo 'em
To suffer wet damnation to run through 'em.
Here's a cheek keeps her colour, let the wind go whistle:
Spout rain, we fear thee not; be hot or cold
Alls one with us. And is not he absurd
Whose fortunes are upon their faces set,
That fear no other God but wind and wet?
HIPPOLITO. Brother, y'ave spoke that right.
Is this the form that living shone so bright?
VINDICI. The very same;
And now methinks I could e'en chide myself
For doting on her beauty, tho' her death
Shall be reveng'd after no common action.
Does the silkworm expend her yellow labours
For thee? For thee does she undo herself?
Are lordships sold to maintain ladyships
For the poor benefit of a bewitching minute?
Why does yon fellow falsify highways
And put his life between the judge's lips
To refine such a thing, keeps horse and men
To beat their valours for her?
Surely we're all mad people, and they
Whom we think are, are not; we mistake those:
'Tis we are mad in sense, they but in clothes.
HIPPOLITO. Faith, and in clothes too we; give us our due.
VINDICI. Does every proud and self-affecting dame
Camphor her face for this, and grieve her maker
In sinful baths of milk, when many an infant starves,
For her superfluous outside fall for this?
Who now bids twenty pound a-night, prepares
Music, perfumes, and sweetmeats? All are hush'd;
Thou mayst lie chaste now! It were fine, methinks,
To have thee seen at revels, forgetful feasts,
And unclean brothels; sure 'twould fright the sinner
And make him a good coward, put a reveller
Out of his antic amble,
And cloy an epicure with empty dishes.
Here might a scornful and ambitious woman
Look through and through herself; see, ladies, with false forms
You deceive men but cannot deceive worms.
Now to my tragic business. Look you, brother,
I have not fashion'd this only for show
And useless property; no, it shall bear a part
E'en in its own revenge.

[Applies poison to the skull's mouth.]

This very skull,
Whose mistress the duke poisoned, with this drug,
The mortal curse of the earth, shall be reveng'd
In the like strain, and kiss his lips to death.
As much as the dumb thing can, he shall feel:
What fails in poison, we'll supply in steel.
HIPPOLITO. Brother, I do applaud thy constant vengeance,
The quaintness of thy malice above thought.
VINDICI. So 'tis laid on. Now come and welcome, duke;
I have her for thee. I protest it, brother:
Methinks she makes almost as fair a sign
As some old gentlewoman in a periwig.
Hide thy face now for shame; thou hadst need have a mask now:
'Tis vain when beauty flows, but when it fleets,
This would become graves better than the streets.
HIPPOLITO. You have my voice in that. Hark, the duke's come!
VINDICI. Peace, let's observe what company he brings,
And how he does absent 'em, for you know
He'll wish all private: brother, fall you back a little
With the bony lady.
HIPPOLITO. That I will.
VINDICI. So, so: now nine years' vengeance crowd into a minute!

[Enter the DUKE *talking to his* GENTLEMEN.]

DUKE. You shall have leave to leave us, with this charge:
Upon your lives, if we be miss'd by th' duchess
Or any of the nobles, to give out
We're privately rid forth.
VINDICI. *[aside.]* Oh, happiness!
DUKE. With some few honourable gentlemen, you may say;
You may name those that are away from court.
FIRST GENTLEMAN. Your will and pleasure shall be done, my lord.

[Exeunt the GENTLEMEN.]

VINDICI. *[aside.]* Privately rid forth!
He strives to make sure work on't.—Your good grace?
DUKE. Piato, well done. Hast brought her? What lady is't?
VINDICI. Faith, my lord, a country lady, a little bashful at first, as most of them are, but
after the first kiss, my lord, the worst is past with them. Your grace knows now what
you have to do; sh'as somewhat a grave look with her, but—
DUKE. I love that best: conduct her.
VINDICI. Have at all.
DUKE. In gravest looks the greatest faults seem less;
Give me that sin that's rob'd in holiness.

VINDICI. [*aside to* HIPPOLITO.] Back with the torch; brother, raise the perfumes.
DUKE. How sweet can a duke breathe? Age has no fault;
    Pleasure should meet in a perfumed mist.
    Lady, sweetly encount'red. I came from court:
    I must be bold with you—

    [*Kisses the skull.*]

    Oh, what's this? Oh!
VINDICI. Royal villain, white devil!
DUKE. Oh!
VINDICI. Brother,
    Place the torch here, that his affrighted eyeballs
    May start into those hollows. Duke, dost know
    Yon dreadful vizard? View it well: 'tis the skull
    Of Gloriana, whom thou poisoned'st last.
DUKE. Oh, 't 'as poisoned me!
VINDICI. Didst not know that till now?
DUKE. What are you two?
VINDICI. Villains all three! The very ragged bone
    Has been sufficiently reveng'd!
DUKE. Oh, Hippolito? Call treason!
HIPPOLITO. Yes, my good lord: treason, treason, treason!

    [*Stamping on him.*]

DUKE. Then I'm betray'd!
VINDICI. Alas, poor lecher in the hands of knaves:
    A slavish duke is baser than his slaves.
DUKE. My teeth are eaten out!
VINDICI. Hadst any left?
HIPPOLITO. I think but few.
VINDICI. Then those that did eat are eaten.
DUKE. Oh, my tongue!
VINDICI. Your tongue? 'Twill teach you to kiss closer,
    Not like a slobbering Dutchman! You have eyes still:
    Look, monster, what a lady hast thou made me,
    My once betrothed wife!
DUKE. Is it thou, villain? Nay, then—
VINDICI. 'Tis I, 'tis Vindici, 'tis I!
HIPPOLITO. And let this comfort thee: our lord and father
    Fell sick upon the infection of thy frowns
    And died in sadness; be that thy hope of life!
DUKE. Oh!
VINDICI. He had his tongue, yet grief made him die speechless.
    Puh, 'tis but early yet; now I'll begin
    To stick thy soul with ulcers, I will make
    Thy spirit grievous sore: it shall not rest,

But like some pestilent man toss in thy breast. Mark me, duke,
    Thou'rt a renowned, high, and mighty cuckold.
DUKE. Oh!
VINDICI. Thy bastard, thy bastard rides a-hunting in thy brow.
DUKE. Millions of deaths!
VINDICI. Nay, to afflict thee more,
    Here in this lodge they meet for damned clips;
    Those eyes shall see the incest of their lips.
DUKE. Is there a hell besides this, villains?
VINDICI. Villain?
    Nay, heaven is just: scorns are the hires of scorns;
    I ne'er knew yet adulterer without horns.
HIPPOLITO. Once ere they die 'tis quitted.

[*Music within.*]

VINDICI. Hark, the music!
    Their banquet is prepar'd; they're coming.
DUKE. Oh, kill me not with that sight!
VINDICI. Thou shalt not lose that sight for all thy dukedom.
DUKE. Traitors, murderers!
VINDICI. What? Is not thy tongue eaten out yet?
    Then we'll invent a silence. Brother, stifle the torch.
DUKE. Treason, murther!
VINDICI. Nay, faith, we'll have you hush'd now with thy dagger.
    Nail down his tongue, and mine shall keep possession
    About his heart: if he but gasp he dies;
    We dread not death to quittance injuries. Brother,
    If he but wink, not brooking the foul object,
    Let our two other hands tear up his lids,
    And make his eyes like comets shine through blood;
    When the bad bleeds, then is the tragedy good.
HIPPOLITO. Whist, brother: music's at our ear, they come.

[*Enter* SPURIO, *the bastard, meeting the* DUCHESS. *They kiss.*]

SPURIO. Had not that kiss a taste of sin, 'twere sweet.
DUCHESS. Why, there's no pleasure sweet but it is sinful.
SPURIO. True, such a bitter sweetness fate hath given;
    Best side to us is the worst side to heaven.
DUCHESS. Push, come: 'tis the old duke thy doubtful father;
    The thought of him rubs heaven in thy way,
    But I protest by yonder waxen fire,
    Forget him or I'll poison him.
SPURIO. Madam, you urge a thought which ne'er had life.
    So deadly do I loathe him for my birth,
    That if he took me hasp'd within his bed,
    I would add murther to adultery,

And with my sword give up his years to death.
DUCHESS. Why, now thou'rt sociable! Let's in and feast.
　　Loud'st music sound: pleasure is banquet's guest.

[*Loud music. Exeunt.*]

DUKE. I cannot brook—

[VINDICI *stabs the* DUKE, *who dies.*]

VINDICI. The brook is turn'd to blood.
HIPPOLITO. Thanks to loud music.
VINDICI. 'Twas our friend indeed:
　　'Tis state in music for a duke to bleed.
　　The dukedom wants a head, tho' yet unknown;
　　As fast as they peep up, let's cut 'em down.

[*Exeunt.*]

SCENE VI. *The prison.*

[*Enter the* DUCHESS' *two sons,* AMBITIOSO *and* SUPERVACUO.]

AMBITIOSO. Was not this execution rarely plotted?
　　We are the duke's sons now.
SUPERVACUO. Ay, you may thank my policy for that.
AMBITIOSO. Your policy for what?
SUPERVACUO. Why, was 't not my invention, brother,
　　To slip the judges, and in lesser compass,
　　Did not I draw the model of his death,
　　Advising you to sudden officers
　　And e'en extemporal execution?
AMBITIOSO. Heart, 'twas a thing I thought on too.
SUPERVACUO. You thought on't too! 'Sfoot, slander not your thoughts
　　With glorious untruth! I know 'twas from you.
AMBITIOSO. Sir, I say 'twas in my head.
SUPERVACUO. Ay, like your brains then,
　　Ne'er to come out as long as you liv'd.
AMBITIOSO. You'd have the honour on't, forsooth, that your wit
　　Led him to the scaffold.
SUPERVACUO. Since it is my due,
　　I'll publish 't, but I'll ha't in spite of you.
AMBITIOSO. Methinks y'are much too bold; you should a little
　　Remember us, brother, next to be honest duke.
SUPERVACUO. Ay, it shall be as easy for you to be duke
　　As to be honest, and that's never, i'faith.
AMBITIOSO. Well, cold he is by this time, and because
　　We're both ambitious, be it our amity,

And let the glory be shar'd equally.

SUPERVACUO. I am content to that.

AMBITIOSO. This night our younger brother shall out of prison;
    I have a trick.

SUPERVACUO. A trick? Prithee, what is't?

AMBITIOSO. We'll get him out by a wile.

SUPERVACUO. Prithee, what wile?

AMBITIOSO. No, sir, you shall not know it till 't be done,
    For then you'd swear 'twere yours.

[*Enter an* OFFICER, *holding a severed head.*]

SUPERVACUO. How now, what's he?

AMBITIOSO. One of the officers.

SUPERVACUO. Desired news.

AMBITIOSO. How now, my friend?

OFFICER. My lords, under your pardon, I am allotted
    To that desertless office, to present you
    With the yet bleeding head.

SUPERVACUO. [*aside to* AMBITIOSO.] Ha, ha, excellent!

AMBITIOSO. [*aside to* SUPERVACUO.] All's sure our own: brother, canst weep,
    think'st thou?
    'Twould grace our flattery much; think of some dame:
    'Twill teach thee to dissemble.

SUPERVACUO. [*aside to* AMBITIOSO.] I have thought;
    Now for yourself.

AMBITIOSO. Our sorrows are so fluent,
    Our eyes o'erflow our tongues; words spoke in tears
    Are like the murmurs of the waters; the sound
    Is loudly heard, but cannot be distinguish'd.

SUPERVACUO. How died he, pray?

OFFICER. Oh, full of rage and spleen!

SUPERVACUO. He died most valiantly then; we're glad to hear it.

OFFICER. We could not woo him once to pray.

AMBITIOSO. He show'd himself a gentleman in that:
    Give him his due.

OFFICER. But in the stead of prayer,
    He drew forth oaths.

SUPERVACUO. Then did he pray, dear heart,
    Although you understood him not.

OFFICER. My lords,
    E'en at his last, with pardon be it spoke,
    He curs'd you both.

SUPERVACUO. He curs'd us? 'Las, good soul!

AMBITIOSO. It was not in our powers, but the duke's pleasure.
    [*aside to* SUPERVACUO.] Finely dissembled a' both sides. Sweet fate,
    Oh, happy opportunity!

[*Enter* LUSSURIOSO.]

LUSSURIOSO. Now, my lords.
AMBITIOSO, SUPERVACUO. Oh!
LUSSURIOSO. Why do you shun me, brothers?
    You may come nearer now;
    The savour of the prison has forsook me.
    I thank such kind lords as yourselves, I'm free.
AMBITIOSO. Alive!
SUPERVACUO. In health!
AMBITIOSO. Releas'd!
    We were both e'en amaz'd with joy to see it.
LUSSURIOSO. I am much to thank you.
SUPERVACUO. Faith, we spar'd no tongue unto my lord the duke.
AMBITIOSO. I know your delivery, brother,
    Had not been half so sudden but for us.
SUPERVACUO. Oh, how we pleaded!
LUSSURIOSO. Most deserving brothers,
    In my best studies I will think of it.

[*Exit* LUSSURIOSO.]

AMBITIOSO. Oh, death and vengeance!
SUPERVACUO. Hell and torments!
AMBITIOSO. Slave, cam'st thou to delude us?
OFFICER. Delude you, my lords?
SUPERVACUO. Ay, villain, where's this head now?
OFFICER. Why, here, my lord.
    Just after his delivery, you both came
    With warrant from the duke to behead your brother.
AMBITIOSO. Ay, our brother, the duke's son.
OFFICER. The duke's son,
    My lord, had his release before you came.
AMBITIOSO. Whose head's that then?
OFFICER. His whom you left command for, your own brother's.
AMBITIOSO. Our brother's? Oh, furies!
SUPERVACUO. Plagues!
AMBITIOSO. Confusions!
SUPERVACUO. Darkness!
AMBITIOSO. Devils!
SUPERVACUO. Fell it out so accursedly?
AMBITIOSO. So damnedly?
SUPERVACUO. Villain, I'll brain thee with it!
OFFICER. Oh, my good lord!

[*Exit* OFFICER, *running.*]

SUPERVACUO. The devil overtake thee!

AMBITIOSO. Oh, fatal!

SUPERVACUO. Oh, prodigious to our bloods!

AMBITIOSO. Did we dissemble?

SUPERVACUO. Did we make our tears women for thee?

AMBITIOSO. Laugh and rejoice for thee?

SUPERVACUO. Bring warrant for thy death?

AMBITIOSO. Mock off thy head?

SUPERVACUO. You had a trick, you had a wile, forsooth!

AMBITIOSO. A murrain meet 'em! There's none of these wiles
    That ever come to good: I see now
    There is nothing sure in mortality but mortality.
    Well, no more words; shalt be reveng'd, i'faith.
    Come, throw off clouds now, brother, think of vengeance
    And deeper-settled hate. Sirrah, sit fast:
    We'll pull down all, but thou shalt down at last.

    [*Exeunt.*]

ACT IV.

SCENE I. *The palace.*

[*Enter* LUSSURIOSO *with* HIPPOLITO.]

LUSSURIOSO. Hippolito.

HIPPOLITO. My lord, has your good lordship
    Ought to command me in?

LUSSURIOSO. I prithee leave us.

HIPPOLITO. [*aside.*] How's this? Come and leave us?

LUSSURIOSO. Hippolito.

HIPPOLITO. Your honour,
    I stand ready for any duteous employment.

LUSSURIOSO. Heart, what mak'st thou here?

HIPPOLITO. [*aside.*] A pretty, lordly humour:
    He bids me to be present, to depart;
    Something has stung his honour.

LUSSURIOSO. Be nearer, draw nearer:
    Ye are not so good, methinks; I'm angry with you.

HIPPOLITO. With me, my lord? I'm angry with myself for't.

LUSSURIOSO. You did prefer a goodly fellow to me.
    'Twas wittily elected, 'twas; I thought
    H'ad been a villain, and he proves a knave,
    To me a knave.

HIPPOLITO. I chose him for the best, my lord.
    'Tis much my sorrow if neglect in him,
    Breed discontent in you.

LUSSURIOSO. Neglect? 'Twas will! Judge of it:
    Firmly to tell of an incredible act,

Not to be thought, less to be spoken of,
'Twixt my stepmother and the bastard, oh,
Incestuous sweets between 'em!
HIPPOLITO. Fie, my lord!
LUSSURIOSO. I, in kind loyalty to my father's forehead,
  Made this a desperate arm, and in that fury
  Committed treason on the lawful bed,
  And with my sword e'en ras'd my father's bosom,
  For which I was within a stroke of death.
HIPPOLITO. Alack, I'm sorry.

[*Enter* VINDICI. *disguised as* PIATO.]

[*aside.*] 'Sfoot, just upon the stroke
  Jars in my brother; 'twill be villainous music.
VINDICI. My honoured lord.
LUSSURIOSO. Away! Prithee forsake us;
  Hereafter we'll not know thee.
VINDICI. Not know me, my lord? Your lordship cannot choose.
LUSSURIOSO. Be gone, I say: thou art a false knave.
VINDICI. Why, the easier to be known, my lord.
LUSSURIOSO. Push, I shall prove too bitter with a word,
  Make thee a perpetual prisoner,
  And lay this ironage upon thee!
VINDICI. Mum,
  For there's a doom would make a woman dumb.
  [*aside.*] Missing the bastard, next him, the wind's come about;
  Now 'tis my brother's turn to stay, mine to go out.

[*Exit* VINDICI.]

LUSSURIOSO. H'as greatly mov'd me.
HIPPOLITO. Much to blame, i'faith.
LUSSURIOSO. But I'll recover to his ruin: 'twas told me lately,
  I know not whether falsely, that you'd a brother.
HIPPOLITO. Who I? Yes, my good lord, I have a brother.
LUSSURIOSO. How chance the court ne'er saw him? Of what nature?
  How does he apply his hours?
HIPPOLITO. Faith, to curse fates,
  Who, as he thinks, ordain'd him to be poor,
  Keeps at home full of want and discontent.
LUSSURIOSO. There's hope in him, for discontent and want
  Is the best clay to mould a villain of.
  Hippolito, wish him repair to us,
  If there be ought in him to please our blood;
  For thy sake we'll advance him and build fair
  His meanest fortunes, for it is in us
  To rear up towers from cottages.

HIPPOLITO. It is so, my lord, he will attend your honour;
  But he's a man in whom much melancholy dwells.
LUSSURIOSO. Why, the better; bring him to court.
HIPPOLITO. With willingness and speed.
  [*aside.*] Whom he cast off e'en now must now succeed.
  Brother, disguise must off;
  In thine own shape now I'll prefer thee to him:
  How strangely does himself work to undo him.

  [*Exit.*]

LUSSURIOSO. This fellow will come fitly; he shall kill
  That other slave that did abuse my spleen
  And made it swell to treason. I have put
  Much of my heart into him; he must die.
  He that knows great men's secrets and proves slight,
  That man ne'er lives to see his beard turn white.
  Ay, he shall speed him; I'll employ the brother:
  Slaves are but nails to drive out one another.
  He being of black condition, suitable
  To want and ill content, hope of preferment
  Will grind him to an edge.

  [*The* NOBLES *enter.*]

FIRST NOBLE. Good days unto your honour.
LUSSURIOSO. My kind lords, I do return the like.
SECOND NOBLE. Saw you my lord the duke?
LUSSURIOSO. My lord and father, is he from court?
FIRST NOBLE. He's sure from court,
  But where, which way his pleasure took, we know not,
  Nor can we hear on't.

  [*Enter the* DUKE's GENTLEMEN.]

LUSSURIOSO. Here come those should tell.
  Saw you my lord and father?
FIRST GENTLEMAN. Not since two hours before noon, my lord,
  And then he privately rid forth.
LUSSURIOSO. Oh, he's rid forth?
FIRST NOBLE. 'Twas wondrous privately.
SECOND NOBLE. There's none i' th' court had any knowledge on't.
LUSSURIOSO. His grace is old and sudden; 'tis no treason
  To say the duke my father has a humour
  Or such a toy about him: what in us
  Would appear light, in him seems virtuous.
FIRST GENTLEMAN. 'Tis oracle, my lord.

[Exeunt.]

SCENE II. *The palace.*

[*Enter* VINDICI *and* HIPPOLITO, VINDICI *out of his disguise.*]

HIPPOLITO. So, so, all's as it should be; y'are yourself.
VINDICI. How that great villain puts me to my shifts!
HIPPOLITO. He that did lately in disguise reject thee
    Shall, now thou art thyself, as much respect thee.
VINDICI. 'Twill be the quainter fallacy; but, brother,
    'Sfoot, what use will he put me to now, think'st thou?
HIPPOLITO. Nay, you must pardon me in that, I know not:
    H'as some employment for you, but what 'tis
    He and his secretary, the devil, knows best.
VINDICI. Well, I must suit my tongue to his desires,
    What colour soe'er they be, hoping at last
    To pile up all my wishes on his breast.
HIPPOLITO. Faith, brother, he himself shows the way.
VINDICI. Now the duke is dead, the realm is clad in clay:
    His death being not yet known, under his name
    The people still are govern'd. Well, thou his son
    Art not long-liv'd; thou shalt not 'joy his death:
    To kill thee then, I should most honour thee,
    For 'twould stand firm in every man's belief
    Thou'st a kind child and only died'st with grief.
HIPPOLITO. You fetch about well, but let's talk in present.
    How will you appear in fashion different,
    As well as in apparel, to make all things possible?
    If you be but once tripp'd, we fall forever.
    It is not the least policy to be doubtful;
    You must change tongue: familiar was your first.
VINDICI. Why, I'll bear me in some strain of melancholy
    And string myself with heavy-sounding wire,
    Like such an instrument, that speaks merry
    Things sadly.
HIPPOLITO. Then 'tis as I meant:
    I gave you out at first in discontent.
VINDICI. I'll turn myself, and then—

[*Enter* LUSSURIOSO.]

HIPPOLITO. [*aside to* VINDICI.] 'Sfoot, here he comes!
    Hast thought upon't?
VINDICI. [*aside to* HIPPOLITO.] Salute him, fear not me.
LUSSURIOSO. Hippolito.
HIPPOLITO. Your lordship.
LUSSURIOSO. What's he yonder?

HIPPOLITO. 'Tis Vindici, my discontented brother,
    Whom 'cording to your will I've brought to court.
LUSSURIOSO. Is that thy brother? Beshrew me, a good presence;
    I wonder h'as been from the court so long. [*To* Vindici.] Come nearer.
HIPPOLITO. Brother, Lord Lussurioso, the duke's son.

[VINDICI *snatches off his hat and makes legs to him.*]

LUSSURIOSO. Be more near to us; welcome, nearer yet.
VINDICI. How don you? God you god den.
LUSSURIOSO. We thank thee.
    How strangely such a coarse, homely salute
    Shows in the palace, where we greet in fire
    Nimble and desperate tongues; should we name
    God in a salutation, 'twould ne'er be stood on't. Heaven!
    Tell me, what has made thee so melancholy?
VINDICI. Why, going to law.
LUSSURIOSO. Why, will that make a man melancholy?
VINDICI. Yes, to look long upon ink and black buckram: I went me to law in *anno quadregesimo secundo*, and I waded out of it in *anno sextagesimo tertio*.
LUSSURIOSO. What, three and twenty years in law?
VINDICI. I have known those that have been five and fifty, and all about pullen and pigs.
LUSSURIOSO. May it be possible such men should breath,
    To vex the terms so much?
VINDICI. 'Tis food to some, my lord. There are old men at the present that are so poisoned with the affectation of law-words, having had many suites canvass'd, that their common talk is nothing but Barbary Latin: they cannot so much as pray but in law, that their sins may be remov'd with a writ of error, and their souls fetch'd up to heaven with a sasarara.
LUSSURIOSO. It seems most strange to me,
    Yet all the world meets round in the same bent:
    Where the heart's set, there goes the tongue's consent.
    How dost apply thy studies, fellow?
VINDICI. Study? Why, to think how a great, rich man lies a-dying, and a poor cobbler tolls the bell for him; how he cannot depart the world, and see the great chest stand before him; when he lies speechless, how he will point you readily to all the boxes; and when he is past all memory, as the gossips guess, then thinks he of forfeitures and obligations; nay, when to all men's hearings he whirls and rattles in the throat, he's busy threat'ning his poor tenants; and this would last me now some seven years thinking or thereabouts. But I have a conceit a-coming in picture upon this: I draw it myself, which, i'faith la, I'll present to your honour; you shall not choose but like it, for your lordship shall give me nothing for it.
LUSSURIOSO. Nay, you mistake me then,
    For I am publish'd bountiful enough;
    Let's taste of your conceit.
VINDICI. In picture, my lord?
LUSSURIOSO. Ay, in picture.
VINDICI. Marry, this it is:

"A usuring father to be boiling in hell,
    And his son and heir with a whore dancing over him."
HIPPOLITO. [*aside*.] H'as par'd him to the quick.
LUSSURIOSO. The conceit's pretty, i'faith,
    But take 't upon my life, 'twill ne'er be lik'd.
VINDICI. No? Why, I'm sure the whore will be lik'd well enough.
HIPPOLITO. [*aside*.] Ay, if she were out a' th' picture, he'd like her then himself.
VINDICI. And as for the son and heir, he shall be an eyesore to no young revellers, for
    he shall be drawn in cloth-of-gold breeches.
LUSSURIOSO. And thou hast put my meaning in the pockets
    And canst not draw that out; my thought was this:
    To see the picture of a usuring father
    Boiling in hell, our rich men would ne'er like it.
VINDICI. Oh, true, I cry you heartily mercy! I know the reason, for some of 'em had
    rather be damn'd indeed than damn'd in colours.
LUSSURIOSO. [*aside*.] A parlous melancholy; h'as wit enough
    To murder any man, and I'll give him means.—
    I think thou art ill-monied.
VINDICI. Money! Ho, ho!
    'T 'as been my want so long, 'tis now my scoff.
    I've e'en forgot what colour silver's of.
LUSSURIOSO. [*aside*.] It hits as I could wish.
VINDICI. I get good clothes
    Of those that dread my humour, and for tableroom,
    I feed on those that cannot be rid of me.
LUSSURIOSO. [*Giving him gold.*] Somewhat to set thee up withal.
VINDICI. Oh, mine eyes!
LUSSURIOSO. How now, man?
VINDICI. Almost struck blind!
    This bright, unusual shine to me seems proud;
    I dare not look till the sun be in a cloud.
LUSSURIOSO. [*aside.*] I think I shall affect his melancholy.—
    How are they now?
VINDICI. The better for your asking.
LUSSURIOSO. You shall be better yet if you but fasten
    Truly on my intent; now y'are both present,
    I will unbrace such a close, private villain
    Unto your vengeful swords, the like ne'er heard of,
    Who hath disgrac'd you much and injur'd us.
HIPPOLITO. Disgraced us, my lord?
LUSSURIOSO. Ay, Hippolito.
    I kept it here till now that both your angers
    Might meet him at once.
VINDICI. I'm covetous
    To know the villain.
LUSSURIOSO. You know him: that slave pander,
    Piato, whom we threatened last
    With iron's perpetual prisonment.

VINDICI. [*aside.*] All this is I.

HIPPOLITO. Is't he, my lord?

LUSSURIOSO. I'll tell you,
    You first preferr'd him to me.

VINDICI. Did you, brother?

HIPPOLITO. I did indeed.

LUSSURIOSO. And the ingrateful villain,
    To quit that kindness, strongly wrought with me,
    Being as you see a likely man for pleasure,
    With jewels to corrupt your virgin sister.

HIPPOLITO. Oh, villain!

VINDICI. He shall surely die that did it.

LUSSURIOSO. Ay, far from thinking any virgin harm,
    Especially knowing her to be as chaste
    As that part which scarce suffers to be touch'd,
    Th' eye would not endure him.

VINDICI. Would you not, my lord?
    'Twas wondrous honourably done.

LUSSURIOSO. But with some [*fine.*] frowns kept him out.

VINDICI. Out, slave!

LUSSURIOSO. What did me he but in revenge of that
    Went of his own free will to make infirm
    Your sister's honour, whom I honour with my soul
    For chaste respect, and not prevailing there,
    As 'twas but desperate folly to attempt it,
    In mere spleen, by the way, waylays your mother,
    Whose honour being a coward as it seems
    Yielded by little force.

VINDICI. Coward indeed!

LUSSURIOSO. He, proud of their advantage, as he thought,
    Brought me these news for happy, but I,
    Heaven forgive me for't—

VINDICI. What did your honour?

LUSSURIOSO. In rage push'd him from me,
    Trampled beneath his throat, spurn'd him, and bruis'd:
    Indeed I was too cruel, to say troth.

HIPPOLITO. Most nobly manag'd.

VINDICI. Has not heaven an ear? Is all lightning wasted?

LUSSURIOSO. If I now were so impatient in a modest cause,
    What should you be?

VINDICI. Full mad: he shall not live
    To see the moon change.

LUSSURIOSO. He's about the palace;
    Hippolito, entice him this way, that thy brother
    May take full mark of him.

HIPPOLITO. Heart, that shall not need, my lord,
    I can direct him so far.

LUSSURIOSO. Yet for my hate's sake,

Go, wind him this way; I'll see him bleed myself.
HIPPOLITO. [*Taking Vindici aside.*] What now, brother?
VINDICI. Nay, e'en what you will: y'are put to't, brother.
HIPPOLITO. An impossible task, I'll swear,
    To bring him hither that's already here.

[*Exit* HIPPOLITO.]

LUSSURIOSO. Thy name, I have forgot it.
VINDICI. Vindici, my lord.
LUSSURIOSO. 'Tis a good name, that.
VINDICI. Ay, a revenger.
LUSSURIOSO. It does betoken courage: thou shouldst be valiant
    And kill thine enemies.
VINDICI. That's my hope, my lord.
LUSSURIOSO. This slave is one.
VINDICI. I'll doom him.
LUSSURIOSO. Then I'll praise thee.
    Do thou observe me best, and I'll best raise thee.

[*Enter* HIPPOLITO.]

VINDICI. Indeed, I thank you.
LUSSURIOSO. Now, Hippolito,
    Where's the slave pander?
HIPPOLITO. Your good lordship
    Would have a loathsome sight of him, much offensive.
    He's not in case now to be seen, my lord;
    The worst of all the deadly sins is in him:
    That beggarly damnation, drunkenness.
LUSSURIOSO. Then he's a double slave.
VINDICI. [*aside to* HIPPOLITO.] 'Twas well convey'd
    Upon a sudden wit.
LUSSURIOSO. What, are you both
    Firmly resolv'd? I'll see him dead myself.
VINDICI. Or else let not us live.
LUSSURIOSO. You may direct
    Your brother to take note of him.
HIPPOLITO. I shall.
LUSSURIOSO. Rise but in this and you shall never fall.
VINDICI. Your honour's vassals.
LUSSURIOSO. [*aside.*] This was wisely carried.
    Deep policy in us makes fools of such:
    Then must a slave die when he knows too much.

[*Exit* LUSSURIOSO.]

VINDICI. Oh, thou almighty patience, 'tis my wonder

That such a fellow, impudent and wicked,
Should not be cloven as he stood,
Or with a secret wind burst open!
Is there no thunder left, or is't kept up
In stock for heavier vengeance? There it goes!
HIPPOLITO. Brother, we lose ourselves.
VINDICI. But I have found it.
'Twill hold, 'tis sure; thanks, thanks to any spirit
That mingled it 'mongst my inventions!
HIPPOLITO. What is't?
VINDICI. 'Tis sound and good, thou shalt partake it:
I'm hir'd to kill myself.
HIPPOLITO. True.
VINDICI. Prithee mark it:
And the old duke being dead but not convey'd,
For he's already miss'd too, and you know
Murder will peep out of the closest husk.
HIPPOLITO. Most true.
VINDICI. What say you then to this device,
If we dress'd up the body of the duke?
HIPPOLITO. In that disguise of yours.
VINDICI. Y'are quick, y'ave reach'd it.
HIPPOLITO. I like it wondrously.
VINDICI. And being in drink, as you have publish'd him,
To lean him on his elbow, as if sleep had caught him,
Which claims most interest in such sluggy men.
HIPPOLITO. Good yet, but here's a doubt:
We, thought by th' duke's son to kill that pander,
Shall when he is known be thought to kill the duke.
VINDICI. Neither. Oh, thanks, it is substantial!
For that disguise being on him, which I wore,
It will be thought I, which he calls the pander,
Did kill the duke and fled away in his apparel,
Leaving him so disguis'd to avoid swift pursuit.
HIPPOLITO. Firmer and firmer.
VINDICI. Nay, doubt not 'tis in grain;
I warrant it hold colour.
HIPPOLITO. Let's about it.
VINDICI. But, by the way too, now I think on't, brother,
Let's conjure that base devil out of our mother.

[*Exeunt.*]

SCENE III. *The palace.*

[*Enter the* DUCHESS *arm in arm with the bastard* SPURIO; *he seemeth lasciviously to her. After them, enter* SUPERVACUO, *running with a rapier, his brother* AMBITIOSO *stops him.*]

SPURIO. Madam, unlock yourself; should it be seen,
　　Your arm would be suspected.
DUCHESS. Who is't that dares suspect, or this or these?
　　May not we deal our favours where we please?
SPURIO. I'm confident you may.

[*Exeunt* DUCHESS *and* SPURIO.]

AMBITIOSO. 'Sfoot, brother, hold!
SUPERVACUO. Woult let the bastard shame us?
AMBITIOSO. Hold, hold, brother;
　　There's fitter time than now.
SUPERVACUO. Now, when I see it!
AMBITIOSO. 'Tis too much seen already.
SUPERVACUO. Seen and known,
　　The nobler she's, the baser is she grown.
AMBITIOSO. If she were bent lasciviously, the fault
　　Of mighty women that sleep soft. Oh, death,
　　Must she needs choose such an unequal sinner
　　To make all worse?
SUPERVACUO. A bastard, the duke's bastard!
　　Shame heap'd on shame!
AMBITIOSO. Oh, our disgrace!
　　Most women have small waist the world throughout,
　　But their desires are thousand miles about.
SUPERVACUO. Come, stay not here, let's after and prevent,
　　Or else they'll sin faster than we'll repent.

SCENE IV. VINDICI'*s house.*

[*Enter* VINDICI *and* HIPPOLITO *bringing out their mother* GRATIANA, *one by one shoulder, and the other by the other, with daggers in their hands.*]

VINDICI. Oh, thou for whom no name is bad enough!
GRATIANA. What means my sons? What, will you murder me?
VINDICI. Wicked, unnatural parent!
HIPPOLITO. Fiend of women!
GRATIANA. Oh! Are sons turn'd monsters? Help!
VINDICI. In vain.
GRATIANA. Are you so barbarous to set iron nipples
　　Upon the breast that gave you suck?

VINDICI. That breast
    Is turned to quarled poison.
GRATIANA. Cut not your days for't: am not I your mother?
VINDICI. Thou dost usurp that title now by fraud,
    For in that shell of mother breeds a bawd.
GRATIANA. A bawd? Oh, name far loathsomer than hell!
HIPPOLITO. It should be so, knew'st thou thy office well.
GRATIANA. I hate it!
VINDICI. Ah, is't possible, you powers on high,
    That women should dissemble when they die?
GRATIANA. Dissemble!
VINDICI. Did not the duke's son direct
    A fellow of the world's condition hither,
    That did corrupt all that was good in thee,
    Made thee uncivilly forget thyself,
    And work our sister to his lust?
GRATIANA. Who, I?
    That had been monstrous! I defy that man
    For any such intent: none lives so pure
    But shall be soil'd with slander.
    Good son, believe it not.
VINDICI. Oh, I'm in doubt,
    Whether I'm myself or no.
    Stay, let me look again upon this face.
    Who shall be sav'd when mothers have no grace?
HIPPOLITO. 'Twould make one half despair.
VINDICI. I was the man.
    Defy me now? Let's see do't modestly.
GRATIANA. Oh, hell unto my soul!
VINDICI. In that disguise, I sent from the duke's son,
    Tried you, you, and found you base metal
    As any villain might have done.
GRATIANA. Oh, no,
    No tongue but yours could have bewitch'd me so.
VINDICI. Oh, nimble in damnation, quick in tune;
    There is no devil could strike fire so soon!
    I am confuted in a word.
GRATIANA. Oh, sons,
    Forgive me; to myself I'll prove more true:
    You that should honour me, I kneel to you.
VINDICI. A mother to give aim to her own daughter.
HIPPOLITO. True, brother, how far beyond nature 'tis,
    Tho' many mothers do't.
VINDICI. Nay, and you draw tears once, go you to bed.
    Wet will make iron blush and change to red:
    Brother, it rains, 'twill spoil your dagger; house it.
HIPPOLITO. 'Tis done.
VINDICI. I'faith, 'tis a sweet shower; it does much good.

The fruitful grounds and meadows of her soul
Has been long dry: pour down thou blessed dew.
Rise, mother; troth, this shower has made you higher.
GRATIANA. Oh, you heavens!
Take this infectious spot out of my soul;
I'll rinse it in seven waters of mine eyes.
Make my tears salt enough to taste of grace.
To weep is to our sex naturally given,
But to weep truly, that's a gift from heaven.
VINDICI. Nay, I'll kiss you now. Kiss her, brother.
Let's marry her to our souls, wherein's no lust,
And honourably love her.
HIPPOLITO. Let it be.
VINDICI. For honest women are so seld and rare,
'Tis good to cherish those poor few that are.
Oh, you of easy wax, do but imagine
Now the disease has left you, how leprously
That office would have cling'd unto your forehead.
All mothers that had any graceful hue
Would have worn masks to hide their face at you;
It would have grown to this: at your foul name
Green-colour'd maids would have turn'd red with shame.
HIPPOLITO. And then our sister, full of hire and baseness—
VINDICI. There had been boiling lead again.
The duke's son's great concubine!
A drab of state, a cloth-a'-silver slut,
To have her train borne up and her soul trail
I' th' dirt: great!
HIPPOLITO. To be miserably great; rich,
To be eternally wretched.
VINDICI. Oh, common madness!
Ask but the thriving'st harlot in cold blood,
She'd give the world to make her honour good.
Perhaps you'll say but only to th' duke's son
In private; why, she first begins with one
Who afterward to thousand proves a whore:
"Break ice in one place, it will crack in more."
GRATIANA. Most certainly applied.
HIPPOLITO. Oh, brother, you forget our business.
VINDICI. And well rememb'red; joy's a subtle elf:
I think man's happiest when he forgets himself.
Farewell, once dried, now holy-wat'red mead;
Our hearts wear feathers that before wore lead.
GRATIANA. I'll give you this, that one I never knew
Plead better for and 'gainst the devil than you.
VINDICI. You make me proud on't.
HIPPOLITO. Commend us in all virtue to our sister.
VINDICI. Ay, for the love of heaven, to that true maid.

GRATIANA. With my best words.
VINDICI. Why, that was motherly said.

[*Exeunt* VINDICI *and* HIPPOLITO.]

GRATIANA. I wonder now what fury did transport me?
    I feel good thoughts begin to settle in me.
    Oh, with what forehead can I look on her
    Whose honour I've so impiously beset?

[*Enter* CASTIZA.]

    And here she comes.
CASTIZA. Now, mother, you have wrought with me so strongly
    That what for my advancement, as to calm
    The trouble of your tongue: I am content.
GRATIANA. Content to what?
CASTIZA. To do as you have wish'd me,
    To prostitute my breast to the duke's son,
    And to put myself to common usury.
GRATIANA. I hope you will not so!
CASTIZA. Hope you I will not?
    That's not the hope you look to be saved in.
GRATIANA. Truth, but it is.
CASTIZA. Do not deceive yourself;
    I am as you e'en out of marble wrought.
    What would you now? Are ye not pleas'd yet with me?
    You shall not wish me to be more lascivious
    Than I intend to be.
GRATIANA. Strike not me cold.
CASTIZA. How often have you charg'd me on your blessing
    To be a cursed woman! When you knew
    Your blessing had no force to make me lewd,
    You laid your curse upon me. That did more;
    The mother's curse is heavy: where that fights,
    Suns set in storm and daughters lose their lights.
GRATIANA. Good child, dear maid, if there be any spark
    Of heavenly intellectual fire within thee,
    Oh, let my breath revive it to a flame!
    Put not all out with woman's wilful follies.
    I am recover'd of that foul disease
    That haunts too many mothers. Kind, forgive me;
    Make me not sick in health: if then
    My words prevail'd when they were wickedness,
    How much more now when they are just and good?
CASTIZA. I wonder what you mean. Are not you she
    For whose infect persuasions I could scarce
    Kneel out my prayers, and had much ado

In three hours reading to untwist so much
Of the black serpent as you wound about me?
GRATIANA. 'Tis unfruitful, held tedious to repeat what's past;
I'm now your present mother.
CASTIZA. Push, now 'tis too late.
GRATIANA. Bethink again, thou know'st not what thou sayst.
CASTIZA. No? Deny advancement, treasure, the duke's son?
GRATIANA. Oh, see,
I spoke those words, and now they poison me!
What will the deed do then?
Advancement? True, as high as shame can pitch.
For treasure, whoe'er knew a harlot rich,
Or could build by the purchase of her sin
An hospital to keep their bastards in?
The duke's son! Oh, when women are young courtiers,
They are sure to be old beggars!
To know the miseries most harlots taste,
Thou'dst wish thyself unborn when thou art unchaste.
CASTIZA. Oh, mother, let me twine about your neck,
And kiss you till my soul melt on your lips:
I did but this to try you.
GRATIANA. Oh, speak truth!
CASTIZA. Indeed, I did not, for no tongue has force
To alter me from honest.
If maidens would, men's words could have no power.
A virgin honour is a crystal tower,
Which being weak is guarded with good spirits:
Until she basely yields no ill inherits.
GRATIANA. Oh, happy child! Faith and thy birth hath saved me.
'Mongst thousands daughters happiest of all others!
Be thou a glass for maids, and I for mothers.

[*Exeunt.*]

ACT V.

SCENE I. *A room in the palace.*

[*Enter* VINDICI *and* HIPPOLITO *with the* DUKE's *corpse in* PIATO's *clothes, which they prop up in chair.*]

VINDICI. So, so, he leans well; take heed you wake him not, brother.
HIPPOLITO. I warrant you, my life for yours.
VINDICI. That's a good lay, for I must kill myself!
Brother, that's I: that sits for me, do you mark it?
And I must stand ready here to make away myself yonder: I must sit to be kill'd, and stand to kill myself. I could vary it not so little as thrice over again, 't 'as some eight returns like Michaelmas Term.

HIPPOLITO. That's enow, a' conscience.

VINDICI. But, sirrah, does the duke's son come single?

HIPPOLITO. No, there's the hell on't, his faith's too feeble to go alone; he brings flesh-flies after him that will buzz against suppertime and hum for his coming out.

VINDICI. Ah, the fly-flop of vengeance beat 'em to pieces! Here was the sweetest occasion, the fittest hour, to have made my revenge familiar with him, show him the body of the duke his father, and how quaintly he died like a politician in huggermugger, made no man acquainted with it, and in catastrophe slain him over his father's breast, and oh, I'm mad to lose such a sweet opportunity!

HIPPOLITO. Nay, push, prithee be content! There's no remedy present; may not hereafter times open in as fair faces as this?

VINDICI. They may if they can paint so well.

HIPPOLITO. Come, now to avoid all suspicion, let's forsake this room, and be going to meet the duke's son.

VINDICI. Content, I'm for any weather.

[*Enter* LUSSURIOSO.]

Heart, step close, here he comes!

HIPPOLITO. My honour'd lord?

LUSSURIOSO. Oh, me; you both present?

VINDICI. E'en newly, my lord, just as your lordship *enter*'d now; about this place we had notice given he should be, but in some loathsome plight or other.

HIPPOLITO. Came your honour private?

LUSSURIOSO. Private enough for this: only a few
    Attend my coming out.

HIPPOLITO. [*aside.*] Death rot those few!

LUSSURIOSO. Stay, yonder's the slave.

VINDICI. Mass, there's the slave indeed, my lord!
    [*aside.*] 'Tis a good child, he calls his father slave.

LUSSURIOSO. Ay, that's the villain, the damn'd villain: softly,
    Tread easy.

VINDICI. Puh, I warrant you, my lord,
    We'll stifle in our breaths.

LUSSURIOSO. That will do well.
    [*aside.*] Base rogue, thou sleepest thy last; 'tis policy
    To have him kill'd in's sleep, for if he wak'd
    He would betray all to them.

VINDICI. But, my lord—

LUSSURIOSO. Ha, what sayst?

VINDICI. Shall we kill him now he's drunk?

LUSSURIOSO. Ay, best of all.

VINDICI. Why, then he will ne'er live to be sober.

LUSSURIOSO. No matter, let him reel to hell.

VINDICI. But being so full of liquor, I fear he will put out all the fire—

LUSSURIOSO. Thou art a mad beast.

VINDICI. And leave none to warm your lordship's golls withal,
    For he that dies drunk falls into hellfire

Like a bucket a' water, qush, qush.
LUSSURIOSO. Come, be ready, nake your swords; think of your wrongs:
    This slave has injur'd you.
VINDICI. [*aside.*] Troth, so he has,
    And he has paid well for't.
LUSSURIOSO. Meet with him now.
VINDICI. You'll bear us out, my lord?
LUSSURIOSO. Puh, am I a lord for nothing think you? Quickly, now.
VINDICI. Sa, sa, sa! [*Stabs the corpse.*] Thump, there he lies.
LUSSURIOSO. Nimbly done. Ha? Oh, villains, murderers,
    'Tis the old duke my father!
VINDICI. That's a jest.
LUSSURIOSO. What stiff and cold already?
    Oh, pardon me to call you from your names;
    'Tis none of your deed: that villain Piato,
    Whom you thought now to kill, has murder'd him
    And left him thus disguis'd.
HIPPOLITO. And not unlikely.
VINDICI. Oh, rascal! Was he not asham'd
    To put the duke into a greasy doublet?
LUSSURIOSO. He has been cold and stiff who knows how long?
VINDICI. [*aside.*] Marry, that do I!
LUSSURIOSO. No words, I pray, of anything intended.
VINDICI. Oh, my lord!
HIPPOLITO. I would fain have your lordship think that we have small reason to prate.
LUSSURIOSO. Faith, thou sayst true; I'll forthwith send to court
    For all the nobles, bastard, duchess, all,
    How here by miracle we found him dead,
    And in his raiment that foul villain fled.
VINDICI. That will be the best way, my lord, to clear us all: let's cast about to be clear.
LUSSURIOSO. Ho, Nencio, Sordido, and the rest!

[*Enter all* LUSSURIOSO's *attendants.*]

SORDIDO. My lord.
NENCIO. My lord.
LUSSURIOSO. Be witnesses of a strange spectacle:
    Choosing for private conference that sad room,
    We found the duke my father 'geal'd in blood.
SORDIDO. My lord, the duke! Run, hie thee, Nencio,
    Startle the court by signifying so much.

[*Exit* NENCIO.]

VINDICI. [*aside to* HIPPOLITO.] Thus much by wit a deep revenger can:
    When murder's known, to be the clearest man.
    We're fardest off, and with as bold an eye
    Survey his body as the standers-by.

LUSSURIOSO. My royal father, too basely let blood
    By a malevolent slave!
HIPPOLITO. [*aside to* VINDICI.] Hark, he calls thee slave again.
VINDICI. [*aside to* HIPPOLITO.] Ha's lost, he may.
LUSSURIOSO. Oh, sight, look hither! See, his lips are gnawn with poison!
VINDICI. How! His lips? By th' mass, they be!
LUSSURIOSO. Oh, villain! Oh, rogue! Oh, slave! Oh, rascal!
HIPPOLITO. [*aside.*] Oh, good deceit! He quits him with like terms.

[*Enter* AMBITIOSO, SUPERVACUO, SPURIO, DUCHESS, *the* DUKE's
    GENTLEMEN, NOBLES, *and* GUARDS.]

FIRST NOBLE. Where?
SECOND NOBLE. Which way?
AMBITIOSO. Over what roof hangs this prodigious comet
    In deadly fire?
LUSSURIOSO. Behold, behold, my lords:
    The duke my father's murder'd by a vassal
    That owes this habit, and here left disguis'd.
DUCHESS. My lord and husband!
SECOND NOBLE. Reverend majesty!
FIRST NOBLE. I have seen these clothes often attending on him.
VINDICI. [*aside.*] That nobleman has been i' th' country, for he does not lie.
SUPERVACUO. [*aside to* AMBITIOSO.] Learn of our mother; let's dissemble too.
    I am glad he's vanish'd; so I hope are you.
AMBITIOSO. [*aside to* SUPERVACUO.] Ay, you may take my word for't.
SPURIO. [*aside.*] Old Dad dead?
    Ay, one of his cast sins will send the fates
    Most hearty commendations by his own son.
    I'll tug the new stream till strength be done.
LUSSURIOSO. Where be those two that did affirm to us
    My lord the duke was privately rid forth?
FIRST GENTLEMAN. Oh, pardon us, my lords, he gave that charge
    Upon our lives if he were miss'd at court
    To answer so; he rode not anywhere,
    We left him private with that fellow here.
VINDICI. [*aside.*] Confirm'd.
LUSSURIOSO. Oh heavens, that false charge was his death!
    Impudent beggars, durst you to our face,
    Maintain such a false answer? Bear him straight
    To execution.
FIRST GENTLEMAN. My lord!
LUSSURIOSO. Urge me no more.
    In this excuse may be call'd half the murther.
VINDICI. [*aside.*] You've sentenc'd well.
LUSSURIOSO. Away, see it be done.

[*Exit the* FIRST GENTLEMAN, *guarded.*]

VINDICI. [*aside.*] Could you not stick? See what confession doth.
    Who would not lie when men are hang'd for truth?
HIPPOLITO. [*aside to* VINDICI.] Brother, how happy is our vengeance?
VINDICI. [*aside to* HIPPOLITO.] Why, it hits,
    Past the apprehension of indifferent wits.
LUSSURIOSO. My lord, let post-horse be sent
    Into all places to entrap the villain.
VINDICI. [*aside.*] Post-horse? Ha, ha!
FIRST NOBLE. My lord, we're something bold to know our duty.
    You father's accidentally departed;
    The titles that were due to him meet you.
LUSSURIOSO. Meet me? I'm not at leisure, my good lord;
    I've many griefs to dispatch out a' th' way.
    [*aside.*] Welcome, sweet titles!—Talk to me, my lords,
    Of sepulchers and mighty emperors' bones,
    That's thought for me.
VINDICI. [*aside.*] So, one may see by this
    How foreign markets go:
    Courtiers have feet a' th' nines and tongues a' th' twelves;
    They flatter dukes and dukes flatter themselves.
FIRST NOBLE. My lord, it is your shine must comfort us.
LUSSURIOSO. Alas, I shine in tears like the sun in April.
FIRST NOBLE. You're now my lord's grace.
LUSSURIOSO. My lord's grace? I perceive you'll have it so.
FIRST NOBLE. 'Tis but your own.
LUSSURIOSO. Then heavens give me grace to be so.
VINDICI. [*aside.*] He prays well for himself.
FIRST NOBLE. Madam, all sorrows
    Must run their circles into joys; no doubt but time
    Will make the murderer bring forth himself.
VINDICI. [*aside.*] He were an ass then, i'faith.
FIRST NOBLE. In the mean season,
    Let us bethink the latest funeral honours
    Due to the duke's cold body, and withal,
    Calling to memory our new happiness,
    Spread in his royal son: lords, gentlemen,
    Prepare for revels.
VINDICI. [*aside.*] Revels!
NOBLE. Time hath several falls.
    Griefs lift up joys, feasts put down funerals.
LUSSURIOSO. Come then, my lords, my favours to you all.
    [*aside.*] The duchess is suspected foully bent;
    I'll begin dukedom with her banishment.

    [*Exeunt Duke* LUSSURIOSO, NOBLES, GENTLEMEN, ATTENDANTS, *and*
    DUCHESS.]

HIPPOLITO. [*aside to* VINDICI.] Revels!
VINDICI. [*aside to* HIPPOLITO.] Ay, that's the word; we are firm yet:
    Strike one strain more and then we crown our wit.

[*Exeunt brothers* VINDICI *and* HIPPOLITO.]

SPURIO. Well, have the fairest mark, so said the duke when he begot me,
    And if I miss his heart or near about,
    Then have at any: a bastard scorns to be out.

[*Exit* SPURIO.]

SUPERVACUO. Not'st thou that Spurio, brother?
AMBITIOSO. Yes, I note him to our shame.
SUPERVACUO. He shall not live; his hair shall not grow much longer: in this time of
    revels, tricks may be set afoot. Seest thou yon new moon? It shall out-live the new
    duke by much; this hand shall dispossess him, then we're mighty.
    A masque is treason's license; that build upon:
    'Tis murder's best face when a vizard's on.

[*Exit* SUPERVACUO.]

AMBITIOSO. Is't so? 'Tis very good.
    And do you think to be duke then, kind brother?
    I'll see fair play: drop one and there lies t'other.

[*Exit* AMBITIOSO.]

SCENE II. VINDICI'*s house.*

[*Enter* VINDICI *and* HIPPOLITO, *with* PIERO *and other* LORDS.]

VINDICI. My lords, be all of music; strike old griefs into other countries
    That flow in too much milk and have faint livers,
    Not daring to stab home their discontents:
    Let our hid flames break out as fire, as lightning,
    To blast this villainous dukedom vex'd with sin;
    Wind up your souls to their full height again.
PIERO. How?
FIRST LORD. Which way?
THIRD LORD. Any way: our wrongs are such,
    We cannot justly be reveng'd too much.
VINDICI. You shall have all enough. Revels are toward,
    And those few nobles that have long suppress'd you
    Are busied to the furnishing of a masque,
    And do affect to make a pleasant tale on't.
    The masquing suits are fashioning; now comes in
    That which must glad us all: we to take pattern

Of all those suits, the colour, trimming, fashion,
E'en to an undistinguish'd hair almost,
Then ent'ring first, observing the true form,
Within a strain or two we shall find leisure
To steal our swords out handsomely,
And when they think their pleasure sweet and good,
In midst of all their joys, they shall sigh blood.
PIERO. Weightily, effectually.
THIRD LORD. Before the t'other masquers come.
VINDICI. We're gone, all done and past.
PIERO. But how for the duke's guard?
VINDICI. Let that alone;
By one and one their strengths shall be drunk down.
HIPPOLITO. There are five hundred gentlemen in the action
That will apply themselves and not stand idle.
PIERO. Oh, let us hug your bosoms!
VINDICI. Come, my lords,
Prepare for deeds; let other times have words.

[*Exeunt.*]

SCENE III. *The palace banqueting hall.*

[*In a dumb show, the possessing of the young duke* LUSSURIOSO *with all his*
NOBLES. *Then sounding music, a furnish'd table is brought forth; then enters
the duke* LUSSURIOSO *and his three* NOBLES *to the banquet. A blazing star
appeareth.*]

FIRST NOBLE. Many harmonious hours and choicest pleasures
Fill up the royal numbers of your years.
LUSSURIOSO. My lords, we're pleas'd to thank you [*aside.*] tho' we know
'Tis but your duty now to wish it so.
FIRST NOBLE. That shine makes us all happy.
THIRD NOBLE. [*aside.*] His grace frowns?
SECOND NOBLE. [*aside.*] Yet we must say he smiles.
FIRST NOBLE. [*aside.*] I think we must.
LUSSURIOSO. [*aside.*] That foul, incontinent duchess we have banish'd;
The bastard shall not live: after these revels
I'll begin strange ones; he and the stepsons
Shall pay their lives for the first subsidies.
We must not frown so soon, else 't 'ad been now.
FIRST NOBLE. My gracious lord, please you prepare for pleasure:
The masque is not far off.
LUSSURIOSO. We are for pleasure.
[*To the comet.*] Beshrew thee, what art thou mad'st me start?
Thou hast committed treason: a blazing star!
FIRST NOBLE. A blazing star? Oh, where, my lord?
LUSSURIOSO. Spy out!

SECOND NOBLE. See, see, my lords: a wondrous, dreadful one.
LUSSURIOSO. I am not pleas'd at that ill-knotted fire,
    That bushing, flaring star. Am not I duke?
    It should not quake me now: had it appear'd
    Before it, I might then have justly fear'd;
    But yet they say, whom art and learning weds,
    When stars [wear.] locks, they threaten great men's heads.
    Is it so? You are read, my lords.
FIRST NOBLE. May it please your grace,
    It shows great anger.
LUSSURIOSO. That does not please our grace.
SECOND NOBLE. Yet here's the comfort, my lord: many times
    When it seems most, it threatens fardest off.
LUSSURIOSO. Faith, and I think so too.
FIRST NOBLE. Beside, my lord,
    You're gracefully establish'd with the loves
    Of all your subjects: and for natural death,
    I hope it will be threescore years a-coming.
LUSSURIOSO. True. No more but threescore years?
FIRST NOBLE. Fourscore I hope, my lord.
SECOND NOBLE. And fivescore, I.
THIRD NOBLE. But 'tis my hope, my lord, you shall ne'er die.
LUSSURIOSO. Give me thy hand; these others I rebuke.
    He that hopes so is fittest for a duke.
    Thou shalt sit next me; take your places, lords:
    We're ready now for sports; let 'em set on.
    [*To the comet.*] You thing, we shall forget you quite anon!
THIRD NOBLE. I hear 'em coming, my lord.

    [*Enter the Masque of* REVENGERS: *the two brothers,* VINDICI *and* HIPPOLITO,
    and *two* LORDS *more.*]

LUSSURIOSO. Ah, 'tis well.
    [*aside.*] Brothers and bastard, you dance next in hell.

    [*The* REVENGERS *dance. At the end, steal out their swords and these four kill the*
    four at the table in their chairs. It thunders.]

VINDICI. Mark thunder?
    Dost know thy cue, thou big-voic'd crier?
    Dukes' groans are thunder's watchwords.
HIPPOLITO. So, my lords, you have enough.
VINDICI. Come, let's away, no ling'ring.
HIPPOLITO. Follow, go.

    [*Exeunt* HIPPOLITO *and the two* LORDS.]

VINDICI. No power is angry when the lustful die;

When thunder claps, heaven likes the tragedy.

[*Exit* VINDICI. *Enter the other masque of intended murderers: stepsons* AMBITIOSO, SUPERVACUO, *bastard* SPURIO, *and a Fourth Man* AMBITIOSO's *henchman, coming in dancing; the duke* LUSSURIOSO *recovers a little in voice and groans, calls, "A guard, treason," at which they all start out of their measure, and turning towards the table, they find them all to be murdered.*]

LUSSURIOSO. Oh, oh!
SPURIO. Whose groan was that?
LUSSURIOSO. Treason, a guard!
AMBITIOSO. How now? All murder'd!
SUPERVACUO. Murder'd!
FOURTH MAN. And those his nobles?
AMBITIOSO. Here's a labour sav'd:
    I thought to have sped him. 'Sblood, how came this?
SUPERVACUO. Then I proclaim myself: now I am duke.
AMBITIOSO. Thou duke! Brother, thou liest.

    [*Kills* SUPERVACUO.]

SPURIO. Slave, so dost thou!

    [*Kills* AMBITIOSO.]

FOURTH MAN. Base villain, hast thou slain my lord and master?

    [*Kills* SPURIO. *Enter the first men* VINDICI, HIPPOLITO, *the two* LORDS.]

VINDICI. Pistols, treason, murder! Help, guard my lord the duke!

    [*Enter* ANTONIO, *guards.*]

HIPPOLITO. Lay hold upon this traitor!

    [*The guards seize the* FOURTH MAN.]

LUSSURIOSO. Oh!
VINDICI. Alas, the duke is murder'd!
HIPPOLITO. And the nobles!
VINDICI. Surgeons, surgeons! Heart, does he breathe so long?
ANTONIO. A piteous tragedy, able to make
    An old man's eyes bloodshot.
LUSSURIOSO. Oh!
VINDICI. Look to my lord the duke! [*aside.*] A vengeance throttle him!
    [*To the* FOURTH MAN.] Confess, thou murd'rous and unhallowed man,
    Didst thou kill all these?

FOURTH MAN. None but the bastard I.

VINDICI. How came the duke slain then?

FOURTH MAN. We found him so.

LUSSURIOSO. Oh, villain!

VINDICI. Hark!

LUSSURIOSO. Those in the masque did murder us.

VINDICI. Law you now, sir.
Oh, marble impudence! Will you confess now?

FOURTH MAN. 'Sblood, 'tis all false!

ANTONIO. Away with that foul monster,
Dipp'd in a prince's blood!

FOURTH MAN. Heart, 'tis a lie!

ANTONIO. Let him have bitter execution.

[*Exit* FOURTH MAN, *guarded.*]

VINDICI. [*aside.*] New marrow! No, I cannot be express'd!—
How fares my lord the duke?

LUSSURIOSO. Farewell to all;
He that climbs highest has the greatest fall.
My tongue is out of office.

VINDICI. Air, gentlemen, air!
[*Whispering.*] Now thou'lt not prate on't, 'twas Vindici murd'red thee—

LUSSURIOSO. Oh!

VINDICI. Murd'red thy father—

LUSSURIOSO. Oh!

VINDICI. And I am he.
Tell nobody. [LUSSURIOSO *dies.*] So, so, the duke's departed.

ANTONIO. It was a deadly hand that wounded him.
The rest, ambitious who should rule and sway,
After his death were so made all away.

VINDICI. My lord was unlikely.

HIPPOLITO. Now the hope
Of Italy lies in your reverend years.

VINDICI. Your hair will make the silver age again,
When there was fewer but more honest men.

ANTONIO. The burden's weighty and will press age down;
May I so rule that heaven [may.] keep the crown.

VINDICI. The rape of your good lady has been quitted
With death on death.

ANTONIO. Just is the law above.
But of all things it puts me most to wonder
How the old duke came murd'red.

VINDICI. Oh, my lord!

ANTONIO. It was the strangeliest carried, I not heard
Of the like.

HIPPOLITO. 'Twas all done for the best, my lord.

VINDICI. All for your grace's good; we may be bold to speak it now,

'Twas somewhat witty carried, tho' we say it.
'Twas we two murd'red him.
ANTONIO. You two?
VINDICI. None else, i'faith, my lord; nay, 'twas well manag'd.
ANTONIO. Lay hands upon those villains!

[GUARDS *seize* Vindici *and* Hippolito.]

VINDICI. How? On us?
ANTONIO. Bear 'em to speedy execution.
VINDICI. Heart, was't not for your good, my lord?
ANTONIO. My good! Away with 'em! Such an old man as he!
    You that would murder him would murder me.
VINDICI. Is't come about?
HIPPOLITO. 'Sfoot, brother, you begun.
VINDICI. May not we set as well as the duke's son?
    Thou hast no conscience: are we not reveng'd?
    Is there one enemy left alive amongst those?
    'Tis time to die when we are ourselves our foes.
    When murders shut deeds close, this curse does seal 'em:
    If none disclose 'em they themselves reveal 'em!
    This murder might have slept in tongueless brass
    But for ourselves, and the world died an ass.
    Now I remember too, here was Piato
    Brought forth a knavish sentence: no doubt, said he,
    But time will make the murderer bring forth himself.
    'Tis well he died; he was a witch.
    And now, my lord, since we are in forever,
    This work was ours which else might have been slipp'd,
    And if we list, we could have nobles clipp'd
    And go for less than beggars, but we hate
    To bleed so cowardly; we have enough. I'faith,
    We're well: our mother turn'd, our sister true,
    We die after a nest of dukes. Adieu.

[*Exeunt* VINDICI *and* HIPPOLITO, *guarded*).]

ANTONIO. How subtly was that murder clos'd! Bear up
    Those tragic bodies; 'tis a heavy season:
    Pray heaven their blood may wash away all treason.

[*Exeunt omnes.*]

FINIS.

THE REVENGE OF BUSSY D'AMBOIS.

By GEORGE CHAPMAN

SOURCES

The story of a plot by Bussy D'Ambois's kinsfolk to avenge his murder is, in the main, of Chapman's own invention. But he had evidently read an account similar to that given later by De Thou of the design entertained for a time by Bussy's sister Renée (whom Chapman calls Charlotte) and her husband, Baligny, to take vengeance on Montsurry. Clermont D'Ambois is himself a fictitious character, but the episodes in which appears in Acts II-IV are drawn from the account of the treacherous proceedings against the Count d'Auvergne in Edward Grimeston's translation of Jean de Serres's *Inventaire Général de l'Histoire de France*. This narrative, however, is not by De Serres, but by Pierre Matthieu, whose *Histoire de France* was one of the sources used by Grimeston for events later than 1598.

The portraiture of Clermont throughout the play as the high-souled philosopher is inspired by Epictetus's delineation in his *Discourses* of the ideal Stoic. But in his reluctance to carry out his duty of revenge he is evidently modeled upon Hamlet. In Act V, Scene I, the influence of Shakespeare's tragedy is specially manifest.

The Scenes in Act V relating to the assassination of Guise are based upon Grimeston's translation of De Serres's *Inventaire Général*.

TO THE RIGHT VIRTUOUS, AND TRULY NOBLE KNIGHT, SR. THOMAS HOWARD,[1] &C.

Sir,

Since works of this kind have been lately esteemed worthy the patronage of some of our worthiest Nobles, I have made no doubt to prefer this of mine to your undoubted virtue and exceeding true noblesse, as containing matter no less deserving your reading, and excitation to heroic life, then any such late dedication. Nor have the greatest Princes of Italy and other countries conceived it any least diminution to their greatness to have their names winged with these tragic plumes, and dispersed by way of patronage through the most noble notices of Europe.

Howsoever, therefore, in the scenic presentation it might meet with some maligners, yet, considering even therein it past with approbation of more worthy judgments, the balance of their side (especially being held by your impartial hand) I hope will to no grain abide the out-weighing. And for the authentic truth of either person or action, who (worth the respecting) will expect it in a poem, whose subject is not truth, but things like truth? Poor envious souls they are that cavil at truths want in these natural fictions: material

---

[1] Thomas Howard, born before 1594, was the second son of the first Earl of Suffolk. He was created a Knight of the Bath in January, 1605, and in May, 1614, was appointed Master of the Horse to Charles, Prince of Wales. In 1622 he became Viscount Andover, and in 1626 Earl of Berkshire. He held a number of posts till the outbreak of the Civil War, and after the Restoration was appointed Gentleman of the Bedchamber to Charles II, and Privy Councilor. He died on July 16, 1669. His daughter Elizabeth married Dryden, and his sixth son, Sir Robert Howard, became distinguished as a dramatic writer and critic. Chapman addresses to this patron one of the Sonnets appended to his translation of the *Iliad*, in which he compares him to Antilochus, and calls him "valiant, and mild, and most ingenious."

instruction, elegant and sententious excitation to virtue, and deflection from her contrary, being the soul, limbs, and limits of an authentic tragedy. But whatsoever merit of your full countenance and favor suffers defect in this, I shall soon supply with some other of more general account; wherein your right virtuous name made famous and preserved to posterity, your future comfort and Honor in your present acceptation and love of all virtuous and divine expression may be so much past others of your rank increased, as they are short of your judicial ingenuity, in their due estimation.

For howsoever those ignoble and sour-browed worldlings are careless of whatsoever future or present opinion spreads of them; yet (with the most divine philosopher,[2] if Scripture did not confirm it) I make it matter of my faith, that we truly retain an intellectual feeling of good or bad after this life, proportionally answerable to the love or neglect we bear here to all virtue and truly-humane instruction: in whose favor and Honor I wish you most eminent, and rest ever,

Your true virtues
most true observer,
Geo. Chapman.

DRAMATIS PERSONAE.

HENRY, *the King.*
MONSIEUR, *his Brother.*
GUISE, *Duke.*
RENEL, *a Marquess.*
MONTSUREAU, *an Earl.*
BALIGNY, *Lord Lieutenant of Cambray.*
CLERMONT D'AMBOIS.
MAILLARD, *a Captain.*
CHALLON, *a Captain.*
AUMAL, *a Captain.*
ESPERNONE.
SOISSONE.
PERRICOT, *an Usher.*
A MESSENGER.
THE GUARD.
SOLDIERS.
SERVANTS.
THE GHOST OF BUSSY.
THE GHOST OF MONSIEUR.
THE GHOST OF GUISE.
THE GHOST OF CARD. GUISE.
THE GHOST OF SHATTILION.
COUNTESS *of Cambray.*
TAMYRA, *wife to Montsureau.*
CHARLOTTE D'AMBOIS, *wife to Baligny.*
RIOVA, *a Servant to the Countess.*

---

[2] The reference is doubtless to Epictetus, the influence of whose *Discourses* appears throughout *The Revenge of Bussy D'Ambois.*

SCENE: *Paris, and in or near Cambrai.*

ACT I.

SCENE I. *A Room at the Court in Paris.*

[*Enter* BALIGNY, RENEL.]

BALIGNY. To what will this declining kingdom turn,
    Swinging in every license, as in this
    Stupid permission of brave D'Ambois Murder?
    Murder made parallel with Law! Murder used
    To serve the kingdom, given by suit to men
    For their advancement! suffered scarecrow-like
    To fright adultery! what will policy
    At length bring under his capacity?
RENEL. All things; for as, when the high births of Kings,
    Deliverances, and coronations,
    We celebrate with all the cities bells
    Jangling together in untuned confusion,
    All ordered clocks are tied up; so, when glory,
    Flattery, and smooth applauses of things ill,
    Uphold th' inordinate swing of down-right power,
    Justice, and truth that tell the bounded use,
    Virtuous and well distinguished forms of time,
    Are gagged and tongue-tide. But we have observed
    Rule in more regular motion: things most lawful
    Were once most royal; Kings sought common good,
    Men's manly liberties, though ne'er so mean,
    And had their own swing so more free, and more.
    But when pride entered them, and rule by power,
    All brows that smiled beneath them, frowned; hearts grieved
    By imitation; virtue quite was vanished,
    And all men studied self-love, fraud, and vice.
    Then no man could be good but he was punished.
    Tyrants, being still more fearful of the good
    Than of the bad, their subjects virtues ever
    Managed with curbs and dangers, and esteemed
    As shadows and detractions to their own.
BALIGNY. Now all is peace, no danger, now what follows?
    Idleness rusts us, since no virtuous labor
    Ends ought rewarded; ease, security,
    Now all the palm wears. We made war before
    So to prevent war; men with giving gifts,
    More than receiving, made our country strong;
    Our matchless race of soldiers then would spend
    In public wars, not private brawls, their spirits;
    In daring enemies, armed with meanest arms,
    Not courting strumpets, and consuming birth-rights

In apishness and envy of attire.
No labor then was harsh, no way so deep,
No rock so steep, but if a bird could scale it,
Up would our youth fly to. A foe in arms
Stirred up a much more lust of his encounter
Than of a mistress never so be-painted.
Ambition then was only scaling walls,
And over-topping turrets; fame was wealth;
Best parts, best deeds, were best nobility;
Honor with worth, and wealth well got or none.
Countries we won with as few men as countries:
Virtue subdued all.
RENEL. Just: and then our nobles
    Loved virtue so, they praised and used it to;
    Had rather do than say; their own deeds hearing
    By others glorified, than be so barren
    That their parts only stood in praising others.
BALIGNY. Who could not do, yet praised, and envied not;
    Civil behavior flourished; bounty flowed;
    Avarice to upland bores, slaves, hang-men banished.
RENEL. 'tis now quite otherwise. But to note the cause
    Of all these foul digressions and revolts
    From our first natures, this 'tis in a word:
    Since good arts fail, crafts and deceits are used:
    Men ignorant are idle; idle men
    Most practice what they most may do with ease,
    Fashion and favor; all their studies aiming
    At getting money, which no wise man ever
    Fed his desires with.
BALIGNY. Yet now none are wise
    That think not heavens true foolish, weighed with that.[3]
    Well, thou most worthy to be greatest Guise,
    Make with thy greatness a new world arise.[4]
    Such depressed nobles (followers of his)
    As you, myself, my lord, will find a time
    When to revenge your wrongs.
RENEL. I make no doubt:
    In mean time, I could wish the wrong were righted
    Of your slain brother in law, brave Bussy D'Ambois.
BALIGNY. That one accident was made my charge.
    My brother Bussy's sister (now my wife)
    By no suite would consent to satisfy
    My love of her with marriage, till I vowed
    To use my utmost to revenge my brother:
    But Clermont D'Ambois (Bussy's second brother)

---

[3] That do not consider heavenly bliss complete folly, when compared with money.
[4] A hypocritical appeal by Baligny to the absent Duke of Guise, of whose ambitious schemes he suspects Renel to be a supporter.

Had, since, his apparition, and excitement
To suffer none but his hand in his wreak;
Which he hath vowed, and so will needs acquit
Me of my vow made to my wife, his sister,
And undertake himself Bussy's revenge.
Yet loathing any way to give it act,
But in the noblest and most manly course,
If the Earle dares take it, he resolves to send
A challenge to him, and myself must bear it;
To which delivery I can use no means,
He is so barricaded in his house,
And armed with guard still.

RENEL. That means lay on me,
Which I can strangely make. My last lands sale,
By his great suite, stands now on price with him,[5]
And he (as you know) passing covetous,
With that blind greediness that follows gain,
Will cast no danger where her sweet feet tread.
Besides, you know, his lady, by his suite
(Wooing as freshly as when first love shot
His faultless arrows from her rosy eyes)
Now lives with him again, and she, I know,
Will join with all helps in her friends revenge.

BALIGNY. No doubt, my lord, and therefore let me pray you
To use all speed; for so on needles points
My wife's heart stands with haste of the revenge,
Being (as you know) full of her brothers fire,
That she imagines I neglect my vow;
Keeps off her kind embraces, and still asks,
"When, when, will this revenge come? when performed
Will this dull vow be?" And, I vow to heaven,
So sternly, and so past her sex she urges
My vows performance, that I almost fear
To see her, when I have awhile been absent,
Not showing her, before I speak, the blood
She so much thirsts for, freckling hands and face.

RENEL. Get you the challenge writ, and look from me
To hear your passage cleared no long time after.

[*Exit* RENEL.]

BALIGNY. All restitution to your worthiest lordship!
Whose errand I must carry to the King,
As having sworn my service in the search
Of all such malcontents and their designs,
By seeming one affected with their faction

---

[5] Is now the subject of bargaining between him and me.

And discontented humors against the state:
Nor doth my brother Clermont escape my counsel
Given to the King about his Guisean greatness,
Which (as I spice it) hath possessed the King,
Knowing his daring spirit, of much danger
Charged in it to his person; though my conscience
Dare swear him clear of any power to be
Infected with the least dishonesty:
Yet that sincerity, we politicians
Must say, grows out of envy since it cannot
Aspire to policies greatness; and the more
We work on all respects of kind and virtue,
The more our service to the King seems great,
In sparing no good that seems bad to him:
And the more bad we make the most of good,
The more our policy searcheth, and our service
Is wondered at for wisdom and sincereness.
'tis easy to make good suspected still,
Where good, and God, are made but cloaks for ill.

[*Enter* HENRY, MONSIEUR, GUISE, CLERMONT, ESPERNONE, SOISSON.
    MONSIEUR *taking leave of the* KING.][6]

See Monsieur taking now his leave for Brabant;[7]
The Guise & his dear minion, Clermont D'Ambois,
Whispering together, not of state affairs,
I durst lay wagers, (though the Guise be now
In chief heat of his faction) but of some thing
Savoring of that which all men else despise,
How to be truly noble, truly wise.
MONSIEUR. See how he hangs upon the ear of Guise,
    Like to his jewel!
EPERNONE. He's now whispering in
    Some doctrine of stability and freedom,
    Contempt of outward greatness, and the guises
    That vulgar great ones make their pride and zeal,
    Being only servile trains, and sumptuous houses,
    High places, offices.
MONSIEUR. Contempt of these
    Does he read to the Guise? 'tis passing needful,
    And he, I think, makes show to affect his doctrine.
EPERNONE. Commends, admires it—
MONSIEUR. And pursues another.
    'Tis fine hypocrisy, and cheap, and vulgar,

---

[6] Henry apparently leaves the stage, after this formal ceremony of farewell, without speaking, for he takes no part in the dialogue, and he is not mentioned among those who *exeunt* at l. 290.
    [7] The expedition of the Duke of Anjou here alluded to is that of 1582, when he was crowned Duke of Brabant at Antwerp.

Known for a covert practice, yet believed
By those abused souls that they teach and govern
No more than wives adulteries by their husbands,
They bearing it with so unmoved aspects,
Hot coming from it, as 'twere not [at] all,
Or made by custom nothing. This same D'Ambois
Hath gotten such opinion of his virtues,
Holding all learning but an art to live well,
And showing he hath learned it in his life,
Being thereby strong in his persuading others,
That this ambitious Guise, embracing him,
Is thought to embrace his virtues.
EPERNONE. Yet in some
His virtues are held false for the others vices:
For 'tis more cunning held, and much more common,
To suspect truth than falsehood: and of both
Truth still fares worse, as hardly being believed,
As 'tis unusual and rarely Known.
MONSIEUR. I'll part engendering virtue. Men affirm,
Though this same Clermont hath a D'Ambois spirit,
And breathes his brothers valour, yet his temper
Is so much past his that you cannot move him:
I'll try that temper in him.—Come, you two
Devour each other with your virtues zeal,
And leave for other friends no fragment of ye:
I wonder, Guise, you will thus ravish him
Out of my bosom, that first gave the life
His manhood breathes spirit, and means, and luster.
What do men think of me, I pray thee, Clermont?
Once give me leave (for trial of that love
That from thy brother Bussy thou inheritest)
To unclasp thy bosom.
CLERMONT. As how, sir?
MONSIEUR. Be a true glass to me, in which I may
Behold what thoughts the many-headed beast
And thou thy self breathes out concerning me,
My ends and new upstarted state in Brabant,
For which I now am bound, my higher aims
Imagined here in France: speak, man, and let
Thy words be borne as naked as thy thoughts.
O were brave Bussy living!
CLERMONT. Living, my lord!
MONSIEUR. 'Tis true thou art his brother, but durst thou
Have braved the Guise; mauger his presence, courted
His wedded lady; emptied even the dregs
Of his worst thoughts of me even to my teeth;
Discerned not me, his rising sovereign,
From any common groom, but let me hear

My grossest faults, as gross-full as they were?
Durst thou do this?
CLERMONT. I cannot tell. A man
    Does never know the goodness of his stomach
    Till he sees meat before him. Were I dared,
    Perhaps, as he was, I durst do like him.
MONSIEUR. Dare then to pour out here thy freest soul
    Of what I am.
CLERMONT. 'Tis stale, he told you it.
MONSIEUR. He only jested, spake of splene and envy;
    Thy soul, more learned, is more ingenuous,
    Searching, judicial; let me then from thee
    Hear what I am.
CLERMONT. What but the sole support,
    And most expectant hope of all our France,
    The toward victor of the whole Low Countries?
MONSIEUR. Tush, thou wilt sing encomiums of my praise!
    Is this like D'Ambois? I must vex the Guise,
    Or never look to hear free truth. Tell me,
    For Bussy lives not; he durst anger me,
    Yet, for my love, would not have feared to anger
    The King himself. Thou understandest me, dost not?
CLERMONT. I shall my lord, with study.
MONSIEUR. Dost understand thy self? I pray thee tell me,
    Dost never search thy thoughts, what my design
    Might be to entertain thee and thy brother?
    What turn I meant to serve with you?
CLERMONT. Even what you please to think.
MONSIEUR. But what thinkest thou?
    Had I no end in it, thinkest?
CLERMONT. I think you had.
MONSIEUR. When I took in such two as you two were,
    A ragged couple of decayed commanders,[8]
    When a French-crown would plentifully serve
    To buy you both to anything in the earth—
CLERMONT. So it would you.
MONSIEUR. Nay bought you both out-right,
    You and your trunks—I fear me, I offend thee.
CLERMONT. No, not a jot.
MONSIEUR. The most renowned soldier,
    Epaminondas (as good authors say)
    Had no more suites than backs, but you two shared
    But one suite twixt you both, when both your studies
    Were not what meat to dine with, if your partridge,
    Your snipe, your wood-cock, lark, or your red herring,

---

[8] Monsieur's description in these and the following lines of Clermont's and Bussy's first appearance at Court is purely fictitious.

But where to beg it; whether at my house,
Or at the Guises (for you know you were
Ambitious beggars) or at some cooks-shop,
To eternize the cooks trust, and score it up.
Dost not offend thee?
CLERMONT. No, sir. Pray proceed.
MONSIEUR. As for thy gentry, I dare boldly take
Thy honorable oath: and yet some say
Thou and thy most renowned noble brother
Came to the Court first in a keel of sea-coal.[9]
Dost not offend thee?
CLERMONT. Never doubt it, sir.
MONSIEUR. Why do I love thee, then? Why have I raked thee
Out of the dung-hill? cast my cast ward-robe on thee?
Brought thee to Court to, as I did thy brother?
Made ye my saucy bon companions?
Taught ye to call our greatest Noblemen
By the corruption of their names—Jack, Tom?
Have I blown both for nothing to this bubble?
Though thou art learned, thast no enchanting wit;
Or, were thy wit good, am I therefore bound
To keep thee for my table?
CLERMONT. Well, sir, 'twere
A good knights place. Many a proud dubbed gallant
Seeks out a poor knight's living[10] from such emrods.
MONSIEUR. Or what use else should I design thee to?
Perhaps you'll answer me—to be my pander.
CLERMONT. Perhaps I shall.
MONSIEUR. Or did the sly Guise put thee
Into my bosom to undermine my projects?
I fear thee not; for, though I be not sure
I have thy heart, I know thy brain-pan yet
To be as empty a dull piece of wainscot
As ever armed the scalp of any courtier;
A fellow only that consists of sinews;
Mere Swisser, apt for any execution.
CLERMONT. But killing of the King!
MONSIEUR. Right: now I see
Thou understandest thy self.
CLERMONT. I, and you better.
You are a Kings son borne.
MONSIEUR. Right.

---

[9] A keel was a flat-bottomed boat, used in the northeast of England, for loading and carrying coal. Afterwards the word was also used of the amount of coal a keel would carry, *i.e.* 8 chaldrons, or 21 tons 4 cwt. Sea-coal was the original term for the fossil coal borne from Newcastle to London by sea, to distinguish it from *char-coal.* Cf. Shakespeare, *Merry Wives of Windsor,* i, iv, 9, "at the latter end of a sea-coal fire."
[10] The knights of Windsor, a small body who had apartments in the Castle, and pensions, were often known as "poor knights."

CLERMONT. And a Kings brother.

MONSIEUR. True.

CLERMONT. And might not any fool have been so too,
    As well as you?

MONSIEUR. A pox upon you!

CLERMONT. You did no princely deeds
    Ere you were born (I take it) to deserve it;
    Nor did you any since that I have heard;
    Nor will do ever any, as all think.

MONSIEUR. The Devil take him! I'll no more of him.

GUISE. Nay: stay, my lord, and hear him answer you.

MONSIEUR. No more, I swear. Farewell.

[*Exeunt* MONSIEUR, ESPERNONE, SOISSON.]

GUISE. No more! Ill fortune!
    I would have given a million to have heard
    His scoffs retorted, and the insolence
    Of his high birth and greatness (which were never
    Effects of his deserts, but of his fortune)
    Made show to his dull eyes beneath the worth
    That men aspire to by their knowing virtues,
    Without which greatness is a shade, a bubble.

CLERMONT. But what one great man dreams of that but you?
    All take their births and birth-rights left to them
    (Acquired by others) for their own worths purchase,
    When many a fool in both is great as they:
    And who would think they could win with their worths
    Wealthy possessions, when, won to their hands,
    They neither can judge justly of their value,
    Nor know their use? and therefore they are puffed
    With such proud tumors as this Monsieur is,
    Enabled only by the goods they have
    To scorn all goodness: none great fill their fortunes;
    But as those men that make their houses greater,
    Their households being less, so Fortune raises
    Huge heaps of out-side in these mighty men,
    And gives them nothing in them.

GUISE. True as truth:
    And therefore they had rather drown their substance
    In superfluities of bricks and stones
    (Like Sysiphus, advancing of them ever,
    And ever pulling down) then lay the cost
    Of any sluttish corner on a man,
    Built with Gods finger, and instilled his temple.

BALIGNY. 'Tis nobly said, my lord.

GUISE. I would have these things
    Brought upon stages, to let mighty misers

See all their grave and serious miseries plaid,
    As once they were in Athens and old Rome.
CLERMONT. Nay, we must now have nothing brought on stages,
    But puppetry, and pied ridiculous antics:
    Men thither come to laugh, and feed fool-fat,
    Check at all goodness there, as being profaned:
    When, wheresoever goodness comes, she makes
    The place still sacred, though with other feet
    Never so much 'tis scandaled and polluted.
    Let me learn anything that fits a man,
    In any stables shown, as well as stages.
BALIGNY. Why, is not all the world esteemed a stage?
CLERMONT. Yes, and right worthily;[11] and stages too
    Have a respect due to them, if but only
    For what the good Greek moralist says of them:
    "Is a man proud of greatness, or of riches?
    Give me an expert actor, I'll show all,
    That can within his greatest glory fall.
    Is a man afraid with poverty and lowness?
    Give me an actor, I'll show every eye
    What he laments so, and so much doth fly,
    The best and worst of both."[12] If but for this than,
    To make the proudest out-side that most swells
    With things without him, and above his worth,
    See how small cause he has to be so blown up;
    And the most poor man, to be grieved with poorness,
    Both being so easily borne by expert actors,
    The stage and actors are not so contemptful
    As every innovating Puritan,
    And ignorant sweater out of zealous envy
    Would have the world imagine. And besides
    That all things have been likened to the mirth
    Used upon stages, and for stages fitted,
    The splenative philosopher,[13] that ever
    Laughed at them all, were worthy the enstaging.
    All objects, were they ne'er so full of tears,[14]
    He so conceited that he could distill thence
    Matter that still fed his ridiculous humor.
    Heard he a lawyer, never so vehement pleading,

---

[11] If this is a complimentary allusion to Jaques' speech in *As You Like It*, ii, vii, 140-166, it is remarkable as coming from the writer whom Shakespeare at an earlier date had probably attacked in his *Sonnets*.

[12] This passage is based upon the *Discourses* of Epictetus, bk. iv, vii, 13, which, however, Chapman completely misinterprets. Epictetus is demonstrating that a reasonable being should be able to bear any lot contentedly. "θέλεις πενίαν? φέρε καὶ γνώσῃ τί ἐστιν πενία τυχοῦσα καλοῦ ὑποκριτοῦ. θέλεις ἀρχάς? φέρε, καὶ πόνους." ὑποκρίτης is used here metaphorically, of one who acts a part in life, not, as Chapman takes it, of an actor in the professional sense.

[13] Democritus.

[14] These lines are suggested by Juvenal's *Satire*, x, ll. 33-55, but they diverge too far from the original to be merely a paraphrase, as they are termed by the editor of the 1873 reprint.

He stood and laughed. Heard he a trades-man swearing,
Never so thriftily selling of his wares,
He stood and laughed. Heard he an holy brother,
For hollow ostentation, at his prayers
Ne'er so impetuously, he stood and laughed.
Saw he a great man never so insulting,
Severely inflicting, gravely giving laws,
Not for their good, but his, he stood and laughed.
Saw he a youthful widow
Never so weeping, wringing of her hands
For her lost lord, still the philosopher laughed.
Now whether he supposed all these presentments
Were only maskeries, and wore false faces,
Or else were simply vain, I take no care;
But still he laughed, how grave so ere they were.
GUISE. And might right well, my Clermont; and for this
Virtuous digression we will thank the scoffs
Of vicious Monsieur. But now for the main point
Of your late resolution for revenge
Of your slain friend.
CLERMONT. I have here my challenge,
Which I will pray my brother Baligny
To bear the murderous Earle.
BALIGNY. I have prepared
Means for access to him, through all his guard.
GUISE. About it then, my worthy Baligny,
And bring us the success.
BALIGNY. I will, my lord.

[*Exeunt.*]

SCENE II. *A Room in* MONTSURRY*'s house.*

[TAMYRA *alone.*].

TAMYRA. Revenge, that ever red sittest in the eyes
Of injured ladies, till we crown thy brows
With bloody laurel, and receive from thee
Justice for all our honors injury;
Whose wings none fly that wrath or tyranny
Have ruthless made and bloody, enter here,
Enter, O enter! and, though length of time
Never lets any escape thy constant justice,
Yet now prevent that length. Fly, fly, and here
Fix thy steel foot-steps; here, O here, where still
Earth (moved with pity) yielded and embraced
My loves faire figure, drawn in his dear blood,
And marked the place, to show thee where was done

The cruelest Murder that ere fled the sun.
O Earth! why keepest thou not as well his spirit,
To give his form life? No, that was not earthly;
That (rarefying the thin and yielding air)
Flew sparkling up into the sphere of fire
Whence endless flames it sheds in my desire.
Here be my daily pallet; here all nights
That can be wrested from thy rivals arms,
O my dear Bussy, I will lie, and kiss
Spirit into thy blood, or breathe out mine
In sighs, and kisses, and sad tunes to thine.

[*She sings.*]

[*Enter* MONTSURRY.]

MONTSURRY. Still on this haunt? Still shall adulterous blood
    Affect thy spirits? Think, for shame, but this,
    This blood, that cockatrice-like thus thou broodest,
    To dry is to breed any quench to thine.
    And therefore now (if only for thy lust
    A little covered with a veil of shame)
    Look out for fresh life, rather than witch-like
    Learn to kiss horror, and with death engender.
    Strange cross in nature, purest virgin shame
    Lies in the blood as lust lies; and together
    Many times mix too; and in none more shameful
    Than in the shamefaced. Who can then distinguish
    Twixt their affections; or tell when he meets
    With one not common? Yet, as worthiest poets
    Shun common and plebeian forms of speech,
    Every illiberal and affected phrase,
    To clothe their matter, and together tie
    Matter and form with art and decency;
    So worthiest women should shun vulgar guises,
    And though they cannot but fly out for change,
    Yet modesty, the matter of their lives,
    Be it adulterate, should be painted true
    With modest out-parts; what they should do still
    Graced with good show, though deeds be ne'er so ill.
TAMYRA. That is so far from all ye seek of us
    That (though your selves be common as the air)
    We must not take the air, we must not fit
    Our actions to our own affections:
    But as geometricians (you still say)
    Teach that no lines, nor superficies,
    Do move themselves, but still accompany
    The motions of their bodies; so poor wives

    Must not pursue, nor have their own affections,
    But to their husbands earnests, and their jests,
    To their austerities of looks, and laughters,
    (Though ne'er so foolish and injurious)
    Like parasites and slaves, fit their disposers.
MONTSURRY. I used thee as my soul, to move and rule me.
TAMYRA. So said you, when you wooed. So soldiers tortured
    With tedious sieges of some well-walled town,
    Propound conditions of most large contents,
    Freedom of laws, all former government;
    But having once set foot within the walls,
    And got the reins of power into their hands,
    Then do they tyrannize at their own rude swings,
    Seize all their goods, their liberties, and lives,
    And make advantage, and their lusts, their laws.
MONTSURRY. But love me, and perform a wife's part yet,
    With all my love before, I swear forgiveness.
TAMYRA. Forgiveness! that grace you should seek of me:
    These tortured fingers and these stabbed-through arms
    Keep that law in their wounds yet unobserved,
    And ever shall.
MONTSURRY. Remember their deserts.
TAMYRA. Those with faire warnings might have been reformed,
    Not these unmanly rages. You have heard
    The fiction of the north wind and the sun,
    Both working on a traveler, and contending
    Which had most power to take his cloak from him:
    Which when the wind attempted, he roared out
    Outrageous blasts at him to force it off,
    That wrapped it closer on: when the calm sun
    (The wind once leaving) charged him with still beams,
    Quiet and fervent, and therein was constant,
    Which made him cast off both his cloak and coat;
    Like whom should men do. If ye wish your wives
    Should leave disliked things, seek it not with rage,
    For that enrages; what ye give, ye have:
    But use calm warnings, and kind manly means,
    And that in wives most prostitute will win
    Not only sure amends, but make us wives
    Better than those that ne'er led faulty lives.

    [*Enter a* SOLDIER.]

SOLDIER. My lord.
MONTSURRY. How now; would any speak with me?
SOLDIER. I, sir.
MONTSURRY. Perverse, and traitorous miscreant!
    Where are your other fellows of my guard?

Have I not told you I will speak with none
But Lord Renel?
SOLDIER. And it is he that stays you.
MONTSURRY. O, is it he? 'tis well: attend him in.

[*Exit* SOLDIER.]

I must be vigilant; the Furies haunt me.
Do you hear, dame?

[*Enter* RENEL, *with the* SOLDIER.]

RENEL. [*aside, to the* SOLDIER]. Be true now, for your ladies injured sake,
　　Whose bounty you have so much cause to Honor:
　　For her respect is chief in this design,
　　And therefore serve it; call out of the way
　　All your confederate fellows of his guard,
　　Till Monsieur Baligny be entered here.
SOLDIER. Upon your Honor, my lord shall be free
　　From any hurt, you say?
RENEL. Free as myself. Watch then, and clear his entry.
SOLDIER. I will not fail, my lord. *Exit Soldier.*
RENEL. God save your lordship!
MONTSURRY. My noblest Lord Renel! past all men welcome!
　　Wife, welcome his lordship.

[*They kiss.*]

RENEL. [*to* TAMYRA.] I much joy
　　In your return here.
TAMYRA. You do more than I.
MONTSURRY. She's passionate still, to think we ever parted
　　By my too stern injurious jealousy.
RENEL. 'Tis well your lordship will confess your error
　　In so good time yet.

[*Enter* BALIGNY, *with a challenge.*]

MONTSURRY. Death! who have we here?
　　Ho! Guard! Villains!
BALIGNY. Why exclaim you so?
MONTSURRY. Negligent traitors! Murder, Murder, Murder!
BALIGNY. Ye are mad. Had mine intent been so, like yours,
　　It had been done ere this.
RENEL. Sir, your intent,
　　And action too, was rude to enter thus.
BALIGNY. Ye are a decayed lord to tell me of rudeness,
　　As much decayed in manners as in means.

RENEL. You talk of manners, that thus rudely thrust
    Upon a man that's busy with his wife!
BALIGNY. And kept your lordship then the door?
RENEL. The door!
MONTSURRY. Sweet lord, forbear. Show, show your purpose, sir,
    To move such bold feet into others roofs.
BALIGNY. This is my purpose, sir; from Clermont D'Ambois
    I bring this challenge.
MONTSURRY. Challenge! I'll touch none.
BALIGNY. I'll leave it here then.
RENEL. Thou shall leave thy life first.
MONTSURRY. Murder, Murder!
RENEL. Retire, my lord; get off.

    [*They all fight and* BALIGNY *drives in* MONTSURRY.]

    Hold, or thy death shall hold thee. Hence, my lord!
BALIGNY. There lie the challenge.

    [*Exit* MONTSURRY.]

RENEL. Was not this well handled?
BALIGNY. Nobly, my lord. All thanks.

    [*Exit* BALIGNY.]

TAMYRA. I'll make him read it.

    [*Exit* TAMYRA.]

RENEL. This was a sleight well masked. O what is man,
    Unless he be a politician! [*Exit.*]

ACT II.

SCENE I. *A Room at the Court.*

[HENRY, BALIGNY.]

HENRY. Come, Baligny, we now are private; say,
    What service bringest thou? make it short; the Guise
    (Whose friend thou seemest) is now in Court, and near,
    And may observe us.
BALIGNY. This, sir, then, in short.
    The faction of the Guise (with which my policy,
    For service to your Highness, seems to join)
    Grows ripe, and must be gathered into hold;
    Of which my brother Clermont being a part

Exceeding capital, deserves to have
A capital eye on him. And (as you may
With best advantage, and your speediest charge)
Command his apprehension: which (because
The Court, you know, is strong in his defense)
We must ask country swing and open fields.
And therefore I have wrought him to go down
To Cambray with me (of which government
Your Highness bounty made me your lieutenant),
Where when I have him, I will leave my house,
And feign some service out about the confines;
When, in the mean time, if you please to give
Command to my lieutenant, by your letters,
To train him to some muster, where he may
(Much to his Honor) see for him your forces
Put into battle, when he comes, he may
With some close stratagem be apprehended:
For otherwise your whole powers there will fail
To work his apprehension: and with that
My hand needs never be discerned therein.
HENRY. Thanks, honest Baligny.
BALIGNY. Your Highness knows
I will be honest, and betray for you
Brother and father; for I know (my lord)
Treachery for Kings is truest loyalty,
Nor is to bear the name of treachery,
But grave, deep policy. All acts that seem
Ill in particular respects are good
As they respect your universal rule:
As in the main sway of the Universe
The supreme Rectors general decrees,
To guard the mighty globes of earth and heaven,
Since they make good that guard to preservation
Of both those in their order and first end,
No mans particular (as he thinks) wrong
Must hold him wronged;[15] no, not though all men's reasons,
All law, all conscience, concludes it wrong.
Nor is comparison a flatterer
To liken you here to the King of Kings;
Nor any mans particular offence
Against the worlds sway, to offence at yours
In any subject; who as little may
Grudge at their particular wrong, if so it seem
For the universal right of your estate,
As, being a subject of the worlds whole sway

---

[15] Since these decrees ensure the performance of that guardianship, so that earth and heaven are kept true to their original order and purpose, in no case must the wrong suffered by an individual man, as he thinks, be considered really a wrong done to him.

As well as yours, and being a righteous man
To whom heaven promises defense, and blessing,
Brought to decay, disgrace, and quite defenseless,
He may complain of heaven for wrong to him.
HENRY. 'Tis true: the simile at all parts holds,
As all good subjects hold, that love our favor.
BALIGNY. Which is our heaven here; and a misery
Incomparable, and most truly hellish,
To live deprived of our Kings grace and countenance,
Without which best conditions are most cursed:
Life of that nature, howsoever short,
Is a most lingering and tedious life;
Or rather no life, but a languishing,
And an abuse of life.
HENRY. 'Tis well conceited.
BALIGNY. I thought it not amiss to yield your Highness
A reason of my speeches; lest perhaps
You might conceive I flattered: which (I know)
Of all ills under heaven you most abhor.
HENRY. Still thou art right, my virtuous Baligny,
For which I thank and love thee. Thy advise
I'll not forget. Haste to thy government,
And carry D'Ambois with thee. So farewell.

[*Exit.*]

BALIGNY. Your Majesty far ever like itself.

[*Enter* GUISE.]

GUISE. My sure friend Baligny!
BALIGNY. Noblest of princes!
GUISE. How stands the state of Cambray?
BALIGNY. Strong, my lord,
And fit for service: for whose readiness
Your creature, Clermont D'Ambois, and myself
Ride shortly down.
GUISE. That Clermont is my love;
France never bred a nobler gentleman
For all parts; he exceeds his brother Bussy.
BALIGNY. I, my lord?
GUISE. Far: because (besides his valour)
He hath the crown of man and all his parts,
Which Learning is; and that so true and virtuous
That it gives power to do as well as say
Whatever fits a most accomplished man;
Which Bussy, for his valor's season, lacked;
And so was wrapped with outrage oftentimes

Beyond decorum; where this absolute Clermont,
Though (only for his natural zeal to right)
He will be fiery, when he sees it crossed,
And in defense of it, yet when he lists
He can contain that fire, as hid in embers.
BALIGNY. No question, he's a true, learned gentleman.
GUISE. He is as true as tides, or any star
    Is in his motion; and for his rare learning,
    He is not (as all else are that seek knowledge)
    Of taste so much depraved that they had rather
    Delight and satisfy themselves to drink
    Of the stream troubled, wandering ne'er so far
    From the clear fount, than of the fount itself.
    In all, Rome's Brutus is revived in him,
    Whom he of industry doth imitate;
    Or rather, as great Troy's Euphorbus[16] was
    After Pithagoras, so is Brutus, Clermont.
    And, were not Brutus a conspirator—
BALIGNY. Conspirator, my lord! Doth that impair him?
    Cæsar began to tyrannize; and when virtue,
    Nor the religion of the Gods, could serve
    To curb the insolence of his proud laws,
    Brutus would be the Gods just instrument.
    What said the Princess, sweet Antigone,[17]
    In the grave Greek tragedian, when the question
    Twixt her and Creon is for laws of Kings?
    Which when he urges, she replies on him
    Though his laws were a Kings, they were not Gods;
    Nor would she value Creons written laws
    With Gods unwritten edicts, since they last not
    This day and the next, but every day and ever,
    Where Kings laws alter every day and hour,
    And in that change imply a bounded power.
GUISE. Well, let us leave these vain disputings what
    Is to be done, and fall to doing something.
    When are you for your government in Cambray?
BALIGNY. When you command, my lord.
GUISE. Nay, that's not fit.
    Continue your designments with the King,
    With all your service; only, if I send,
    Respect me as your friend, and love my Clermont.
BALIGNY. Your Highness knows my vows.
GUISE. I, 'tis enough.

---

[16] Son of Panthous, a Trojan hero, who first wounded Patroclus, but was afterwards slain by Menelaus. Pythagoras, as part of his doctrine of the transmigration of souls, is said to have claimed to have been formerly Euphorbus.

[17] The reference is to Sophocles' *Antigone*, 446-457, where the Princess justifies herself for burying her brother's body in defiance of Creon's edict.

[*Exit* GUISE. BALIGNY *remains.*]

Ἀμήχανον δὲ παντὸς, &c.

Impossible est viri cognoscere mentem ac voluntatem, priusquam in Magistratibus
    apparet.—Sopho. Antig.

BALIGNY. Thus must we play on both sides, and thus hearten
    In any ill those men whose good we hate.
    Kings may do what they list, and for Kings, subjects,
    Either exempt from censure or exception;
    For, as no mans worth can be justly judged
    But when he shines in some authority,
    So no authority should suffer censure
    But by a man of more authority.[18]
    Great vessels into less are emptied never,
    There's a redundancy past their continent ever.
    These *virtuosi*[19] are the poorest creatures;
    For look how spinners weave out of themselves
    Webs, whose strange matter none before can see;
    So these, out of an unseen good in virtue,
    Make arguments of right and comfort in her,
    That clothe them like the poor web of a spinner.

    [*Enter* CLERMONT.]

CLERMONT. Now, to my challenge. What's the place, the weapon?
BALIGNY. Soft, sir! let first your challenge be received.
    He would not touch, nor see it.
CLERMONT. Possible!
    How did you then?
BALIGNY. Left it, in his despite.
    But when he saw me enter so expectless,
    To hear his base exclaims of "Murder, Murder,"
    Made me think noblesse lost, in him quick buried.

Quo mollius degunt, eo servilius.—Epict.

CLERMONT. They are the breathing sepulchers of noblesse:
    No trulier noble men than lions pictures,

---

[18] The lines here paraphrased, to which Chapman gives a marginal reference, are from the *Antigone*, 175-
7.

Ἀμήχανον δὲ παντὸς ἀνδρὸς ἐκμαθεῖν
ψυχήν τε καὶ φρόνημα καὶ γνώμην, πρὶν ἂν
ἀρχαῖς τε καὶ νόμοισιν ἐντριβὴς φανῇ.
[19] The word is here used not in the sense of *connoisseurs*, but of *devotees of virtue*. The editor has not
been able to trace any other instance of this.

Hung up for signs, are lions. Who knows not
That lions the more soft kept, are more servile?
And look how lions close kept, fed by hand,
Lose quite the innative fire of spirit and greatness
That lions free breathe, foraging for prey,[20]
And grow so gross that mastiffs, curs, and mongrels
Have spirit to cow them: so our soft French Nobles
Chained up in ease and numbed security
(Their spirits shrunk up like their covetous fists,
And never opened but Domitian-like,
And all his base, obsequious minions
When they were catching though it were but flies),
Besotted with their pheasants love of gain,
Rusting at home, and on each other preying,
Are for their greatness but the greater slaves,
And none is noble but who scrapes and saves.

BALIGNY. 'Tis base, 'tis base; and yet they think them high.

CLERMONT. So children mounted on their hobby-horse
Think they are riding, when with wanton toile
They bear what should bear them. A man may well
Compare them to those foolish great-spleened camels,
That to their high heads begged of Jove horns higher;
Whose most uncomely and ridiculous pride
When he had satisfied, they could not use,
But where they went upright before, they stooped,
And bore their heads much lower for their horns: *(Similarly.)*[21]

As these high men do, low in all true grace,
Their height being privilege to all things base.
And as the foolish poet that still writ
All his most self-loved verse in paper royal,
Or parchment ruled with lead, smoothed with the pumice,
Bound richly up, and strung with crimson strings;
Never so blest as when he writ and read
The ape-loved issue of his brain; and never
But joining in himself, admiring ever:
Yet in his works behold him, and he showed
Like to a ditcher. So these painted men,
All set on out-side, look upon within,
And not a pheasants entrails you shall find
More foul and mezeled, nor more starved of mind.

BALIGNY. That makes their bodies fat. I feign would know
How many millions of our other Nobles

---

[20] Adapted and expanded from the *Discourses* of Epictetus, bk. iv, i, 25. The original of the words quoted marginally by Chapman in a Latin version is, οὐχὶ δ' ὅσῳ μαλακώτερον διεξάγει, τοσούτῳ δουλικώτερον?

[21] By this marginal reference Chapman seems to indicate that ll. 176-181 are drawn from the same source—the *Discourses* of Epictetus—as ll. 157-160, to which the previous marginal note refers. But no such passage occurs in the *Discourses*.

Would make one Guise. There is a true tenth Worthy,
Who, did not one act only blemish him—
CLERMONT. One act! what one?
BALIGNY. One that (though years past done)
Sticks by him still, and will distain him ever.
CLERMONT. Good heaven! wherein? what one act can you name
Supposed his stain that I'll not prove his luster?
BALIGNY. To satisfy you, 'twas the Massacre.
CLERMONT. The Massacre! I thought 'twas some such blemish.
BALIGNY. O, it was heinous!
CLERMONT. To a brutish sense,
But not a manly reason. We so tender
The vile part in us that the part divine
We see in hell, and shrink not. Who was first
Head of that Massacre?
BALIGNY. The Guise.
CLERMONT. 'tis nothing so.
Who was in fault for all the slaughters made
In Ilion, and about it? Were the Greeks?
Was it not Paris ravishing the Queen
Of Lacædemon; breach of shame and faith,
And all the laws of hospitality?
This is the beastly slaughter made of men,
When truth is over-thrown, his laws corrupted;
When souls are smothered in the flattered flesh,
Slain bodies are no more than oxen slain.
BALIGNY. Differ not men from oxen?
CLERMONT. Who says so?
But see wherein; in the understanding rules
Of their opinions, lives, and actions;
In their communities of faith and reason.
Was not the wolf that nourished Romulus
More humane than the men that did expose him?
BALIGNY. That makes against you.
CLERMONT. Not, sir, if you note
That by that deed, the actions difference make
Twixt men and beasts, and not their names nor forms.
Had faith, nor shame, all hospitable rights
Been broke by Troy, Greece had not made that slaughter.
Had that been said (says a philosopher)
The Iliads and Odysseys had been lost.[22]
Had Faith and true Religion been preferred
Religious Guise had never massacred.
BALIGNY. Well, sir, I cannot, when I meet with you,
But thus digress a little, for my learning,
From any other business I intend.

---

[22] Freely adapted and transposed from the *Discourses* of Epictetus, i, xxviii, 11-20.

But now the voyage we resolved for Cambray,
I told the Guise, begins; and we must haste.
And till the Lord Renel hath found some mean
(Conspiring with the Countess) to make sure
Your sworn wreak on her husband, though this failed,
In my so brave command we'll spend the time,
Sometimes in training out in skirmishes
And battles all our troops and companies;
And sometimes breathe your brave Scotch running horse,[23]
That great Guise gave you, that all the horse in France
Far over-runs at every race and hunting
Both of the hare and deer. You shall be honored
Like the great Guise himself, above the King.
And (can you but appease your great-spleened sister
For our delayed wreak of your brothers slaughter)
At all parts you'll be welcomed to your wonder.
CLERMONT. I'll see my lord the Guise again before
    We take our journey?
BALIGNY. O, sir, by all means;
    You cannot be too careful of his love,
    That ever takes occasion to be raising
    Your virtues past the reaches of this age,
    And ranks you with the best of the ancient Romans.
CLERMONT. That praise at no part moves me, but the worth
    Of all he can give others sphered in him.
BALIGNY. He yet is thought to entertain strange aims.
CLERMONT. He may be well; yet not, as you think, strange.
    His strange aims are to cross the common custom
    Of servile Nobles; in which he's so ravished,
    That quite the earth he leaves, and up he leaps
    On Atlas shoulders, and from thence looks down,
    Viewing how far off other high ones creep;
    Rich, poor of reason, wander; all pale looking,
    And trembling but to think of their sure deaths,
    Their lives so base are, and so rank their breaths.
    Which I teach Guise to heighten, and make sweet
    With life's dear odors, a good mind and name;
    For which he only loves me, and deserves
    My love and life, which through all deaths I vow:
    Resolving this (whatever change can be)
    Thou hast created, thou hast ruined me.

    [*Exit.*]

---

[23] Count of Auvergne's "Scottish horse (which Vitry had given him) the which would have outrun all the horses of France."

ACT III.

SCENE I. *A Parade-Ground near Cambrai.*

[*A march of* CAPTAINS *over the Stage.* MAILLARD, CHALLON, AUMAL *following with* SOLDIERS.]

MAILLARD. These troops and companies come in with wings:
    So many men, so armed, so gallant horse,
    I think no other government in France
    So soon could bring together. With such men
    Me thinks a man might pass the insulting Pillars[24]
    Of Bacchus and Alcides.
CHALLON. I much wonder
    Our Lord Lieutenant brought his brother down
    To feast and Honor him, and yet now leaves him
    At such an instance.
MAILLARD. 'Twas the Kings command;
    For whom he must leave brother, wife, friend, all things.
AUMAL. The confines of his government, whose view
    Is the pretext of his command, hath need
    Of no such sudden expedition.
MAILLARD. We must not argue that. The Kings command
    Is need and right enough: and that he serves,
    (As all true subjects should) without disputing.
CHALLON. But knows not he of your command to take
    His brother Clermont?
MAILLARD. No: the Kings will is
    Expressly to conceal his apprehension
    From my Lord Governor. Observed ye not?
    Again peruse the letters. Both you are
    Made my assistants, and have right and trust
    In all the weighty secrets like myself.
AUMAL. 'Tis strange a man that had, through his life past,
    So sure a foot in virtue and true knowledge
    As Clermont D'Ambois, should be now found tripping,
    And taken up thus, so to make his fall
    More steep and head-long.
MAILLARD. It is Virtues fortune,
    To keep her low, and in her proper place;
    Height hath no room for her. But as a man
    That hath a fruitful wife, and every year
    A child by her, hath every year a month
    To breathe himself, where he that gets no childe

---

[24] These "Pillars" are mentioned together by Strabo (bk. iii, vi), who relates that during Alexander's expedition to India the Macedonians did not see them, but identified those places with them, where they found records of the god or the hero.

Hath not a nights rest (if he will do well);
So, let one marry this same barren Virtue,
She never lets him rest, where fruitful Vice
Spares her rich drudge, gives him in labor breath,
Feeds him with bane, and makes him fat with death.
CHALLON. I see that good lives never can secure
    Men from bad livers. Worst men will have best
    As ill as they, or heaven to hell they'll wrest.
AUMAL. There was a merit for this, in the fault
    That Bussy made, for which he (doing penance)
    Proves that these foul adulterous guilts will run
    Through the whole blood, which not the clear can shun.
MAILLARD. I'll therefore take heed of the bastarding
    Whole innocent races; 'tis a fearful thing.
    And as I am true bachelor, I swear,
    To touch no woman (to the coupling ends)
    Unless it be mine own wife or my friends;
    I may make bold with him.
AUMAL. 'Tis safe and common.
    The more your friend dares trust, the more deceive him.
    And as through dewy vapors the suns form
    Makes the gay rainbow girdle to a storm,
    So in hearts hollow, friendship (even the sun
    To all good growing in society)
    Makes his so glorious and divine name hold
    Colors for all the ill that can be told.

[*Trumpets within.*]

MAILLARD. Hark! our last troops are come.
CHALLON. [*Drums beat.*] Hark! our last foot.
MAILLARD. Come, let us put all quickly into battle,
    And send for Clermont, in whose Honor all
    This martial preparation we pretend.
CHALLON. We must bethink us, ere we apprehend him,
    (Besides our main strength) of some stratagem
    To make good our severe command on him,
    As well to save blood as to make him sure:
    For if he come on his Scotch horse, all France
    Put at the heels of him will fail to take him.
MAILLARD. What think you if we should disguise a brace
    Of our best soldiers in faire lackeys coats,
    And send them for him, running by his side,
    Till they have brought him in some ambuscado
    We close may lodge for him, and suddenly
    Lay sure hand on him, plucking him from horse?
AUMAL. It must be sure and strong hand; for if once
    He feels the touch of such a stratagem,

'Tis not choicest brace of all our bands
Can manacle or quench his fiery hands.
MAILLARD. When they have seized him, the ambush shall make in.
AUMAL. Do as you please; his blameless spirit deserves
(I dare engage my life) of all this, nothing.
CHALLON. Why should all this stir be, then?
AUMAL. Who knows not
The bombast polity thrusts into his giant,
To make his wisdom seem of size as huge,
And all for sleight encounter of a shade,
So he be touched, he would have heinous made?[25]
MAILLARD. It may be once so; but so ever, never.
Ambition is abroad, on foot, on horse;
Faction chokes every corner, street, the Court;
Whose faction 'tis you know, and who is held
The fautors right hand: how high his aims reach
Nought but a crown can measure. This must fall
Past shadows weights, and is most capital.
CHALLON. No question; for since he is come to Cambray,
The malcontent, decayed Marquess Renel,
Is come, and new arrived; and made partaker
Of all the entertaining shows and feasts
That welcomed Clermont to the brave virago,
His manly sister. Such we are esteemed
As are our consorts. Marquess malcontent
Comes where he knows his vain hath safest vent.
MAILLARD. Let him come at his will, and go as free;
Let us ply Clermont, our whole charge is he.

[*Exeunt.*]

SCENE II. *A Room in the* GOVERNOR'*s Castle at Cambrai.*

[*Enter a Gentleman* USHER *before* CLERMONT: RENEL, CHARLOTTE, *with two*
women Attendants, *with others: shows having past within.*]

CHARLOTTE. This for your lordships welcome into Cambray.
RENEL. Noblest of ladies, 'tis beyond all power
(Were my estate at first full) in my means
To quit or merit.
CLERMONT. You come something latter
From Court, my lord, than I: and since news there
Is every day increasing with the affaires,
Must I not ask now, what the news is there?
Where the Court lies? what stir? change? what avise

---

[25] Who is unaware that crafty policy pads out the giant that does his will, so that his wisdom may seem
commensurate with his bulk, though it is merely for a trifling encounter with what, when touched, proves a
shadow, though policy makes it out to be a monster.

From England, Italy?
RENEL. You must do so,
    If you'll be called a gentleman well qualified,
    And wear your time and wits in those discourses.
CLERMONT. The Locrian princes[26] therefore were brave rulers;
    For whosoever there came new from country,
    And in the city asked, "What news?" was punished:
    Since commonly such brains are most delighted
    With innovations, gossips tales, and mischiefs.
    But as of lions it is said and eagles,
    That, when they go, they draw their seers and talons
    Close up, to shun rebating of their sharpness:
    So our wits sharpness, which we should employ
    In noblest knowledge, we should never waste
    In vile and vulgar admirations.
RENEL. 'Tis right; but who, save only you, performs it,
    And your great brother? Madam, where is he?
CHARLOTTE. Gone, a day since, into the countries confines,
    To see their strength, and readiness for service.
RENEL. 'Tis well; his favor with the King hath made him
    Most worthily great, and live right royally.
CLERMONT. I: would he would not do so! Honor never
    Should be esteemed with wise men as the price
    And value of their virtuous services,
    But as their sign or badge; for that betrays
    More glory in the outward grace of goodness
    Than in the good itself; and then 'tis said,
    Who more joy takes that men his good advance
    Than in the good itself, does it by chance.
CHARLOTTE. My brother speaks all principle. What man
    Is moved with your soul? or hath such a thought
    In any rate of goodness?
CLERMONT. 'Tis their fault.
    We have examples of it, clear and many.
    Demetrius Phalerius,[27] an orator,
    And (which not oft meet) a philosopher,
    So great in Athens grew that he erected
    Three hundred statues of him; of all which,
    No rust nor length of time corrupted one;
    But in his life time all were overthrown.
    And Demades[28] (that past Demosthenes

---

[26] The inhabitants of Locri, a settlement near the promontory of Zephyrium, were celebrated for the excellence of their code of laws, drawn up by Zaleucus.

[27] Demetrius Phalerius, born about b. c. 345, was a follower of Phocion, and on the death of the latter in b. c. 317, became head of the Athenian administration. The citizens, in gratitude for his services, erected 360 statues to him, but afterwards turned against him. In b. c. 307 he was driven from Athens, sentence of death was passed on him, and the statues were demolished.

[28] Demades, a contemporary of Demosthenes, who, by his genius for extempore oratory, raised himself to a predominant position in Athens as a champion of the Macedonian influence, but afterwards incurred the

For all extemporal orations)
Erected many statues, which (he living)
Were broke, and melted into chamber-pots.
Many such ends have fallen on such proud honors,
No more because the men on whom they fell
Grew insolent and left their virtues state,
Than for their hugeness, that procured their hate:
And therefore little pomp in men most great
Makes mightily and strongly to the guard
Of what they win by chance or just reward.
Great and immodest braveries again,
Like statues much too high made for their bases,
Are overturned as soon as given their places.

[*Enter a* MESSENGER *with a Letter.*]

MESSENGER. Here is a letter, sir, delivered me
    Now at the fore-gate by a gentleman.
CLERMONT. What gentleman?
MESSENGER. He would not tell his name;
    He said, he had not time enough to tell it,
    And say the little rest he had to say.
CLERMONT. That was a merry saying; he took measure
    Of his dear time like a most thrifty husband.
CHARLOTTE. What news?
CLERMONT. Strange ones, and fit for a novation;
    Weighty, unheard of, mischievous enough.
RENEL. Heaven shield! what are they?
CLERMONT. Read them, good my lord.
RENEL. "You are betrayed into this country." Monstrous!
CHARLOTTE. How's that?
CLERMONT. Read on.
RENEL. "Maillard, your brothers Lieutenant, that yesterday invited you to see his musters, hath letters and strict charge from the King to apprehend you."
CHARLOTTE. To apprehend him!
RENEL. "Your brother absents himself of purpose."
CLERMONT. That's a sound one.
CHARLOTTE. That's a lie.
RENEL. "Get on your Scotch horse, and retire to your strength; you know where it is, and there it expects you. Believe this as your best friend had sworn it. Farewell if you will. Anonymous." What's that?
CLERMONT. Without a name.
CHARLOTTE. And all his notice, too, without all truth.
CLERMONT. So I conceive it, sister: I'll not wrong
    My well Known brother for Anonymous.
CHARLOTTE. Some fool hath put this trick on you, yet more

---

penalty of ἀτιμία.

To uncover your defect of spirit and valour,
First shown in lingering my dear brothers wreak.
See what it is to give the envious world
Advantage to diminish eminent virtue.
Send him a challenge. Take a noble course
To wreak a Murder, done so like a villain.
CLERMONT. Shall we revenge a villain with villain.
CHARLOTTE. Is it not equal?
CLERMONT. Shall we equal be with villains?
   Is that your reason?
CHARLOTTE. Cowardice evermore
   Flies to the shield of reason.
CLERMONT. Nought that is
   Approved by reason can be cowardice.
CHARLOTTE. Dispute, when you should fight! Wrong, wreakless sleeping,
   Makes men die honorless; one borne, another
   Leaps on our shoulders.
CLERMONT. We must wreak our wrongs
   So as we take not more.
CHARLOTTE. One wreaked in time
   Prevents all other. Then shines virtue most
   When time is found for facts; and found, not lost.
CLERMONT. No time occurs to Kings, much less to virtue;
   Nor can we call it virtue that proceeds
   From vicious fury. I repent that ever
   (By any instigation in the appearance
   My brothers spirit made, as I imagined)
   That ever I yielded to revenge his Murder.
   All worthy men should ever bring their blood
   To bear all ill, not to be wreaked with good.
   Do ill for no ill; never private cause
   Should take on it the part of public laws.
CHARLOTTE. A D'Ambois bear in wrong so tame a spirit!
RENEL. Madam, be sure there will be time enough
   For all the vengeance your great spirit can wish.
   The course yet taken is allowed by all,
   Which being noble, and refused by the Earle,
   Now makes him worthy of your worst advantage:
   And I have cast a project with the Countess
   To watch a time when all his wariest guards
   Shall not exempt him. Therefore give him breath;
   Sure death delayed is a redoubled death.
CLERMONT. Good sister, trouble not yourself with this:
   Take other ladies care; practice your face.
   There's the chaste matron, Madam Perigot,
   Dwells not far hence; I'll ride and send her to you.
   She did live by retailing maiden-heads
   In her minority; but now she deals

In whole-sale altogether for the Court.
I tell you, she's the only fashion-monger,
For your complexion, powdering of your hair,
Shadows, rebatos, wires, tires, and such tricks,
That Cambray or, I think, the Court affords.
She shall attend you, sister, and with these
Womanly practices imply your spirit;
This other suites you not, nor fits the fashion.
Though she be dear, lay it on, spare for no cost;
Ladies in these have all their bounties lost.
RENEL. Madam, you see, his spirit will not Check
At any single danger, when it stands
Thus merrily firm against an host of men,
Threatened to be [in] arms for his surprise.
CHARLOTTE. That's a mere bug-bear, an impossible mock.
If he, and him I bound by nuptial faith,
Had not been dull and drossy in performing
Wreak of the dear blood of my matchless brother,
What Prince, what King, which of the desperatest ruffings,
Outlaws in Arden, durst have tempted thus
One of our blood and name, be it true or false?
CLERMONT. This is not caused by that; twill be as sure
As yet it is not, though this should be true.
CHARLOTTE. True, 'tis past thought false.
CLERMONT. I suppose the worst,
Which far I am from thinking; and despise
The army now in battle that should act it.
CHARLOTTE. I would not let my blood up to that thought,
But it should cost the dearest blood in France.
CLERMONT. Sweet sister, [*They kiss.*] far be both off as the fact
Of my feigned apprehension.
CHARLOTTE. I would once
Strip off my shame with my attire, and try
If a poor woman, votist of revenge,
Would not perform it with a president
To all you bungling, foggy-spirited men.
But for our birth-rights Honor, do not mention
One syllable of any word may go
To the begetting of an act so tender
And full of sulfur as this letters truth:
It comprehends so black a circumstance
Not to be named, that but to form one thought,
It is or can be so, would make me mad.
Come, my lord, you and I will fight this dream
Out at the chess.
RENEL. Most gladly, worthiest lady.

[*Exeunt* CHARLOTTE *and* RENEL.]

[*Enter a* MESSENGER.]

MESSENGER. Sir, my Lord Governors Lieutenant prays
    Access to you.
CLERMONT. Himself alone?
MESSENGER. Alone, sir.
CLERMONT. Attend him in. [*Exit* MESSENGER.] Now comes this plot to trial;
    I shall discern (if it be true as rare)
    Some sparks will fly from his dissembling eyes.
    I'll sound his depth.

[*Enter* MAILLARD *with the* MESSENGER.]

MAILLARD. Honor, and all things noble!
CLERMONT. As much to you, good Captain. What's the affair?
MAILLARD. Sir, the poor Honor we can add to all
    Your studied welcome to this martial place,
    In presentation of what strength consists
    My lord your brothers government, is ready.
    I have made all his troops and companies
    Advance and put themselves in battalion,
    That you may see both how well armed they are
    How strong is every troop and company,
    How ready, and how well prepared for service.
CLERMONT. And must they take me?
MAILLARD. Take you, sir! O heaven!
MESSENGER. [*aside, to* CLERMONT.] Believe it, sir, his countenance changed in
    turning.
MAILLARD. What do you mean, sir?
CLERMONT. If you have charged them,
    You being charged yourself, to apprehend me,
    Turn not your face; throw not your looks about so.
MAILLARD. Pardon me, sir. You amaze me to conceive
    From whence our wills to Honor you should turn
    To such dishonor of my lord, your brother.
    Dare I, without him, undertake your taking?
CLERMONT. Why not? by your direct charge from the King.
MAILLARD. By my charge from the King! would he so much
    Disgrace my lord, his own Lieutenant here,
    To give me his command without his forfeit?
CLERMONT. Acts that are done by Kings, are not asked why.
    I'll not dispute the case, but I will search you.[29]

---

[29] This episode is suggested by the following passage concerning the Count of Auvergne "He was ready to call the two brothers of Murat into his cabinet, and to cause them to be searched, for that he was well advertised that they always carried the Kings letters and his commandments. But a great resolution, thinking that there is no more harm in fearing, then in the thing that causeth fear, fears extremely to make show that he hath any fear."

MAILLARD. Search me! for what?

CLERMONT. For letters.

MAILLARD. I beseech you,
Do not admit one thought of such a shame
To a commander.

CLERMONT. Go to! I must do it.
Stand and be searched; you know me.

MAILLARD. You forget
What 'tis to be a captain, and yourself.

CLERMONT. Stand, or I vow to heaven, I'll make you lie,
Never to rise more.

MAILLARD. If a man be mad,
Reason must bear him.

CLERMONT. So coy to be searched?

MAILLARD. Is death, sir, use a captain like a carrier!

CLERMONT. Come, be not furious; when I have done,
You shall make such a carrier of me,
If it be your pleasure: you're my friend, I know,
And so am bold with you.

MAILLARD. You'll nothing find
Where nothing is.

CLERMONT. Swear you have nothing.

MAILLARD. Nothing you seek, I swear. I beseech you,
Know I desired this out of great affection,
To the end my lord may know out of your witness
His forces are not in so bad estate
As he esteemed them lately in your hearing;
For which he would not trust me with the confines,
But went himself to witness their estate.

CLERMONT. I heard him make that reason, and am sorry
I had no thought of it before I made
Thus bold with you, since 'tis such ruberb to you.
I'll therefore search no more. If you are charged
(By letters from the King, or otherwise)
To apprehend me, never spice it more
With forced terms of your love, but say: I yield;
Hold, take my sword, here; I forgive thee freely;
Take; do thine office.

MAILLARD. Is foot! you make me a hang-man;
By all my faith to you, there's no such thing.

CLERMONT. Your faith to me!

MAILLARD. My faith to God; all's one:
Who hath no faith to men, to God hath none.

CLERMONT. In that sense I accept your oath, and thank you.
I gave my word to go, and I will go.

[*Exit* CLERMONT.]

MAILLARD. I'll watch you whither.

[*Exit* MAILLARD.]

MESSENGER. If he goes, he proves
    How vain are men's foreknowledges of things,
    When heaven strikes blind their powers of note and use,
    And makes their way to ruin seem more right
    Than that which safety opens to their sight.
    Cassandra's prophecy had no more profit
    With Troyes blind citizens, when she foretold
    Troyes ruin; which, succeeding, made her use
    This sacred exclamation: "God" (said she)
    "Would have me utter things uncredited;
    For which now they approve what I presaged;
    They count me wise, that said before, I raged."

[*Exit.*]

SCENE III. *A Camp near Cambrai.*

[*Enter* CHALLON *with two* SOLDIERS.]

CHALLON. Come, soldiers: you are downwards fit for lackeys;
    Give me your pieces, and take you these coats,
    To make you complete foot men, in whose forms
    You must be complete soldiers: you two only
    Stand for our army.
1st SOLDIER. That were much.
CHALLON. 'tis true;
    You two must do, or enter, what our army
    Is now in field for.
2nd SOLDIER. I see then our guerdon
    Must be the deed itself, twill be such Honor.
CHALLON. What fight soldiers most for?
1st SOLDIER. Honor only.
CHALLON. Yet here are crowns beside.
AMBOIS. We thank you, Captain.
2nd SOLDIER. Now, sir, how show we?
CHALLON. As you should at all parts.
    Go now to Clermont D'Ambois, and inform him,
    Two battles are set ready in his Honor,
    And stay his presence only for their signal,
    When they shall join; and that, to attend him hither
    Like one we so much Honor, we have sent him—
1st SOLDIER. Us two in person.
CHALLON. Well, sir, say it so;
    And having brought him to the field, when I

Fall in with him, saluting, get you both
Of one side of his horse, and pluck him down,
And I with the ambush laid will second you.
1st SOLDIER. Nay, we shall lay on hands of too much strength
To need your secondings.
2nd SOLDIER. I hope we shall.
Two are enough to encounter Hercules.[30]
CHALLON. 'Tis well said, worthy soldiers; hast, and hast him.

[*Exeunt.*]

SCENE IV. *A Room in the Governor's Castle at Cambrai.*

[*Enter* CLERMONT, MAILLARD *close following him.*]

CLERMONT. My Scotch horse to their army—
MAILLARD. Please you, sir?
CLERMONT. Is death! you're passing diligent.
MAILLARD. Of my soul,
'Tis only in my love to Honor you
With what would grace the King: but since I see
You still sustain a jealous eye on me,
I'll go before.
CLERMONT. 'Tis well; I'll come; my hand.
MAILLARD. Your hand, sir! Come, your word; your choice be used.

[*Exit.*]

[CLERMONT *alone.*]

CLERMONT. I had an aversation to this voyage,
When first my brother moved it, and have found
That native power in me was never vain;
Yet now neglected it. I wonder much
At my inconstancy in these decrees
I every hour set down to guide my life.
When Homer made Achilles passionate,
Wrathful, revengeful, and insatiate
In his affections, what man will deny
He did compose it all of industry
To let men see that men of most renown,
Strongest, noblest, fairest, if they set not down
Decrees within them, for disposing these,[31]
Of judgment, resolution, uprightness,
And certain knowledge of their use and ends,

---

[30] A proverbial expression.
[31] For regulating these gifts of fame, strength, noble birth, and beauty. *These* is used loosely to qualify the nouns implied by the adjectives, *Strong'st, noblest, fairest*, in l. 19.

Mishap and misery no less extends
To their destruction, with all that they prized,
Than to the poorest and the most despised?[32]

[*Enter* RENEL.]

RENEL. Why, how now, friend, retired! take heed you prove not
    Dismayed with this strange fortune. All observe you:
    Your government's as much marked as the Kings.
    What said a friend to Pompey?
CLERMONT. What?
RENEL. The people
    Will never know, unless in death thou try,
    That thou knowest how to bear adversity.
CLERMONT. I shall approve how vile I value fear
    Of death at all times; but to be too rash,
    Without both will and care to shun the worst,
    (It being in power to do well and with cheer)
    Is stupid negligence and worse than fear.
RENEL. Suppose this true now.
CLERMONT. No, I cannot do it.
    My sister truly said, there hung a tail
    Of circumstance so black on that supposure,
    That to sustain it thus abhorred our metal.
    And I can shun it too, in spite of all,
    Not going to field; and there to, being so mounted
    As I will, since I go.
RENEL. You will then go?
CLERMONT. I am engaged both in my word and hand.
    But this is it that makes me thus retired,
    To call myself to account, how this affaire
    Is to be managed, if the worst should chance:
    With which I note, how dangerous it is
    For any man to press beyond the place
    To which his birth, or means, or knowledge ties him.
    For my part, though of noble birth, my birthright
    Had little left it, and I know 'tis better
    To live with little, and to keep within
    A man's own strength still, and in mans true end,
    Than run a mixed course. Good and bad hold never
    Anything common; you can never find
    Things outward care, but you neglect your mind.[33]

---

[32] The editor of the 1873 edition of Chapman's Plays points out that "these twelve lines headed *Of great men* appear, with a few unimportant verbal differences, among the Epigrams printed at the end of Chapman's Petrarch in 1612."

[33] If the text is correct, the lines mean: you can never find means to give attention to externals without neglecting the improvement of your mind. Mr. Brereton has suggested to the editor that the true reading may be, *Things out worth care*, in which case "out" = "outward."

God hath the whole world perfect made and free;
His parts to the use of the All. Men, then, that are
Parts of that All, must, as the general sway
Of that importeth, willingly obey
In everything without their power to change.
He that, unpleased to hold his place, will range,
Can in no other be contained that's fit,
And so resisting the All is crushed with it:
But he that knowing how divine a frame
The whole world is, and of it all can name
(Without self-flattery) no part so divine
As he himself; and therefore will confine
Freely his whole powers in his proper part,
Goes on most God-like. He that strives to invert
The Universals course with his poor way,
Not only dust-like shivers with the sway,
But crossing God in his great work, all earth
Bears not so cursed and so damned a birth.[34]

RENEL. Go on; I'll take no care what comes of you;
Heaven will not see it ill, how ere it show.
But the pretext to see these battles ranged
Is much your Honor.[35]

CLERMONT. As the world esteems it.
But to decide that, you make me remember
An accident of high and noble note,
And fits the subject of my late discourse
Of holding on our free and proper way.
I over-took, coming from Italy,
In Germany a great and famous Earle
Of England, the most goodly fashioned man
I ever saw; from head to foot in form
Rare and most absolute; he had a face
Like one of the most ancient Honored Romans
From whence his noblest family was derived;
He was beside of spirit passing great,
Valiant, and learned, and liberal as the sun,
Spoke and writ sweetly, or of learned subjects,
Or of the discipline of public weals;
And 'twas the Earle of Oxford:[36] and being offered

---

[34] A free paraphrase of the *Discourses* of Epictetus, bk. iv, vii, 6-11.

[35] But the reason alleged, to see these battalions in review order, is a great compliment to you.

[36] The subject of this remarkable encomium was Edward de Vere (1550-1604), seventeenth Earl of Oxford. He was educated at Cambridge, and from an early age became a prominent figure at the Court of Elizabeth, who, it was said in 1573, "delighteth more in his personage, and his dancing and valiantness, than any other." In 1575 he paid a visit to Italy, and it is apparently to an episode on his return journey in the spring of 1576 that reference is made here, and in the following lines. The portrait here drawn of him is too flattering, as he was violent in temper and extravagant, but the Earl's literary gifts merited the praise of Chapman. Puttenham and Meres speak highly of him as a writer of comedy, and Webbe pays a tribute to his excellence in "the rare devises of poetry." Over twenty of his lyrics survive, chiefly in anthologies.

At that time, by Duke Cassimere, the view
Of his right royal army then in field,
Refused it, and no foot was moved to stir
Out of his own free fore-determined course.
I, wondering at it, asked for it his reason,
It being an offer so much for his Honor.
He, all acknowledging, said 'twas not fit
To take those honors that one cannot quit.[37]
RENEL. 'Twas answered like the man you have described.
CLERMONT. And yet he cast it only in the way,
    To stay and serve the world. Nor did it fit
    His own true estimate how much it weighed;
    For he despised it, and esteemed it freer
    To keep his own way straight, and swore that he
    Had rather make away his whole estate
    In things that crossed the vulgar than he would
    Be frozen up stiff (like a Sir John Smith,[38]
    His countryman) in common Nobles fashions;
    Affecting, as it the end of noblesse were,
    Those servile observations.
RENEL. It was strange.
CLERMONT. O 'tis a vexing sight to see a man,
    Out of his way, stalk proud as he were in;
    Out of his way, to be officious,
    Observant, wary, serious, and grave,
    Fearful, and passionate, insulting, raging,
    Labor with iron flails to thresh down feathers
    Flitting in air.
RENEL. What one considers this,
    Of all that are thus out? or once endeavors,
    Erring, to enter on mans right-hand path?
CLERMONT. These are too grave for brave wits; give them toys;
    Labor bestowed on these is harsh and thriftless.
    If you would Consul be (says one) of Rome,
    You must be watching, starting out of sleeps;
    Every way whisking; glorifying Plebeians;
    Kissing Patricians hands,[39] rot at their doors;

---

[37] The *Duke Cassimere* here spoken of was John Casimir, Count Palatine, who in the autumn of 1575 entered into alliance with the Huguenots and invaded France, but, after suffering a check at the hands of the Duke of Guise, made a truce and retired. The incident here spoken of apparently took place in the spring of the next year (cf. the previous note). Why, however, does Chapman introduce it here, and how did he know of it? Can he, immediately after leaving Oxford, which he entered, according to Wood, "in 1574 or thereabouts," have gone in Oxford's train to the Continent?

[38] Though alluded to in so contemptuous a way, this Sir John Smith appears to be the noted soldier of fortune, diplomatist, and military writer, who lived from about 1534 to 1607. After serving for many years in continental armies, in 1574 he became an agent of the English government, and took part in various diplomatic missions. In 1590 he published "Certain Discourses concerning the forms and effects of divers sorts of Weapons" and dedicated the work to the English nobility, whom he calls in one part of his "proeme" the "very eyes, ears and language of the king, and the body of the watch, and redress of the Commonwealth." Hence perhaps the allusion in l. 113 to "common Nobles fashions."

Speak and do basely; every day bestow
Gifts and observance upon one or other:
And what's the event of all? Twelve rods before thee;
Three or four times sit for the whole tribunal;[40]
Exhibit Circean games; make public feasts;
And for these idle outward things (says he)
Wouldest thou lay on such cost, toile, spend thy spirits?
And to be void of perturbation,
For constancy,[41] sleep when thou wouldest have sleep,
Wake when thou wouldest wake, fear nought, vex for nought,
No pains wilt thou bestow? no cost? no thought?[42]

RENEL. What should I say? As good consort with you
    As with an angel; I could hear you ever.

CLERMONT. Well, in, my lord, and spend time with my sister,
    And keep her from the field with all endeavor.
    The soldiers love her so, and she so madly
    Would take my apprehension, if it chance,
    That blood would flow in rivers.

RENEL. Heaven forbid!
    And all with Honor your arrival speed!

[*Exit.*]

[*Enter* MESSENGER *with two* SOLDIERS *like Lackeys.*]

MESSENGER. Here are two lackeys, sir, have message to you.

CLERMONT. What is your message? and from whom, my friends?

1st SOLDIER. From the Lieutenant, Colonel,[43] and the Captains,
    Who sent us to inform you that the battles
    Stand ready ranged, expecting but your presence
    To be their honored signal when to join,
    And we are charged to run by, and attend you.

CLERMONT. I come. I pray you see my running horse
    Brought to the back-gate to me.

MESSENGER. Instantly.

[*Exit* MESSENGER.]

CLERMONT. Chance what can chance me, well or ill is equal
    In my acceptance, since I joy in neither,
    But go with sway of all the world together.

---

[39] Epictetus has simply, τὰς χεῖρας καταφιλῆσαι.

[40] A mistranslation of ἐρὶ βῆμα καθίσαι, i. e. "sit on the tribunal."

[41] An obscure rendering of ὑπὲρ ἀπαθείας οὖν, ὑπὲρ ἀταραξίας. For constancy = for the sake of tranquility of mind.

[42] A translation of the *Discourses* of Epictetus, bk. iv, x, 20-22.

[43] Clermont seems to be addressed by this title because of the statement that "D'Eurre entreated the coun of Auvergne to see [the muster] to the end . . . that all his companions should be wonderfully honored with the presence of their coronel."

In all successes Fortune and the day
To me alike are; I am fixed, be she
Never so fickle; and will there repose,
Far past the reach of any die she throws.

[*Exit with* MESSENGER.]

ACT IV.

SCENE I. *A Parade-Ground near Cambrai.*

[*Alarm within: Excursions over the Stage.*]

[*The* SOLDIERS *disguised as Lackeys running,* MAILLARD *following them.*]

MAILLARD. Villains, not hold him when ye had him down!
1st SOLDIER. Who can hold lightning? Is death a man as well
    Might catch a canon bullet in his mouth,
    And spit it in your hands, as take and hold him.
MAILLARD. Pursue, enclose him! stand or fall on him,
    And ye may take him. Is death! they make him guards. *Exit.*

[*Alarm still, and enter* CHALLON.]

CHALLON. Stand, cowards, stand; strike, send your bullets at him.
1st SOLDIER. We came to entertain him, sir, for Honor.
2nd SOLDIER. Did ye not say so?
CHALLON. Slaves, he is a traitor;
    Command the horse troops to over-run the traitor.

[*Exeunt.*]

[*Shouts within. Alarum still, and Chambers shot off. Then enter* AUMAL.]

AUMAL. What spirit breathes thus in this more than man,
    Turns flesh to air possessed, and in a storm
    Tears men about the field like autumn leaves?
    He turned wild lightning in the lackeys hands,
    Who, though their sudden violent twitch unhorsed him,
    Yet when he bore himself, their saucy fingers
    Flew as too hot off, as he had been fire.
    The ambush then made in, through all whose force
    He drove as if a fierce and fire-given canon
    Had spit his iron vomit out amongst them.
    The battles then in two half-moons enclosed him,
    In which he showed as if he were the light,
    And they but earth, who, wondering what he was,
    Shrunk their steel horns and gave him glorious pass.

And as a great shot from a town besieged
At foes before it flies forth black and roaring,
But they too far, and that with weight oppressed
(As if disdaining earth) doth only grass,
Strike earth, and up again into the air,
Again sinks to it, and again doth rise,
And keeps such strength that when it softliest moves
It piece-meal shivers any let it proves—
So flew brave Clermont forth, till breath forsook him,
Then fell to earth; and yet (sweet man) even then
His spirits convulsions made him bound again
Past all their reaches; till, all motion spent,
His fixed eyes cast a blaze of such disdain,
All stood and stared, and untouched let him lie,
As something sacred fallen out of the sky.[44]

[*A cry within.*]

O now some rude hand hath laid hold on him!

[*Enter* MAILLARD, CHALLON *leading* CLERMONT, CAPTAINS *and*
SOLDIERS *following.*]

See, prisoner led, with his bands Honored more
Than all the freedom he enjoyed before.
MAILLARD. At length we have you, sir.
CLERMONT. You have much joy too;
I made you sport. Yet, but I pray you tell me,
Are not you perjured?
MAILLARD. No: I swore for the King.
CLERMONT. Yet perjury, I hope, is perjury.
MAILLARD. But thus forswearing is not perjury.
You are no politician: not a fault,
How foul so ever, done for private ends,
Is fault in us sworn to the public good:
We never can be of the damned crew;
We may impolitic ourselves (as 'twere)
Into the kingdoms body politic,
Whereof indeed we're members; you miss terms.
CLERMONT. The things are yet the same.
MAILLARD. 'Tis nothing so; the property is altered:
Ye are no lawyer. Or say that oath and oath
Are still the same in number, yet their species
Differ extremely, as, for flat example,
When politic widows try men for their turn,

---

[44] This account of Clermont's desperate struggle to avoid capture is an invention of Chapman. P. Matthieu says of the Count of Auvergne: "It was feared that he would not have suffered himself to be taken so easily nor so quietly."

Before they wed them, they are harlots then,
But when they wed them, they are honest women:
So private men, when they foreswear, betray,
Are perjured treachers, but being public once,
That is, sworn-married to the public good—
CLERMONT. Are married women public?
MAILLARD. Public good;
    For marriage makes them, being the public good,
    And could not be without them: so I say
    Men public, that is, being sworn-married
    To the good public, being one body made
    With the realms body politic, are no more
    Private, nor can be perjured, though foresworn,
    More than a widow married, for the act
    Of generation is for that an harlot,
    Because for that she was so, being unmarried:
    An argument *a paribus*.
CHALLON. 'Tis a shrewd one.
CLERMONT. "Who hath no faith to men, to God hath none:"
    Retain you that, sir? who said so?
MAILLARD. 'Twas I.
CLERMONT. Thy own tongue damn thy infidelity!
    But, Captains all, you know me nobly borne;
    Use ye to assault such men as I with lackeys?
CHALLON. They are no lackeys, sir, but soldiers
    Disguised in lackeys coats.
1st SOLDIER. Sir, we have seen the enemy.
CLERMONT. Avant! ye rascals, hence!
MAILLARD. Now leave your coats.
CLERMONT. Let me not see them more.
AUMAL. I grieve that virtue lives so undistinguished
    From vice in any ill, and though the crown
    Of sovereign law, she should be yet her footstool,
    Subject to censure, all the shame and pain
    Of all her rigor.
CLERMONT. Yet false policy
    Would cover all, being like offenders hid,
    That (after notice taken where they hide)
    The more they crouch and stir, the more are spied.
AUMAL. I wonder how this chanced you.
CLERMONT. Some informer,
    Blood-hound to mischief, usher to the hang-man,
    Thirsty of Honor for some huge state act,
    Perceiving me great with the worthy Guise,
    And he (I know not why) held dangerous,
    Made me the desperate organ of his danger,[45]

---

[45] Instrument of his dangerous designs.

    Only with that poor color: 'tis the common
    And more than whore-like trick of treachery
    And vermin bred to rapine and to ruin,
    For which this fault is still to be accused;
    Since good acts fail, crafts and deceits are used.
    If it be other, never pity me.
AUMAL. Sir, we are glad, believe it, and have hope
    The King will so conceit it.
CLERMONT. At his pleasure.
    In mean time, what's your will, Lord Lieutenant?
MAILLARD. To leave your own horse, and to mount the trumpets.
CLERMONT. It shall be done. This heavily prevents
    My purposed recreation in these parts;
    Which now I think on, let me beg you, sir,
    To lend me some one captain of your troops,
    To bear the message of my hapless service
    And misery to my most noble mistress,
    Countess of Cambray; to whose house this night
    I promised my repair, and know most truly,
    With all the ceremonies of her favor,
    She sure expects me.
MAILLARD. Think you now on that?
CLERMONT. On that, sir? I, and that so worthily,
    That if the King, in spite of your great service,
    Would send me instant promise of enlargement,
    Condition I would set this message by,
    I would not take it, but had rather die.
AUMAL. Your message shall be done, sir: I, myself,
    Will be for you a messenger of ill.
CLERMONT. I thank you, sir, and doubt not yet to live
    To quite your kindness.
AUMAL. Mean space use your spirit
    And knowledge for the cheerful patience
    Of this so strange and sudden consequence.
CLERMONT. Good sir, believe that no particular torture
    Can force me from my glad obedience
    To anything the high and general Cause,
    To match with his whole fabric, hath ordained;
    And know ye all (though far from all your aims,
    Yet worth them all, and all men's endless studies)
    That in this one thing, all the discipline
    Of manners and of manhood is contained:—
    A man to join himself with the Universe
    In his main sway, and make (in all things fit)
    One with that all, and go on round as it;
    Not plucking from the whole his wretched part,
    And into straits, or into nought revert,
    Wishing the complete Universe might be

Subject to such a rag of it as he;
But to consider great Necessity
All things, as well refract as voluntary,
Reduceth to the prime celestial cause;
Which he that yields to with a man's applause,
And cheek by cheek goes, crossing it no breath,
But like Gods image follows to the death,
That man is truly wise, and every thing
(Each cause and every part distinguishing)
In nature with enough art understands,
And that full glory merits at all hands
That doth the whole world at all parts adorn,
And appertains to one celestial borne.

[*Exeunt omnes.*]

SCENE II. *A Room at the Court in Paris.*

[*Enter* BALIGNY, RENEL.]

BALIGNY. So foul a scandal never man sustained,
    Which caused by the King is rude and tyrannous:
    Give me a place, and my Lieutenant make
    The filler of it!
RENEL. I should never look
    For better of him; never trust a man
    For any justice, that is wrapped with pleasure;
    To order arms well, that makes smocks his ensigns,
    And his whole governments sails: you heard of late
    He had the four and twenty ways of venery
    Done all before him.
BALIGNY. 'Twas abhorred and beastly.
RENEL. 'Tis more than natures mighty hand can do
    To make one humane and a lecher too.
    Look how a wolf doth like a dog appear,
    So like a friend is an adulterer;
    Voluptuaries, and these belly-gods,
    No more true men are than so many toads.
    A good man happy is a common good;
    Vile men advanced live of the common blood.
BALIGNY. Give, and then take, like children!
RENEL. Bounties are
    As soon repented as they happen rare.
BALIGNY. What should Kings do, and men of eminent places,
    But, as they gather, sow gifts to the graces?
    And where they have given, rather give again
    (Being given for virtue) than, like babes and fools,
    Take and repent gifts? why are wealth and power?

RENEL. Power and wealth move to tyranny, not bounty;
    The merchant for his wealth is swollen in mind,
    When yet the chief lord of it is the wind.
BALIGNY. That may so chance to our state-merchants too;
    Something performed, that hath not far to go.[46]
RENEL. That's the main point, my lord; insist on that.
BALIGNY. But doth this fire rage further? hath it taken
    The tender tinder of my wife's sere blood?
    Is she so passionate?
RENEL. So wild, so mad,
    She cannot live and this unwreaked sustain.
    The woes are bloody that in women reign.
    The Sicily gulf keeps fear in less degree;
    There is no tiger not more tame than she.
BALIGNY. There is no looking home, then?
RENEL. Home! Medea
    With all her herbs, charms, thunders, lightning,
    Made not her presence and black haunts more dreadful.
BALIGNY. Come, to the King; if he reform not all,
    Mark the event, none stand where that must fall. *Exeunt.*

SCENE III. *A Room in the House of the Countess of Cambrai.*

[*Enter* COUNTESS, RIOVA, *and an* USHER.]

USHER. Madam, a captain come from Clermont D'Ambois
    Desires access to you.
COUNTESS. And not himself?
USHER. No, madam.
COUNTESS. That's not well. Attend him in.

[*Exit* USHER.]

The last hour of his promise now run out!
And he break, some brack's in the frame of nature
That forceth his breach.

[*Enter* USHER *and* AUMAL.]

AUMALE. Save your ladyship!
COUNTESS. All welcome! Come you from my worthy servant?
AUMAL. I, madam, and confer such news from him—
COUNTESS. Such news! what news?
AUMAL. News that I wish some other had the charge of.
COUNTESS. O, what charge? what news?

---

[46] An obscure line. It seems to mean that, as the wealth of merchants may be scattered by storms, so the performances of "state-merchants" or rulers may be cut short before obtaining their end.

AUMAL. Your ladyship must use some patience,
    Or else I cannot do him that desire
    He urged with such affection to your graces.
COUNTESS. Do it, for heavens love, do it! if you serve
    His kind desires, I will have patience.
    Is he in health?
AUMAL. He is.
COUNTESS. Why, that's the ground
    Of all the good estate we hold in earth;
    All our ill built upon that is no more
    Than we may bear, and should; express it all.
AUMAL. Madam, 'tis only this; his liberty—
COUNTESS. His liberty! Without that health is nothing.
    Why live I, but to ask in doubt of that?
    Is that bereft him?
AUMAL. You'll again prevent me.
COUNTESS. No more, I swear; I must hear, and together
    Come all my misery! I'll hold, though I burst.
AUMAL. Then, madam, thus it fares; he was invited,
    By way of Honor to him, to take view
    Of all the powers his brother Baligny
    Hath in his government; which ranged in battles,
    Maillard, Lieutenant to the Governor,
    Having received strict letters from the King,
    To train him to the musters and betray him
    To their surprise; which, with Challon in chief,
    And other captains (all the field put hard
    By his incredible valour for his escape)
    They haplessly and guiltlessly performed;
    And to Bastille he's now led prisoner.
COUNTESS. What change is here! how are my hopes prevented!
    O my most faithful servant, thou betrayed!
    Will Kings make treason lawful? Is society
    (To keep which only Kings were first ordained)
    Less broke in breaking faith twixt friend and friend
    Than twixt the King and subject? let them fear
    Kings presidents in license lack no danger.[47]
    Kings are compared to Gods, and should be like them,
    Full in all right, in nought superfluous,
    Nor nothing straining past right for their right.
    Reign justly, and reign safely. Policy
    Is but a guard corrupted, and a way
    Ventured in deserts, without guide or path.
    Kings punish subjects errors with their own.
    Kings are like archers, and their subjects, shafts:

---

[47] Let them be afraid that the precedents set by Kings in violating obligations may prove a dangerous example.

For as when archers let their arrows fly,
They call to them, and bid them fly or fall,
As if 'twere in the free power of the shaft
To fly or fall, when only 'tis the strength,
Straight shooting, compass given it by the archer,
That makes it hit or miss; and doing either,
He's to be praised or blamed, and not the shaft:
So Kings to subjects crying, "Do, do not this,"
Must to them by their own examples strength,
The straightness of their acts, and equal compass,
Give subjects power to obey them in the like;
Not shoot them forth with faulty aim and strength,
And lay the fault in them for flying amiss.

AUMAL. But for your servant, I dare swear him guiltless.

COUNTESS. He would not for his kingdom traitor be;
His laws are not so true to him, as he.
O knew I how to free him, by way forced
Through all their army, I would fly, and do it:
And had I of my courage and resolve
But ten such more, they should not all Retain him.
But I will never die, before I give
Maillard an hundred slashes with a sword,
Challon an hundred breaches with a pistol.
They could not all have taken Clermont D'Ambois
Without their treachery; he had bought his bands out
With their slave bloods: but he was credulous;
He would believe, since he would be believed;
Your noblest natures are most credulous.
Who gives no trust, all trust is apt to break;
Hate like hell mouth who think not what they speak.

AUMAL. Well, madam, I must tender my attendance
On him again. Will it please you to return
No service to him by me?

COUNTESS. Fetch me straight
My little cabinet.

[*Exit* RIOVA.]

'Tis little, tell him,
And much too little for his matchless love:
But as in him the worths of many men
Are close contracted, [*Enter* RIOVA.] so in this are jewels
Worth many cabinets. Here, with this (good sir)
Commend my kindest service to my servant,
Thank him, with all my comforts, and, in them,
With all my life for them; all sent from him
In his remembrance of me and true love.
And look you tell him, tell him how I lie

[*She kneels down at his feet.*]

Prostrate at feet of his accursed misfortune,
Pouring my tears out, which shall ever fall,
Till I have poured for him out eyes and all.
AUMAL. O madam, this will kill him; comfort you
With full assurance of his quick acquittal;
Be not so passionate; rise, cease your tears.
COUNTESS. Then must my life cease. Tears are all the vent
My life hath to escape death. Tears please me better
Than all life's comforts, being the natural seed
Of hearty sorrow. As a tree fruit bears,
So doth an undissembled sorrow, tears.

[*He raises her, and leads her out. Exeunt.*]

USHER. This might have been before, and saved much charge.[48]

[*Exit.*]

SCENE IV. *A Room at the Court in Paris.*

[*Enter* HENRY, GUISE, BALIGNY, ESPERNONE, SOISSON. PERICOT *with pen, ink, and paper.*]

GUISE. Now, sir, I hope you're much abused eyes see
In my word for my Clermont, what a villain
He was that whispered in your jealous ear
His own black treason in suggesting Clermont's,
Colored with nothing but being great with me.
Sign then this writ for his delivery;
Your hand was never urged with worthier boldness:
Come, pray, sir, sign it. Why should Kings be prayed
To acts of justice? 'tis a reverence
Makes them despised, and shows they stick and tire
In what their free powers should be hot as fire.
HENRY. Well, take your will, sir;—I'll have mine ere long.—[*Turned.*]
But wherein is this Clermont such a rare one?
GUISE. In his most gentle and unwearied mind,
Rightly to virtue framed in very nature;
In his most firm inexorable spirit
To be removed from anything he chooseth
For worthiness; or bear the lest persuasion
To what is base, or fitteth not his object;

---

[48] The thrifty Usher is apparently deploring that the Countess, before retiring, had sent so rich a gift of jewels to Clermont.

In his contempt of riches, and of greatness
In estimation of the idolatrous vulgar;
His scorn of all things servile and ignoble,
Though they could gain him never such advancement;
His liberal kind of speaking what is truth,
In spite of temporizing; the great rising
And learning of his soul so much the more
Against ill fortune, as she set her self
Sharpe against him or would present most hard,
To shun the malice of her deadliest charge;
His detestation of his special friends,
When he perceived their tyrannous will to do,
Or their abjection basely to sustain
Any injustice that they could revenge;
The flexibility of his most anger,
Even in the main career and fury of it,
When any object of desertful pity
Offers itself to him; his sweet disposure,
As much abhorring to behold as do
Any unnatural and bloody action;
His just contempt of jesters, parasites,
Servile observers, and polluted tongues—
In short, this Senecal man is found in him,
He may with heavens immortal powers compare,[49]
To whom the day and fortune equal are;
Come faire or foul, whatever chance can fall,
Fixed in himself, he still is one to all.
HENRY. Shows he to others thus?
ALL. To all that know him.
HENRY. And apprehend I this man for a traitor?
GUISE. These are your Machiavellian villains,
    Your bastard Teucers, that, their mischiefs done,
    Run to your shield for shelter; Cacusses[50]
    That cut their too large murderous thieveries
    To their dens length still. Woe be to that state
    Where treachery guards, and ruin makes men great!
HENRY. Go, take my letters for him, and release him.
ALL. Thanks to your Highness; ever live your Highness! *Exeunt.*
BALIGNY. Better a man were buried quick than live
    A property for state and spoil to thrive.[51]

[*Exit.*]

---

[49] He is so completely a Senecal man that he may be compared with, etc.

[50] The legend of the Italian shepherd and robber Cacus, who carried his plunder to his cave or "den," is told by Ovid (*Fasti*, i, 544 ff.), Virgil (*Æneid*, viii, 190 ff.), and other writers.

[51] Iit were better for a man to be buried alive than exist as a mere property for a despoliating government to grow rich upon.

SCENE V. *A Country Road, between Cambrai and Paris.*

[*Enter* CLERMONT, MAILLARD, CHALLON *with* SOLDIERS.]

MAILLARD. We joy you take a chance so ill, so well.
CLERMONT. Who ever saw me differ in acceptance
    Of either fortune?
CHALLON. What, love bad like good!
    How should one learn that?
CLERMONT. To love nothing outward,
    Or not within our own powers to command;
    And so being sure of everything we love,
    Who cares to lose the rest? if any man
    Would neither live nor die in his free choice,
    But as he sees necessity will have it
    (Which if he would resist, he strives in vain)
    What can come near him that he doth not well?
    And if in worst events his will be done,
    How can the best be better? all is one.
MAILLARD. Me thinks 'tis pretty.
CLERMONT. Put no difference
    If you have this, or not this; but as children
    Playing at coits ever regard their game,
    And care not for their coits, so let a man
    The things themselves that touch him not esteem,
    But his free power in well disposing them.
CHALLON. Pretty, from toys!
CLERMONT. Me thinks this double disticke
    Seems prettily too to stay superfluous longings:
    "Not to have want, what riches doth exceed?
    Not to be subject, what superior thing?
    He that to nought aspires, doth nothing need;
    Who breaks no law is subject to no King."
MAILLARD. This goes to mine ear well, I promise you.
CHALLON. O, but 'tis passing hard to stay one thus.
CLERMONT. 'Tis so; rank custom raps men so beyond it.
    And as 'tis hard so well men's doors to bar
    To keep the cat out and the adulterer:
    So 'tis as hard to curb affections so
    We let in nought to make them over-flow.
    And as of Homers verses, many critics
    On those stand of which times old moth hath eaten
    The first or last feet, and the perfect parts
    Of his unmatched poem sink beneath,
    With upright gasping and sloth dull as death:
    So the unprofitable things of life,
    And those we cannot compass, we affect;

All that doth profit and we have, neglect,
Like covetous and basely getting men
That, gathering much, use never what they keep;
But for the least they lose, extremely weep.
MAILLARD. This pretty talking, and our horses walking
Down this steep hill, spends time with equal profit.
CLERMONT. 'Tis well bestowed on ye; meat and men sick
Agree like this and you: and yet even this
Is the end of all skill, power, wealth, all that is.
CHALLON. I long to hear, sir, how your mistress takes this.

[*Enter* AUMAL *with a cabinet.*]

MAILLARD. We soon shall know it; see Aumal returned.
AUMAL. Ease to your bands, sir!
CLERMONT. Welcome, worthy friend!
CHALLON. How took his noblest mistress your sad message?
AUMAL. As great rich men take sudden poverty.
I never witnessed a more noble love,
Nor a more ruthful sorrow: I well wished
Some other had been master of my message.
MAILLARD. Ye are happy, sir, in all things, but this one
Of your unhappy apprehension.
CLERMONT. This is to me, compared with her much mone,
As one tear is to her whole passion.
AUMAL. Sir, she commends her kindest service to you,
And this rich cabinet.
CHALLON. O happy man!
This may enough hold to redeem your bands.
CLERMONT. These clouds, I doubt not, will be soon blown over.

[*Enter* BALIGNY, *with his discharge:* RENEL, *and others.*]

AUMAL. Your hope is just and happy; see, sir, both
In both the looks of these.
BALIGNY. Here's a discharge
For this your prisoner, my good Lord Lieutenant.
MAILLARD. Alas, sir, I usurp that stile, enforce it,
And hope you know it was not my aspiring.
BALIGNY. Well, sir, my wrong aspired past all men's hopes.
MAILLARD. I sorrow for it, sir.
RENEL. You see, sir, there
Your prisoners discharge authentically.
MAILLARD. It is, sir, and I yield it him with gladness.
BALIGNY. Brother, I brought you down to much good purpose.
CLERMONT. Repeat not that, sir; the amends makes all.
RENEL. I joy in it, my best and worthiest friend;
O, ye have a princely fautor of the Guise.

BALIGNY. I think I did my part to.

RENEL. Well, sir, all
    Is in the issue well: and (worthiest friend)
    Here's from your friend, the Guise; here from the Countess,
    Your brothers mistress, the contents whereof
    I know, and must prepare you now to please
    The unrested spirit of your slaughtered brother,
    If it be true, as you imagined once,
    His apparition showed it. The complot
    Is now laid sure betwixt us; therefore haste
    Both to your great friend (who hath some use weighty
    For your repair to him) and to the Countess,
    Whose satisfaction is no less important.

CLERMONT. I see all, and will haste as it importeth.
    And good friend, since I must delay a little
    My wished attendance on my noblest mistress,
    Excuse me to her, with return of this,
    And endless protestation of my service;
    And now become as glad a messenger,
    As you were late a woeful.

AUMAL. Happy change!
    I ever will salute thee with my service.

    [*Exit.*]

BALIGNY. Yet more news, brother; the late jesting Monsieur
    Makes now your brothers dying prophesy equal
    At all parts, being dead as he presaged.

RENEL. Heaven shield the Guise from seconding that truth
    With what he likewise prophesied on him![52]

CLERMONT. It hath enough, 'twas graced with truth in one;
    To'th other falsehood and confusion!
    Lead to the Court, sir.

BALIGNY. You I'll lead no more;
    It was to ominous and foul before.

    [*Exeunt.*]

---

[52] It is singular that Bussy D'Ambois contains no such "dying prophesy" as is here alluded to, unless the reference is to v, iv, 76-78. Bussy, as he dies, forgives his murderers (v, iv, 112).

ACT V.

SCENE I. *A Room in the Palace of the Duke of* GUISE.

[*Enter the* GHOST OF BUSSY.]

GHOST OF BUSSY. Up from the chaos of eternal night
    (To which the whole digestion of the world
    Is now returning) once more I ascend,
    And bide the cold damp of this piercing air,
    To urge the justice whose almighty word
    Measures the bloody acts of impious men
    With equal penance, who in the act itself
    Includes the infliction, which like chained shot
    Batter together still; though (as the thunder
    Seems, by men's duller hearing than their sight,
    To break a great time after lightning forth,
    Yet both at one time tear the laboring cloud)
    So men think penance of their ills is slow,
    Though the ill and penance still together go.
    Reform, ye ignorant men, your manless lives
    Whose laws ye think are nothing but your lusts;
    When leaving (but for supposition sake)
    The body of felicity, religion,
    Set in the midst of Christendom, and her head
    Cleft to her bosom, one half one way swaying,
    Another the other, all the Christian world
    And all her laws whose observation
    Stands upon faith, above the power of reason—
    Leaving (I say) all these, this might suffice
    To fray ye from your vicious swing in ill
    And set you more on fire to do more good;
    That since the world (as which of you denies?)
    Stands by proportion, all may thence conclude
    That all the joints and nerves sustaining nature
    As well may break, and yet the world abide,
    As any one good unrewarded die,
    Or any one ill escape his penalty.

[*The* GHOST *stands close.*]

[*Enter* GUISE, CLERMONT.]

GUISE. Thus (friend) thou seest how all good men would thrive,
    Did not the good thou promptest me with prevent
    The jealous ill pursuing them in others.
    But now thy dangers are dispatched, note mine.

Hast thou not heard of that admired voice
That at the barricades spake to me,
(No person seen) "Let's lead my lord to Reimes"?
CLERMONT. Nor could you learn the person?
GUISE. By no means.
CLERMONT. 'Twas but your fancy, then, a waking dream:
    For as in sleep, which binds both the outward senses
    And the sense common to, the imagining power
    (Stirred up by forms hid in the memories store,
    Or by the vapors of o'er-flowing humors
    In bodies full and foul, and mixed with spirits)
    Feigns many strange, miraculous images,
    In which act it so painfully applies
    Itself to those forms that the common sense
    It actuates with his motion, and thereby
    Those fictions true seem and have real act:
    So, in the strength of our conceits awake,
    The cause alike doth[53] [oft] like fictions make.
GUISE. Be what it will, 'twas a presage of something
    Weighty and secret, which the advertisements
    I have received from all parts, both without
    And in this kingdom, as from Rome and Spain,
    Lorraine and Savoy, gives me cause to think,
    All writing that our plots catastrophe,
    For propagation of the Catholic cause,
    Will bloody prove, dissolving all our counsels.
CLERMONT. Retire, then, from them all.
GUISE. I must not do so.
    The Arch-Bishop of Lions tells me plain
    I shall be said then to abandon France
    In so important an occasion;
    And that mine enemies (their profit making
    Of my faint absence) soon would let that fall,
    That all my pains did to this height exhale.
CLERMONT. Let all fall that would rise unlawfully!
    Make not your forward spirit in virtues right
    A property for vice, by thrusting on
    Further than all your powers can fetch you off.
    It is enough, your will is infinite
    To all things virtuous and religious,
    Which, within limits kept, may without danger
    Let virtue some good from your graces gather.
    Avarice of all is ever nothings father.
GHOST. Danger (the spur of all great minds) is ever
    The curb to your tame spirits; you respect not
    (With all your holiness of life and learning)

---

[53] The same cause doth.

More than the present, like illiterate vulgars;
Your mind (you say) kept in your fleshes bounds
Shows that man's will must ruled be by his power:
When by true doctrine you are taught to live
Rather without the body than within,
And rather to your God still than yourself.
To live to Him is to do all things fitting
His image in which like Himself we live;
To be His image is to do those things
That make us deathless, which by death is only
Doing those deeds that fit eternity;[54]
And those deeds are the perfecting that justice
That makes the world last, which proportion is
Of punishment and wreak for every wrong,
As well as for right a reward as strong:
Away, then! use the means thou hast to right
The wrong I suffered. What corrupted law
Leaves unperformed in Kings, do thou supply,
And be above them all in dignity.

[*Exit.*]

GUISE. Why standest thou still thus, and applyest thine ears
    And eyes to nothing?
CLERMONT. Saw you nothing here?
GUISE. Thou dreamest awake now;[55] what was here to see?
CLERMONT. My brothers spirit, urging his revenge.
GUISE. Thy brothers spirit! pray thee mock me not.
CLERMONT. No, by my love and service.
GUISE. Would he rise,
    And not be thundering threats against the Guise?
CLERMONT. You make amends for enmity to him,
    With ten parts more love and desert of me;
    And as you make your hate to him no let
    Of any love to me, no more bears he
    (Since you to me supply it) hate to you.
    Which reason and which justice is performed
    In spirits ten parts more than fleshy men;
    To whose fore-sights our acts and thoughts lie open:
    And therefore, since he saw the treachery
    Late practiced by my brother Baligny,
    He would not honor his hand with the justice
    (As he esteems it) of his bloods revenge,
    To which my sister needs would have him sworn,
    Before she would consent to marry him.

---

[54] To be His image is to do the deeds that confer immortality, which, owing to the existence of death, consists only in doing the deeds that befit eternal life.

[55] Guise here turns Clermont's own words in l. 41 against him.

GUISE. O Baligny!—who would believe there were
    A man that (only since his looks are raised
    Upwards, and have but sacred heaven in sight)
    Could bear a mind so more than devilish?
    As for the painted glory of the countenance,
    Flitting in Kings, doth good for nought esteem,
    And the more ill he does, the better seem.
CLERMONT. We easily may believe it, since we see
    In this worlds practice few men better be.
    Justice to live doth nought but justice need,
    But policy must still on mischief feed.
    Untruth, for all his ends, truths name doth sue in;
    None safely live but those that study ruin.
    A good man happy is a common good;
    Ill men advanced live of the common blood.
GUISE. But this thy brothers spirit startles me,
    These spirits seld or never haunting men
    But some mishap ensues.
CLERMONT. Ensue what can;
    Tyrants may kill but never hurt a man;
    All to his good makes, spite of death and hell.

    [*Enter* AUMAL.]

AUMAL. All the desert of good renown your Highness!
GUISE. Welcome, Aumal!
CLERMONT. My good friend, friendly welcome!
    How took my noblest mistress the changed news?
AUMAL. It came too late sir, for those loveliest eyes
    (Through which a soul looked so divinely loving,
    Tears nothing uttering her distress enough)
    She wept quite out, and, like two falling stars,
    Their dearest sights quite vanished with her tears.[56]
CLERMONT. All good forbid it!
GUISE. What events are these!
CLERMONT. All must be borne, my lord; and yet this chance
    Would willingly enforce a man to cast off
    All power to bear with comfort, since he sees
    In this our comforts made our miseries.
GUISE. How strangely thou art loved of both the sexes;
    Yet thou lovest neither, but the good of both.
CLERMONT. In love of women my affection first
    Takes fire out of the frail parts of my blood;
    Which, till I have enjoyed, is passionate
    Like other lovers; but, fruition past,

---

[56] A much more overwhelming calamity than that which befell the lady in the original narrative, where it
s stated that owing to her "passion . . . she lost the sight of one eye for a time."

I then love out of judgment, the desert
Of her I love still sticking in my heart,
Though the desire and the delight be gone,
Which must chance still, since the comparison
Made upon trial twixt what reason loves,
And what affection, makes in me the best
Ever preferred, what most love, valuing lest.
GUISE. Thy love being judgment then, and of the mind,
Marry thy worthiest mistress now being blind.
CLERMONT. If there were love in marriage, so I would;
But I deny that any man doth love,
Affecting wives, maids, widows, any women:
For neither flies love milk, although they drown
In greedy search thereof; nor doth the bee
Love honey, though the labor of her life
Is spent in gathering it; nor those that fat
On beasts, or fowls, do anything therein
For any love: for as when only nature
Moves men to meat, as far as her power rules,
She doth it with a temperate appetite,
The too much men devour abhorring nature,
And in our most health is our most disease:
So, when humanity rules men and women,
'Tis for society confined in reason.
But what excites the beds desire in blood,
By no means justly can be construed love;
For when love kindles any knowing spirit,
It ends in virtue and effects divine,
And is in friendship chaste and masculine.
GUISE. Thou shalt my mistress be; me thinks my blood
Is taken up to all love with thy virtues.
And howsoever other men despise
These paradoxes strange and too precise,
Since they hold on the right way of our reason,
I could attend them ever. Come, away;
Perform thy brothers thus importuned wreak;
And I will see what great affaires the King
Hath to employ my counsel which he seems
Much to desire, and more and more esteems.

[*Exeunt.*]

SCENE II. *A Room at the Court.*

[*Enter* HENRY, BALIGNY, *with six of the guard.*]

HENRY. Saw you his saucy forcing of my hand
    To D'Ambois freedom?
BALIGNY. Saw, and through mine eyes
    Let fire into my heart, that burned to bear
    An insolence so giantly austere.
HENRY. The more Kings bear at subjects hands, the more
    Their lingering justice gathers; that resembles
    The weighty and the goodly-bodied eagle,
    Who (being on earth) before her shady wings
    Can raise her into air, a mighty way
    Close by the ground she runs; but being aloft,
    All she commands, she flies at; and the more
    Death in her seres bears, the more time she stays
    Her thundery stoop from that on which she preys.
BALIGNY. You must be then more secret in the weight
    Of these your shady counsels, who will else
    Bear (where such sparks fly as the Guise and D'Ambois)
    Powder about them. Counsels (as your entrails)
    Should be unpierced and sound kept; for not those
    Whom you discover you neglect;[57] but ope
    A ruinous passage to your own best hope.
HENRY. We have spies set on us, as we on others;
    And therefore they that serve us must excuse us,
    If what we most hold in our hearts take wind;
    Deceit hath eyes that see into the mind.
    But this plot shall be quicker than their twinkling,
    On whose lids Fate with her dead weight shall lie,
    And confidence that lightens ere she die.
    Friends of my Guard, as ye gave oath to be
    True to your Sovereign, keep it manfully.
    Your eyes have witnessed oft the ambition
    That never made access to me in Guise
    But treason ever sparkled in his eyes;
    Which if you free us of, our safety shall
    You not our subjects but our patrons call.
ALL. Our duties bind us; he is now but dead.
HENRY. We trust in it, and thank ye. Baligny,
    Go lodge their ambush, and thou God, that art
    Fautor of princes, thunder from the skies
    Beneath his hill of pride this giant Guise.

---

[57] For the counsels that you disclose you do not render of no account.

[*Exeunt.*]

SCENE III. *A Room in* MONTSURRY's *House.*

[*Enter* TAMYRA *with a letter,* CHARLOTTE *in mans attire.*]

TAMYRA. I see ye are servant, sir, to my dear sister,
    The lady of her loved Baligny.
CHARLOTTE. Madam, I am bound to her virtuous bounties
    For that life which I offer, in her service,
    To the revenge of her renowned brother.
TAMYRA. She writes to me as much, and much desires
    That you may be the man, whose spirit she knows
    Will cut short off these long and dull delays
    Hitherto bribing the eternal Justice:
    Which I believe, since her unmatched spirit
    Can judge of spirits that have her sulfur in them.
    But I must tell you that I make no doubt
    Her living brother will revenge her dead,
    On whom the dead imposed the task, and he,
    I know, will come to effect it instantly.
CHARLOTTE. They are but words in him; believe them not.
TAMYRA. See; this is the vault where he must enter;
    Where now I think he is.

[*Enter* RENEL *at the vault, with the* COUNTESS *being blind.*]

RENEL. God save you, lady!
    What gentleman is this, with whom you trust
    The deadly weighty secret of this hour?
TAMYRA. One that yourself will say I well may trust.
RENEL. Then come up, madam.

[*He helps the* COUNTESS *up.*]

    See here, Honored lady,
    A Countess that in loves mishap doth equal
    At all parts your wronged self, and is the mistress
    Of your slain servants brother; in whose love,
    For his late treacherous apprehension,
    She wept her faire eyes from her ivory brows,
    And would have wept her soul out, had not I
    Promised to bring her to this mortal quarry,[58]
    That by her lost eyes for her servants love
    She might conjure him from this stern attempt,

---

[58] This deadly attack. *Quarry* is generally used of slaughtered game, but it also signifies the attack or swoop of the bird or beast of prey on its victim, and here we have an extension of this sense.

In which (by a most ominous dream she had)
  She knows his death fixed, and that never more
  Out of this place the sun shall see him live.
CHARLOTTE. I am provided, then, to take his place
  And undertaking on me.
RENEL. You sir, why?
CHARLOTTE. Since I am charged so by my mistress,
  His mournful sister.
TAMYRA. See her letter, sir.

[*He reads.*]

Good madam, I rue your fate more than mine,
  And know not how to order these affaires,
  They stand on such occurrence.
RENEL. This, indeed,
  I know to be your lady mistress hand;
  And know besides, his brother will and must
  Endure no hand in this revenge but his.

[*Enter* GHOST OF BUSSY.]

GHOST OF BUSSY. Away, dispute no more; get up, and see!
  Clermont must author this just tragedy.
COUNTESS. Who's that?
RENEL. The spirit of Bussy.
TAMYRA. O my servant!
  Let us embrace.
GHOST OF BUSSY. Forebear! The air, in which
  My figures likeness is impressed, will blast.
  Let my revenge for all loves satisfy,
  In which, dame, fear not, Clermont shall not die.
  No word dispute more; up, and see the event.

[*Exeunt Ladies.*]

Make the guard sure, Renel; and then the doors
Command to make fast, when the Earle is in.

[*Exit* RENEL.]

The black soft-footed hour is now on wing,
Which, for my just wreak, ghosts shall celebrate
With dances dire and of infernal state. *Exit.*

SCENE IV. *An Ante-room to the Council-Chamber.*

[*Enter* GUISE.]

GUISE. Who says that death is natural, when nature
    Is with the only thought of it dismayed?
    I have had lotteries set up for my death,
    And I have drawn beneath my trencher one,
    Knit in my hand-kerchief another lot,
    The word being, "Ye are a dead man if you enter";[59]
    And these words this imperfect blood and flesh
    Shrink at in spite of me, their solidest part
    Melting like snow within me with cold fire.
    I hate myself, that, seeking to rule Kings,
    I cannot curb my slave. Would any spirit
    Free, manly, princely, wish to live to be
    Commanded by this masse of slavery,
    Since reason, judgment, resolution,
    And scorn of what we fear, will yield to fear?
    While this same sink of sensuality swells,
    Who would live sinking in it? and not spring
    Up to the stars, and leave this carrion here,
    For wolves, and vultures, and for dogs to tear?
    O Clermont D'Ambois, wert thou here to chide
    This softness from my flesh, far as my reason,
    Far as my resolution not to stir
    One foot out of the way for death and hell!
    Let my false man by falsehood perish here;
    There's no way else to set my true man clear.

[*Enter* MESSENGER.]

MESSENGER. The King desires your Grace to come to Council.
GUISE. I come. It cannot be; he will not dare
    To touch me with a treachery so profane.
    Would Clermont now were here, to try how he
    Would lay about him, if this plot should be:
    Here would be tossing souls into the sky.
    Who ever knew blood saved by treachery?
    Well, I must on, and will; what should I fear?
    Not against two, Alcides; against two,
    And Hercules to friend, the Guise will go.[60]

[*He takes up the Arras, and the* GUARD *enters upon him: he draws.*]

---

[59] Chapman here combines two episodes assigned by De Serres to different days.

[60] Taken in conjunction with iii, iii, 24, this means: Hercules is no match for two foes, but Guise will encounter two, though with Hercules as their ally.

GUISE. Hold, murderers!

[*They strike him down.*]

So then, this is confidence
In greatness, not in goodness. Where is the King?

[*The* KING *comes in sight with* ESPERNONE, SOISSON, *& others.*]

Let him appear to justify his deed,
In spite of my betrayed wounds; ere my soul
Take her flight through them, and my tongue hath strength
To urge his tyranny.
HENRY. See, sir, I am come
To justify it before men and God,
Who knows with what wounds in my heart for woe
Of your so wounded faith I made these wounds,
Forced to it by an insolence of force
To stir a stone; nor is a rock, opposed
To all the billows of the churlish sea,
More beat and eaten with them than was I
With your ambitious, mad idolatry;
And this blood I shed is to save the blood
Of many thousands.
GUISE. That's your white pretext;
But you will find one drop of blood shed lawless
Will be the fountain to a purple sea.
The present lust and shift made for Kings lives,
Against the pure form and just power of law,
Will thrive like shifters purchases; there hangs
A black star in the skies, to which the sun
Gives yet no light, will rain a poisoned shower
Into your entrails, that will make you feel
How little safety lies in treacherous steel.
HENRY. Well, sir, I'll bear it; ye have a brother to
Bursts with like threats, the scarlet Cardinal—
Seek, and lay hands on him;[61] and take this hence,
Their bloods, for all you, on my conscience!

[*Exit.*]

GUISE. So, sir, your full swing take; mine death hath curbed.
Clermont, farewell! O didst thou see but this!
But it is better; see by this the ice

---

[61] Louis de Lorraine, youngest brother of the Duke of Guise, became Archbishop of Rheims in 1574, and Cardinal in 1578.

Broke to thine own blood, which thou wilt despise
When thou hearest mine shed. Is there no friend here
Will bear my love to him?
AUMAL. I will, my lord.
GUISE. Thanks with my last breath: recommend me, then,
 To the most worthy of the race of men.

 [*Dies. Exeunt.*]

SCENE V. A *Room in* MONTSURRY'*s House.*

 [*Enter* MONTSURRY *and* TAMYRA.]

MONTSURRY. Who have you let into my house?
TAMYRA. I? none.
MONTSURRY. 'Tis false; I savor the rank blood of foes
 In every corner.
TAMYRA. That you may do well;
 It is the blood you lately shed you smell.
MONTSURRY. Is death! the vault opens.

 [*The gulf opens.*]

TAMYRA. What vault? hold your sword.

 [CLERMONT *ascends.*]

CLERMONT. No, let him use it.
MONTSURRY. Treason! Murder! Murder!
CLERMONT. Exclaim not; 'tis in vain, and base in you,
 Being one to only one.
MONTSURRY. O bloody strumpet!
CLERMONT. With what blood charge you her? it may be mine
 As well as yours; there shall not any else
 Enter or touch you: I confer no guards,
 Nor imitate the murderous course you took,
 But single here will have my former challenge
 Now answered single; not a minute more
 My brothers blood shall stay for his revenge,
 If I can act it; if not, mine shall ad
 A double conquest to you, that alone
 Put it to fortune now, and use no odds.
 Storm not, nor beat yourself thus against the doors,
 Like to a savage vermin in a trap:
 All doors are sure made, and you cannot escape
 But by your valour.
MONTSURRY. No, no, come and kill me.
CLERMONT. If you will die so like a beast, you shall;

But when the spirit of a man may save you,
  Do not so shame man, and a Nobleman.
MONTSURRY. I do not show this baseness that I fear thee,
  But to prevent and shame thy victory,
  Which of one base is base, and so I'll die.
CLERMONT. Here, then.
MONTSURRY. Stay, hold! One thought hath hardened me,

[*He starts up.*]

And since I must afford thee victory,
  It shall be great and brave, if one request
  Thou wilt admit me.
CLERMONT. What's that?
MONTSURRY. Give me leave
  To fetch and use the sword thy brother gave me,
  When he was bravely giving up his life.[62]
CLERMONT. No; I'll not fight against my brothers sword;
  Not that I fear it, but since 'tis a trick
  For you to show your back.
MONTSURRY. By all truth, no:
  Take but my honorable oath, I will not.
CLERMONT. Your honorable oath! Plain truth no place has
  Where oaths are honorable.
TAMYRA. Trust not his oath.
  He will lie like a lapwing; when she flies
  Far from her sought nest, still "Here 'tis" she cries.[63]
MONTSURRY. Out on thee, damn of devils! I will quite
  Disgrace thy bravos conquest, die, not fight.

[*Lies down.*]

TAMYRA. Out on my fortune, to wed such an abject!
  Now is the peoples voice the voice of God;
  He that to wound a woman vaunts so much,
  As he did me, a man dares never touch.
CLERMONT. Revenge your wounds now, madam; I resign him
  Up to your full will, since he will not fight.
  First you shall torture him (as he did you,
  And justice wills) and then pay I my vow.

---

[62] Cf. Bussy D'Ambois, v, iv, 114-118.

[63] This habit of the lapwing gave the bird an evil reputation as a symbol of deceitfulness. Cf. *Measure for Measure*, i, iv, 32.

> Though 'tis my familiar sin
> With maids to seem the lapwing and to jest,
> Tongue far from heart.

For a sarcastic hit at a different trick of the lapwing, cf. *Hamlet*, v, ii, 174.

Here, take this poniard.

MONTSURRY. Sink earth, open heaven,
    And let fall vengeance!

TAMYRA. Come sir, good sir, hold him.

MONTSURRY. O shame of women, whither art thou fled!

CLERMONT. Why (good my lord) is it a greater shame
    For her than you? come, I will be the bands
    You used to her, profaning her faire hands.

MONTSURRY. No, sir, I'll fight now, and the terror be
    Of all you champions to such as she.
    I did but thus far dally; now observe.
    O all you aching fore-heads that have robbed
    Your hands of weapons and your hearts of valour,
    Join in me all your rages and rebutters,
    And into dust ram this same race of Furies;
    In this one relic of the Ambois gall,
    In his one purple soul shed, drown it all.

    [*Fight.*]

MONTSURRY. Now give me breath awhile.

CLERMONT. Receive it freely.

MONTSURRY. What think ye a this now?

CLERMONT. It is very noble,
    Had it been free, at least, and of yourself;
    And thus we see (where valour most doth vaunt)
    What 'tis to make a coward valiant.

MONTSURRY. Now I shall grace your conquest.

CLERMONT. That you shall.

MONTSURRY. If you obtain it.

CLERMONT. True, sir, 'tis in fortune.

MONTSURRY. If you were not a D'Ambois, I would scarce
    Change lives with you, I feel so great a change
    In my tall spirits breathed, I think, with the breath
    A D'Ambois breathes here; and necessity
    (With whose point now pricked on, and so whose help
    My hands may challenge) that doth all men conquer,
    If she except not you of all men only,
    May change the case here.

CLERMONT. True, as you are changed;
    Her power, in me urged, makes ye another man
    Than yet you ever were.

MONTSURRY. Well, I must on.

CLERMONT. Your lordship must by all means.

MONTSURRY. Then at all.

    [*Fights, and* D'AMBOIS *hurts him.*]

[*Enter* RENEL, *the* COUNTESS, *and* CHARLOTTE *above.*][64]

CHARLOTTE. Death of my father, what a shame is this!
    Stick in his hands thus!

[*She gets down.*]

RENEL. [*trying to stop her.*] Gentle sir, forebear!
COUNTESS. Is he not slain yet?
RENEL. No, madam, but hurt
    In divers parts of him.
MONTSURRY. Ye have given it me,
    And yet I feel life for another vennie.

[*Enter* CHARLOTTE *below.*]

CLERMONT. What would you, sir?
CHARLOTTE. I would perform this combat.
CLERMONT. Against which of us?
CHARLOTTE. I care not much if 'twere
    Against thy self; thy sister would have shamed
    To have thy brothers wreak with any man
    In single combat stick so in her fingers.
CLERMONT. My sister! know you her?
TAMYRA. I, sir, she sent him
    With this kind letter, to perform the wreak
    Of my dear servant.
CLERMONT. Now, alas! good sir,
    Think you you could do more?
CHARLOTTE. Alas! I do;
    And were it not I, fresh, sound, should charge a man
    Weary and wounded, I would long ere this
    Have proved what I presume on.
CLERMONT. Ye have a mind
    Like to my sister, but have patience now;
    If next charge speed not, I'll resign to you.
MONTSURRY. Pray thee, let him decide it.
CLERMONT. No, my lord,
    I am the man in fate; and since so bravely
    Your lordship stands me, escape but one more charge,
    And, on my life, I'll set your life at large.
MONTSURRY. Said like a D'Ambois, and if now I die,
    Sit joy and all good on thy victory!

---

[64] The addition of the bracketed words is necessary, as the Q gives no indication of the entrance of these two characters. They appear with Charlotte "above," i. e. in a gallery at the back of the stage. When Charlotte, enraged at Clermont's slowness in dispatching Montsurry, "gets downe" (l. 87), they remain in the gallery unobserved.

[*Fights, and falls down.*]

MONTSURRY. Farewell! I heartily forgive thee; wife,
    And thee; let penitence spend thy rest of life.

[*He gives his hand to* CLERMONT *and his wife.*]

CLERMONT. Noble and Christian!
TAMYRA. O, it breaks my heart.
CLERMONT. And should; for all faults found in him before
    These words, this end, makes full amends and more.
    Rest, worthy soul; and with it the dear spirit
    Of my loved brother rest in endless peace!
    Soft lie thy bones; Heaven be your souls abode;
    And to your ashes be the earth no lode!

[*Music, and the* GHOST OF BUSSY *enters, leading the* GHOSTS *of the* GUISE,
    MONSIEUR, CARDINAL GUISE, *and* SHATTILION; *they dance about the
    dead body, and exeunt.*]

CLERMONT. How strange is this! The Guise amongst these spirits,
    And his great brother Cardinal, both yet living!
    And that the rest with them with joy thus celebrate
    This our revenge! This certainly presages
    Some instant death both to the Guise and Cardinal.
    That the Shattilion's ghost to should thus join
    In celebration of this just revenge
    With Guise that bore a chief stroke in his death,[65]
    It seems that now he doth approve the act;
    And these true shadows of the Guise and Cardinal,
    Fore-running thus their bodies, may approve
    That all things to be done, as here we live,
    Are done before all times in the other life.
    That spirits should rise in these times yet are fables;
    Though learnedest men hold that our sensive spirits
    A little time abide about the graves
    Of their deceased bodies, and can take,
    In cold condensed air, the same forms they had
    When they were shut up in this bodies shade.

[*Enter* AUMAL.]

AUMAL. O sir, the Guise is slain!
CLERMONT. Avert it heaven!
AUMAL. Sent for to Council by the King, an ambush

---

[65] Gaspar de Chatillon, better known as Admiral de Coligny, the champion of the Huguenot party, was murdered during "the Massacre of St. Bartholomew," on Aug. 24, 1572, at the instigation of the Duke of Guise.

(Lodged for the purpose) rushed on him, and took
 His princely life; who sent (in dying then)
 His love to you, as to the best of men.
CLERMONT. The worst and most accursed of things creeping
 On earths sad bosom. Let me pray ye all
 A little to forebear, and let me use
 Freely mine own mind in lamenting him.
 I'll call ye straight again.
AUMAL. We will forebear,
 And leave you free, sir.

 [*Exeunt.*]

CLERMONT. Shall I live, and he
 Dead, that alone gave means of life to me?
 There's no disputing with the acts of Kings;
 Revenge is impious on their sacred persons.
 And could I play the worldling (no man loving
 Longer than gain is reaped or grace from him)
 I should survive; and shall be wondered at
 Though (in mine own hands being) I end with him:
 But friendship is the cement of two minds,
 As of one man the soul and body is,
 Of which one cannot sever but the other
 Suffers a needful separation.
RENEL. I fear your servant, madam: let's descend.[66]

 [*Descend* RENEL & COUNTESS.]

CLERMONT. Since I could skill of man, I never lived
 To please men worldly, and shall I in death
 Respect their pleasures, making such a jar
 Betwixt my death and life, when death should make
 The consort sweetest, the end being proof and crown
 To all the skill and worth we truly own?
 Guise, O my lord, how shall I cast from me
 The bands and coverts hindering me from thee?
 The garment or the cover of the mind
 The humane soul is; of the soul, the spirit
 The proper robe is; of the spirit, the blood;
 And of the blood, the body is the shroud.
 With that must I begin then to unclothe,
 And come at the other. Now, then, as a ship
 Touching at strange and far removed shores,
 Her men a shore go, for their several ends,

---

[66] Renel and the Countess have overheard from the gallery Clermont's speech, and Renel, realizing that it foreshadows suicide, descends in the hope of preventing this. But, as he has to lead his blind companion, his progress is slow, and when they "enter" the main stage (l. 203), it is too late.

Fresh water, victuals, precious stones, and pearl,
All yet intentive, when the master calls,
The ship to put off ready, to leave all
Their greediest labors, lest they there be left
To thieves or beasts, or be the countries slaves:
So, now my master calls, my ship, my venture
All in one bottom put, all quite put off,
Gone under sail, and I left negligent
To all the horrors of the vicious time,
The far removed shores to all virtuous aims,
None favoring goodness, none but he respecting
Piety or man-hood—shall I here survive,
Not cast me after him into the sea,
Rather than here live, ready every hour
To feed thieves, beasts, and be the slave of power?
I come, my lord! Clermont, thy creature, comes.

[*He kills himself.*]

[*Enter* AUMAL, TAMYRA, CHARLOTTE.]

AUMAL. What! lie and languish, Clermont! Cursed man,
    To leave him here thus! he hath slain himself.
TAMYRA. Misery on misery! O me wretched dame,
    Of all that breath! all heaven turn all his eyes
    In hearty envy thus on one poor dame.
CHARLOTTE. Well done, my brother! I did love thee ever,
    But now adore thee: loose of such a friend
    None should survive, of such a brother [none.]
    With my false husband live, and both these slain!
    Ere I return to him, I'll turn to earth.

[*Enter* RENEL *leading the* COUNTESS.]

RENEL. Horror of humane eyes! O Clermont D'Ambois!
    Madam, we staid too long, your servant's slain.
COUNTESS. It must be so; he lived but in the Guise,
    As I in him. O follow life mine eyes!
TAMYRA. Hide, hide thy snaky head; to cloisters fly;
    In penance pine; too easy 'tis to die.
CHARLOTTE. It is. In cloisters then let's all survive.
    Madam, since wrath nor grief can help these fortunes,
    Let us forsake the world in which they reign,
    And for their wished amends to God complain.
COUNTESS. 'Tis fit and only needful: lead me on;
    In heavens course comfort seek, in earth is none.

[*Exeunt.*]

[*Enter* HENRY, ESPERNONE, SOISSONE, *and others.*]

HENRY. We came indeed too late, which much I rue,
    And would have kept this Clermont as my crown.
    Take in the dead, and make this fatal room
    (The house shut up) the famous D'Ambois tomb.

    [*Exeunt.*]

FINIS.

THE ATHEIST'S TRAGEDY

OR, THE HONEST MAN'S REVENGE.

By CYRIL TOURNEUR.

DRAMATIS PERSONAE.

MONTFERRERS, *a Baron.*
BELFOREST, *a Baron.*
D'AMVILLE, *brother to Montferrers.*
LEUIDULCIA, *lady to Belforest.*
CASTABELLA, *daughter to Belforest.*
CHARLEMONT, *son to Montferrers.*
ROUSARD, *elder son to D'amville.*
SEBASTIAN, *younger son to D'amville.*
LANGUEBEAU SNUFFE, *a Puritan; Chaplain to Belforest.*
BORACHIO, *D'amville's instrument.*
CATAPLASMA, *a maker of Periwigs and Attires.*
SOQUETTE, *a seeming Gentlewoman to Cataplasma.*
FRESCO, *Servant to Cataplasma.*
Other servants.
Sergeant in war.
Soldiers.
Watchmen.
Officers.
Judges.

ACT I.

SCENE I.

[*Enter* D'AMVILLE, BORACHIO, *attended.*]

D'AMVILLE. I saw my Nephew Charlemont but now
    Part from his Father.
    Tell him I desire
    To speak with him.

[*Exit* SERVANT.]

    Borachio, thou art read
    In Nature and her large Philosophy.
    Observest thou not the very self same course
    Of revolution, both in Man and Beast?

BORACHIO. The same, for birth, growth, state, decay and death;
    Only a man's beholding to his Nature
    For the better composition of the two.
D'AMVILLE. But where that favor of his Nature is
    Not full and free, you see a man becomes
    A fool, as little-knowing as a beast.
BORACHIO. That shows there's nothing in a Man above
    His nature; if there Were, considering 'tis
    His being's excellency, 'twould not yield
    To Nature's weakness.
D'AMVILLE. Then, if Death casts up
    Our total sum of joy and happiness,
    Let me have all my senses feasted in
    The abundant fullness of delight at once,
    And, with a sweet insensible increase
    Of pleasing surfet, melt into my dust.
BORACHIO. That revolution is too short, me thinks.
    If this life comprehends our happiness,
    How foolish to desire to die so soon!
    And if our time runs home unto the length
    Of Nature, how improvident it were
    To spend our substance on a minute's pleasure,
    And after, live an age in misery!
D'AMVILLE. So thou concludest that pleasure only flows
    Upon the stream of riches?
BORACHIO. Wealth is Lord
    Of all felicity.
D'AMVILLE. 'Tis, Oracle.
    For what's a man that's honest without wealth?

BORACHIO. Both miserable and contemptible.
D'AMVILLE. He's worse, Borachio. For if Charity
    Be an essential part of Honesty,
    And should be practiced first upon ourselves,
    Which must be granted, then your honest man
    That's poor, is most dishonest, for he is
    Uncharitable to the man whom he
    Should most respect. But what doth this touch me
    That seem to have enough?—thanks industry.
    'Tis true, had not my Body spread itself
    Into posterity, perhaps I should
    Desire no more increase of substance, then
    Would hold proportion with mine own dimensions.
    Yet even in that sufficiency of state,
    A man has reason to provide and add.
    For what Is he hath such a present eye,
    And so prepared a strength, that can fore-see,
    And fortify his substance and himself
    Against those accidents, the least whereof
    May rob him of an age's husbandry?
    And for my children, they are as near to me
    As branches to the tree whereon they grow;
    And may as numerously be multiplied.
    As they increase, so should my providence;
    For from my substance they receive the sap,
    Whereby they live and flourish.
BORACHIO. Sir, enough.
    I understand the mark whereat you aim.

[*Enter* CHARLEMONT.]

D'AMVILLE. Silence, we are interrupted. Charlemont!
CHARLEMONT. Good morrow, Uncle.
D'AMVILLE. Noble Charlemont,
    Good morrow. Is not this the honored day
    You purposed to set forward to the war?
CHARLEMONT. My inclination did intend it so.
D'AMVILLE. And not your resolution?
CHARLEMONT. Yes, my Lord;
    Had not my Father contradicted it.
D'AMVILLE. O noble war! Thou first original
    Of all man's honour, how dejectedly
    The baser Spirit of our present time
    Hath cast itself below the ancient worth
    Of our forefathers! From whose noble deeds
    Ignobly we derive our pedigrees.
CHARLEMONT. Sir, tax not me for his unwillingness.

By the command of his authority
My disposition's forced against itself.

D'AMVILLE. Nephew, you are the honour of our blood.
The troop of Gentry, whose inferior worth
Should second your example, are become
Your Leaders; and the scorn of their discourse
Turns smiling back upon your backwardness.

CHARLEMONT. You need not urge my spirit by disgrace,
'Tis free enough; my Father hinders it
To curb me, he denies me maintenance
To put me in the habit of my rank.
Unbind me from that strong necessity,—
And call me Coward, if I stay behind.

D'AMVILLE. For want of means? Borachio, where's the gold?
I'd disinherit my posterity
To purchase honour. 'Tis an interest
I prize above the principal of wealth.
I'm glad I had the occasion to make known
How readily my substance shall unlock
Itself to serve you. Here's a thousand Crowns.

CHARLEMONT. My worthy uncle, in exchange for this
I leave my bond; so I am doubly bound;
By that, for the repayment of this gold,
And by this gold, to satisfy your love.

D'AMVILLE. Sir, 'tis a witness only of my love,
And love doth always satisfy itself.
Now to your Father, labor his consent,
My importunity shall second yours.
We will obtain it.

CHARLEMONT. If entreaty fail,
The force of reputation shall prevail.

   [*Exit.*]

D'AMVILLE. Go call my sons, that they may take their leaves
Of noble Charlemont. Now, my Borachio!

BORACHIO. The substance of our former argument
Was wealth.

D'AMVILLE. The question, how to compass it.

BORACHIO. Young Charlemont is going to the war.

D'AMVILLE. O, thou beginest to take me!

BORACHIO. Mark me then.
Me thinks the pregnant wit of Man might make
The happy absence of this Charlemont
A subject of commodious providence.
He has a wealthy Father, ready even
To drop into his grave. And no man's power,
When Charlemont is gone, can interpose

'Twixt you and him.
D'AMVILLE. Thou hast apprehended both
    My meaning and my love. Now let thy trust,
    For undertaking and for secrecy
    Hold measure with thy amplitude of wit;
    And thy reward shall parallel thy worth.
BORACHIO. My resolution has already bound
    Me to your service.
D'AMVILLE. And my heart to thee.

[*Enter* ROUSARD *and* SEBASTIAN.]

Here are my Sons.————
There's my eternity. My life in them
And their succession shall for ever live.
And in my reason dwells the providence
To add to life as much of happiness.
Let all men lose, so I increase my gain,
I have no feeling of another's pain.

[*Exeunt.*]

SCENE II.

[*Enter Old* MONTFERRERS *and* CHARLEMONT.]

MONTFERRERS. I prithee, let this current of my tears
    Divert thy inclination from the war,
    For of my children thou art only left
    To promise a succession to my house.
    And all the honour thou canst get by arms
    Will give but vain addition to thy name;
    Since from thy ancestors thou dost derive
    A dignity sufficient, and as great
    As thou hast substance to maintain and bear.
    I prithee, stay at home.
CHARLEMONT. My noble Father,
    The weakest sigh you breathe hath power to turn
    My strongest purpose, and your softest tear
    To melt my resolution to as soft
    Obedience; but my affection to the war
    Is as hereditary as my blood
    To every life of all my ancestry.
    Your predecessors were your presidents,
    And you are my example. Shall I serve
    For nothing but a vain Parenthesis
    In the honored story of your Family?
    Or hang but like an empty Escutcheon

230

Between the trophies of my predecessors,
And the rich Arms of my posterity?
There's not a French-man of good blood and youth,
But either out of spirit or example
Is turned a Soldier. Only Charlemont
Must be reputed that same heartless thing
That Cowards will be bold to play upon.

[*Enter* D'AMVILLE, ROUSARD, *and* SEBASTIAN.]

D'AMVILLE. Good morrow, my Lord.
MONTFERRERS. Morrow, good brother.
CHARLEMONT. Good morrow, Uncle.
D'AMVILLE. Morrow, kind Nephew.
    What, have you washed your eyes wi' tears this morning?
    Come, by my soul, his purpose does deserve
    Your free consent;—your tenderness dissuades him.
    What to the Father of a Gentleman
    Should be more tender then the maintenance
    And the increase of honour to his house?
    My Lord, here are my Boys. I should be proud
    That either this were able, or that inclined
    To be my Nephew's brave competitor.
MONTFERRERS. Your importunities have overcome.
    Pray God my forced grant prove not ominous!
D'AMVILLE. We have obtained it—Ominous! in what?
    It cannot be in anything but death.
    And I am of a confident belief
    That even the time, place, manner of our deaths
    Do follow Fate with that necessity
    That makes us sure to die. . And in a thing
    Ordained so certainly unalterable,
    What can the use of providence prevail?

[*Enter* BELFOREST, LEUIDULCIA, CASTABELLA, *attended.*]

BELFOREST. Morrow, my Lord Montferrers, Lord D'amville.
    Good morrow, Gentlemen. Cousin Charlemont,
    Kindly good morrow. Troth, I was afraid
    I should have come too late to tell you that
    I wish your undertakings a success
    That may deserve the measure of their worth.
CHARLEMONT. My Lord, my duty would not let me go
    Without receiving your commandments.
BELFOREST. Complements are more for ornament
    Then use. We should employ no time in them
    But what our serious business will admit.
MONTFERRERS. Your favor had by his duty been prevented,

If we had not with-held him in the way.
D'AMVILLE. He was a coming to present his service;
    But now no more. The book invites to breakfast.
    Wilt please your Lordship enter?—Noble Lady!

[CHARLEMONT *and* CASTABELLA *remain.*]

CHARLEMONT. My noble Mistress, this accomplement
    Is like an elegant and moving speech,
    Composed of many sweet persuasive points,
    Which second one another, with a fluent
    Increase and confirmation of their force,
    Reserving still the best until the last,
    To crown the strong impulsion of the rest
    With a full conquest of the hearer's sense:
    Because the impression of the last we speak
    Doth always longest and most constantly
    Possess the entertainment of remembrance;
    So all that now salute my taking leave
    Have added numerously to the love
    Wherewith I did receive their courtesy.
    But you, dear Mistress, being the last and best
    That speaks my farewell, like the imperious close
    Of a most sweet Oration, wholly have
    Possessed my liking, and shall ever live
    Within the soul of my true memory.
    So, Mistress, with this kiss I take my leave.
CASTABELLA. My worthy Servant, you mistake the intent
    Of kissing. 'Twas not meant to separate
    A pair of Lovers, but to be the seal
    Of Love; importing by the joining of
    Our mutual and incorporated breaths,
    That we should breathe but one contracted life.
    Or stay at home, or let me go with you.
CHARLEMONT. My Castabella, for myself to stay,
    Or you to go, would either tax my youth
    With a dishonorable weakness, or
    Your loving purpose with immodesty.

[*Enter* LANGUEBEAU SNUFFE.]

    And, for the satisfaction of your love,
    Here comes a man whose knowledge I have made
    A witness to the contract of our vows,
    Which my return, by marriage, shall confirm.
LANGUEBEAU. I salute you both with the spirit of copulation, already informed of your
    matrimonial purposes, and will testimony to the integrity—
CASTABELLA. O the sad trouble of my fearful soul!

My faithful servant, did you never hear
That when a certain great man went to the war,
The lovely face of heaven was masked with sorrow,
The sighing winds did moue the breast of earth,
The heavy clouds hung down their mourning heads,
And wept sad showers the day that he went hence;
As if that day presaged some ill success
That fatally should kill his happiness.
And so it came to pass. Me thinks my eyes
(Sweet Heaven forbid!) are like those weeping clouds,
And as their showers presaged, so do my tears.
Some sad event will follow my sad fears.

CHARLEMONT. Fie, superstitious! Is it bad to kiss?

CASTABELLA. May all my fears hurt me no more than this!

LANGUEBEAU. Fie, fie, fie! these carnal kisses do stir up the
Concupiscences of the flesh.

[*Enter* BELFOREST *and* LEUIDULCIA.]

LEUIDULCIA. O! here's your daughter under her servant's lips.

CHARLEMONT. Madame, there is no cause you should mistrust
The kiss I gave; 'twas but a parting one."

LEUIDULCIA. A lusty blood! Now by the lip of Love,
Were I to choose your joining one for me—

BELFOREST. Your Father stays to bring you on the way.
Farewell. The great Commander of the war
Prosper the course you undertake! Farewell.

CHARLEMONT. My Lord, I humbly take my leave.—Madame,
I kiss your hand.—And your sweet lip.—
Farewell.

[*Exeunt.*]

[CHARLEMONT *and* LANGUEBEAU *remains.*]

Her power to speak is perished in her tears.
Something within me would persuade my stay,
But Reputation will not yield unto it.
Dear Sir, you are the man whose honest trust
My confidence hath chosen for my friend.
I fear my absence will discomfort her.
You have the power and opportunity
To moderate her passion. Let her grief
Receive that friendship from you, and your Love
Shall not repent itself of courtesy.

LANGUEBEAU. Sir, I want words and protestation to insinuate into your credit; but in
plainness and truth, I will qualify her grief with the spirit of consolation.

CHARLEMONT. Sir, I will take your friendship up at use,

And fear not that your profit shall be small;
Your interest shall exceed your principal.

[*Exit* CHARLEMONT.]

[*Enter* D'AMVILLE *and* BORACHIO.]

D'AMVILLE. Monsieur Languebeau! happily encountered. The honesty of your conversation makes me request more interest in your familiarity.

LANGUEBEAU. If your Lordship will be pleased to salute me without ceremony, I shall be willing to exchange my service for your favor; but this worshipping kind of entertainment is a superstitious vanity; in plainness and truth, I love it not.

D'AMVILLE. I embrace your disposition, and desire to give you as liberal assurance of my love as my Lord Belforest, your deserved favorer.

LANGUEBEAU. His Lordship is pleased with my plainness and truth of conversation.

D'AMVILLE. It cannot displease him. In the behavior of his noble daughter Castabella a man may read her worth and your instruction.

LANGUEBEAU. That Gentlewoman is most sweetly modest, fair, honest, handsome, wise, well-borne, and rich.

D'AMVILLE. You have given me her picture in small.

LANGUEBEAU. She's like your Diamond; a temptation in every man's eye, yet not yielding to any light impression herself.

D'AMVILLE. The praise is hers, but the comparison your own.

[*Gives him the Ring.*]

LANGUEBEAU. You shall forgive me that, Sir.

D'AMVILLE. I will not do so much at your request as forgive you it I will only give you it, Sir. By —— You will make me swear.

LANGUEBEAU. O! by no means. Profane not your lips with the foulness of that sin. I will rather take it. To save your oath, you shall lose your Ring.—Verily, my Lord, my praise came short of her worth. She exceeds a Jewell. This is but only for ornament: she both for ornament and use.

D'AMVILLE. Yet unprofitably kept without use. She deserves a worthy Husband, Sir. I have often wished a match between my elder son and her. The marriage would join the houses of Belforest and D'amville into a noble alliance.

LANGUEBEAU. And the unity of Families is a work of love and charity.

D'AMVILLE. And that work an employment well becoming the goodness of your disposition.

LANGUEBEAU. If your Lordship please to impose it upon me, I will carry it without any second end; the surest way to satisfy your wish.

D'AMVILLE. Most joyfully accepted.—*Rousard!* Here are Letters to my Lord Belforest, touching my desire to that purpose.

[*Enter* ROUSARD *sickly.*]

Rousard, I send you a suitor to Castabella. To this Gentleman's discretion I commit the managing of your suite. His good success shall be most thankful to your trust. Follow his instructions; he will be your leader.

LANGUEBEAU. In plainness and truth.

ROUSARD. My leader! Does your Lordship think me too weak to give the on-set myself?

LANGUEBEAU. I will only assist your proceedings.

ROUSARD. To say true, so I think you had need; for a sick man can hardly get a woman's good will without help.

LANGUEBEAU. Charlemont, thy gratuity and my promises were both
But words, and both, like words, shall vanish into air.
For thy poor empty hand I must be mute;
This gives me feeling of a better suite.

[*Exeunt* LANGUEBEAU *and* ROUSARD.]

D'AMVILLE. Borachio, didst precisely note this man?

BORACHIO. His own profession would report him pure.

D'AMVILLE. And seems to know if any benefit
Arises of religion after death.
Yet but compare 's profession with his life;—
They so directly contradict themselves,
As if the end of his instructions were
But to divert the world from sin, that he
More easily might engross it to himself.
By that I am confirmed an Atheist.
Well! Charlemont is gone; and here thou seest
His absence the foundation of my plot.

BORACHIO. He is the man whom Castabella loves.

D'AMVILLE. That was the reason I propounded him
Employment, fixed upon a foreign place,
To draw his inclination out of the way.

BORACHIO. 'Thas left the passage of our practice free.

D'AMVILLE. This Castabella is a wealthy heir;
And by her marriage with my elder Son
My house is honored and my state increased.
This work alone deserves my industry;
But if it prosper, thou shalt see my brain
Make this but an induction to a point
So full of profitable policy,
That it would make the soul of honesty
Ambitious to turn villain.

BORACHIO. I bespeak
Employment in it. I'll be an instrument
To grace performance with dexterity.

D'AMVILLE. Thou shalt. No man shall rob thee of the honour.
Go presently and buy a crimson Scarf
Like Charlemont's: prepare thee a disguise

In the habit of a Soldier, hurt and lame;
And then be ready at the wedding feast,
Where thou shalt have employment in a work
Will please thy disposition.
BORACHIO. As I vowed,
Your instrument shall make your project proud.
D'AMVILLE. This marriage will bring wealth. If that succeed,
I will increase it though my Brother bleed.

[*Exeunt.*]

SCENE III.

[*Enter* CASTABELLA *avoiding the importunity of* ROUSARD.]

CASTABELLA. Nay, good Sir; in troth if you knew how little it pleases me, you would forbear it.
ROUSARD. I will not leave thee till thou 'st entertained me for thy servant.
CASTABELLA. My servant! You are sick you say. You would tax me of indiscretion to entertain one that is not able to do me service.
ROUSARD. The service of a Gentlewoman consists most in chamber work, and sick men are fittest for the chamber. I prithee give me a favor.
CASTABELLA. Me thinks you have a very sweet favor of your own.
ROUSARD. I lack but your black eye.
CASTABELLA. If you go to buffets among the Boys, they'll give you one.
ROUSARD. Nay, if you grow bitter Ill dispraise your black eye.
The gray eyed Morning makes the fairest day.
CASTABELLA. Now that you dissemble not, I could be willing to give you a favor. What favor would you have?
ROUSARD. Any toy, any light thing.
CASTABELLA. Fie! Will you be so uncivil to ask a light thing at a Gentlewoman's hand?
ROUSARD. Wilt give me a bracelet of thy hair then?
CASTABELLA. Do you want hair, Sir.
ROUSARD. No faith, I'll want no hair, so long as I can have it for money.
CASTABELLA. What would you do with my hair then?
ROUSARD. Wear it for thy sake, sweet heart.
CASTABELLA. Do you think I love to have my hair worn off?
ROUSARD. Come, you are so witty now and so sensible.

[*Kisses her.*]

CASTABELLA. Tush, I would I wanted one of ray senses now!
ROUSARD. Bitter again? What's that? Smelling?
CASTABELLA. No, no, no. Why now ye are satisfied I hope. I have given you a favor.
ROUSARD. What favor? A kiss? I prithee give me another.
CASTABELLA. Show me that I gave it you then.
ROUSARD. How should I show it?

CASTABELLA. You are unworthy of a favor if you will not bestow the keeping of it one minute.

ROUSARD. Well, in plain terms, dost love me? That's the purpose of my coming.

CASTABELLA. Love you? Yes, very well.

ROUSARD. Give me thy hand upon it.

CASTABELLA. Nay, you mistake me. If I love you very well I must not love you now. For now ye are not very well, ye are sick.

ROUSARD. This Equivocation is for the jest now.

CASTABELLA. I speak it as 'tis now in fashion, in earnest. But I shall not be in quiet for you I perceive, till I have given you a favor. Do you love me?

ROUSARD. With all my heart.

CASTABELLA. Then with all my hart I'll give you a Jewell to hang in your ear.—Hark ye—I can never love you.

[*Exit.*]

ROUSARD. Call you this a Jewell to hang in mine ear? 'Tis no light favor, for I'll be sworn it comes somewhat heavily to me. Well, I will not leave her for all this. Me thinks it animates a man to stand to it, when a woman desires to be rid of him at the first sight.

[*Exit.*]

SCENE IV.

[*Enter* BELFOREST *and* LANGUEBEAU SNUFFE.]

BELFOREST. I entertain the offer of this match
    With purpose to confirm it presently.
    I have already moved it to my daughter.
    Her soft excuses savored at the first,
    Me-thought, but of a modest innocence
    Of blood, whose unmoved stream was never drawn
    Into the current of affection. But when I
    Replied with more familiar arguments,
    Thinking to make her apprehension bold,—
    Her modest blush fell to a pale dislike,
    And she reissued it with such confidence,
    As if she had been prompted by a love
    Inclining firmly to some other man;
    And in that obstinacy she remains.

LANGUEBEAU. Verily, that disobedience doth not become a Child. It proceedeth from an unsanctified liberty. You will be accessory to your own dishonor if you suffer it.

BELFOREST. Your honest wisdom has advised me well.
    Once more I'll moue her by persuasive means.
    If she resist, all mildness set apart,
    I will make use of my authority.

LANGUEBEAU. And instantly, lest fearing your constraint

Her contrary affection teach her some
Devise that may prevent you.
BELFOREST. To cut off every opportunity
Procrastination may assist her with
This instant night she shall be married.
LANGUEBEAU. Best.

[*Enter* CASTABELLA.]

CASTABELLA. Please it your Lordship, my mother attends
In the Gallery, and desires your conference.

[*Exit* BELFOREST.]

This means I used to bring me to your ear.
[*To* LANGUEBEAU.] Time cuts off circumstance; I must be brief.
To your integrity did Charlemont
Commit the contract of his love and mine;
Which now so strong a hand seeks to divide,
That if your grave advice assist me not,
I shall be forced to violate my faith.
LANGUEBEAU. Since Charlemont's absence I have weighed his love with the spirit of
consideration; and in sincerity I find it to be frivolous and vain. With-draw your
respect; his affection deserveth it not.
CASTABELLA. Good sir, I know your heart cannot profane
The holiness you make profession of
With such a vicious purpose as to break
The vow your own consent did help to make.
LANGUEBEAU. Can he deserve your love who in neglect
Of your delightful conversation and
In obstinate contempt of all your prayers
And tears, absents himself so far from your
Sweet fellowship, and with a purpose so
Contracted to that absence that you see
He purchases your separation with
The hazard of his blood and life, fearing to want
Pretence to part your companies.—
'Tis rather hate that doth division moue.
Love still desires the presence of his Love.—
Verily he is not of the Family of Love.
CASTABELLA. O do not wrong him! 'Tis a generous mind
That lead his disposition to the war:
For gentle love and noble courage are
So near allied, that one begets another;
Or Love is Sister and Courage is the Brother.
Could I affect him better than before,
His Soldier's heart would make me love him more.
LANGUEBEAU. But, Castabella—

[*Enter* LEUIDULCIA.]

LEUIDULCIA. Tush, you mistake the way into a woman.
    The passage lies not through her reason but her blood.

[*Exit* LANGUEBEAU. CASTABELLA *about to follow.*]

    Nay, stay! How wouldst thou call the child,
    That being raised with cost and tenderness
    To full ability of body and means,
    Denies relief unto the parents who
    Bestowed that bringing up?
CASTABELLA. Unnatural.
LEUIDULCIA. Then Castabella is unnatural.
    Nature, the loving mother of us all,
    Brought forth a woman for her own relief
    By generation to revive her age;
    Which, now thou hast ability and means
    Presented, most unkindly dost deny.
CASTABELLA. Believe me, Mother, I do love a man.
LEUIDULCIA. Preferrest the affection of an absent Love
    Before the sweet possession of a man;
    The barren mind before the fruitful body,
    Where our creation has no reference
    To man but in his body, being made
    Only for generation; which (unless
    Our children can be gotten by conceit)
    Must from the body come? If Reason were
    Our counselor, we would neglect the work
    Of generation for the prodigal
    Expense it draws us too of that which is
    The wealth of life. Wise Nature, therefore, hath
    Reserved for an inducement to our sense
    Our greatest pleasure in that greatest work;
    Which being offered thee, thy ignorance
    Refuses, for the imaginary joy
    Of an unsatisfied affection to
    An absent man whose blood once spent in the war
    Then he'll come home sick, lame, and impotent,
    And wed thee to a torment, like the pain
    Of Tantalus, continuing thy desire
    With fruitless presentation of the thing
    It loves, still moved, and still unsatisfied.

[*Enter* BELFOREST, D'AMVILLE, ROUSARD, SEBASTIAN, LANGUEBEAU,
    & *c.*]

BELFOREST. Now, Leuidulcia, hast thou yet prepaid
    My Daughter's love to entertain this Man
    Her husband, here?
LEUIDULCIA. I'm but her mother in law;
    Yet if she were my very flesh and blood
    I could advise no better for her good.
ROUSARD. Sweet wife,
    Thy joyful husband thus salutes thy cheek
CASTABELLA. My husband? O! I am betrayed.———
    Dear friend of Charlemont, your purity
    Professes a divine contempt of the world;
    O be not bribed by that you so neglect,
    In being the world's hated instrument,
    To bring a just neglect upon yourself!—

[*Kneels from one to another.*]

    Dear Father, let me but examine my
    Affection.———Sir, your prudent judgment can
    Persuade your son that 'tis improvident
    To marry one whose disposition he
    Did ne'er observe.———Good sir, I may be of
    A nature so unpleasing to your mind,
    Perhaps you'll curse the fatal hour wherein
    You rashly married me.
D'AMVILLE. My Lord Belforest,
    I would not have her forced against her choice.
BELFOREST. Passion of me, thou peevish girl! I charge
    Thee by my blessing, and the authority
    I have to claim the obedience, marry him.
CASTABELLA. Now Charlemont! O my presaging tears!
    This sad event hath followed my sad fears.
SEBASTIAN. A rape, a rape, a rape!
BELFOREST. How now!
D'AMVILLE. What's that?
SEBASTIAN. Why what is it but a Rape to force a wench
    To marry, since it forces her to lie
    With him she would not?
LANGUEBEAU. Verily his Tongue is an unsanctified member.
SEBASTIAN. Verily
    Your gratuity becomes your perished soul
    As hoary moldiness does rotten fruit.
BELFOREST. Cousin, ye are both uncivil and profane.
D'AMVILLE. Thou disobedient villain, get thee out of my sight.
    Now, by my Soule, I'll plague thee for this rudeness.
BELFOREST. Come, set forward to the Church.

[*Exeunt.*]

[SEBASTIAN *remains.*]

SEBASTIAN. And verify the Proverb—The nearer the Church, the further from God.— Poor wench! For thy sake may his ability die in his appetite, that thou beest not troubled with him thou lovest not! May his appetite moue thy desire to another man, so he shall help to make himself Cuckold! And let that man be one that he pays wages to; so thou shalt profit by him thou hatest. Let the Chambers be matted, the hinges oiled, the curtain rings silenced, and the chamber-maid hold her peace at his own request, that he may sleep the quietlier; and in that sleep let him be soundly cuckolded. And when he knows it, and seeks to sue a divorce, let him have no other satisfaction then this: *He lay by and slept: the Law will take no hold of her because he winked at it.*

[*Exit.*]

ACT II.

SCENE I. *Music. A banquet. In the night.*

[*Enter* D'AMVILLE, BELFOREST, LEUIDULCIA, ROUSARD, CASTABELLA, LANGUEBEAU SNUFFE, *at one door. At the other door* CATAPLASMA *and* SOQUETTE, *ushered by* FRESCO.]

LEUIDULCIA. Mistress Cataplasma, I expected you an hour since.
CATAPLASMA. Certain Ladies at my house, Madame, detained me; otherwise I had attended your Ladyship sooner.
LEUIDULCIA. We are beholding to you for your company. My Lord, I pray you bid these Gentlewomen welcome; they're my invited friends.
D'AMVILLE. Gentlewomen, ye are welcome. Pray sit down.
LEUIDULCIA. Fresco, by my Lord D'amville's leave I prithee go into the Buttry. Thou shalt find some of my men there. If they bid thee not welcome they are very Loggerheads.
FRESCO. If your Loggerheads will not, your Hogsheads shall, Madame, if I get into the Buttry.

[*Exit.*]

D'AMVILLE. That fellow's disposition to mirth should be our present example. Let's be grave and meditate when our affaires require our seriousness. 'Tis out of season to be heavily disposed.
LEUIDULCIA. We should be all wound up into the key of Mirth.
D'AMVILLE. The Music there.
BELFOREST. Where's my Lord Montferrers? Tell him here's a room attends him.

[*Enter* MONTFERRERS.]

MONTFERRERS. Heaven give your marriage that I am deprived of, joy!

D'AMVILLE. My Lord Belforest, Castabella's health!

[D'AMVILLE *drinks.*]

Set ope' the Cellar doors, and let this health
Go freely round the house.—Another to
Your Son, my Lord; to noble Charlemont—
He is a Soldier—Let the Instruments
Of war congratulate his memory.

[*Drums and trumpets.*]

[*Enter a* SERVANT.]

SERVANT. My Lord, here's one, in the habit of a Soldier, says he is newly returned from
Ostend, and has some business of import to speak.
D'AMVILLE. Ostend! let him come in. My soul foretells
He brings the news will make our Music full.
My brother's joy would do it, and here comes he
Will raise it.

[*Enter* BORACHIO *disguised.*]

MONTFERRERS. O my spirit, it does dissuade
My tongue to question him, as if it knew
His answer would displease.

D'AMVILLE. Soldier, what news?
We heard a rumor of a blow you gave
The Enemy.
BORACHIO. Tis very true, my Lord.
BELFOREST. Canst thou relate it?
BORACHIO. Yes.
D'AMVILLE. I Prithee do.
BORACHIO. The Enemy, defeated of a fair
Advantage by a flattering stratagem,
Plants all the Artillery against the Towne;
Whose thunder and lightning made our bulwarks shake
And threatened in that terrible report
The storm wherewith they meant to second it.
The assault was general. But, for the place
That promised most advantage to be forced—
The pride of all their Army was drawn forth
And equally divided into Front
And Rear. They marched, and coming to a stand,
Ready to pass our Channel at an ebb,
W' advised it for our safest course, to draw
Our sluices up and make it impassable.

Our Governor opposed and suffered them
To charge us home even to the Rampier's foot.
But when their front was forcing up our breach
At push of pike, then did his policy
Let go the sluices, and tripped up the heels
Of the whole body of their troupe that stood
Within the violent current of the stream.
Their front, beleaguered 'twixt the water and
The Towne, seeing the flood was grown too deep
To promise them a safe retreat, exposed
The force of all their spirits, (like the last
Expiring gasp of a strong hearted man)
Upon the hazard of one charge, but were
Oppressed, and fell. The rest that could not swim
Were only drowned; but those that thought to escape
By swimming, were by murderers that flanked
The level of the flood, both drowned and slain.

D'AMVILLE. Now, by my soul, Soldier, a brave service.

MONTFERRERS. O what became of my dear Charlemont?

BORACHIO. Walking next day upon the fatal shore,
Among the slaughtered bodies of their men
Which the full-stomached Sea had cast upon
The sands, it was m' unhappy chance to light
Upon a face, whose favor when it lived,
My astonished mind informed me I had seen.
He lay in his Armor, as if that had been
His Coffin; and the weeping Sea, like one
Whose milder temper doth lament the death
Of him whom in his rage he slew, runs up
The Shore, embraces him, kisses his cheek,
Goes back again, and forces up the Sands
To bury him. and every time it parts
Sheds tears upon him, till at last (as if
It could no longer endure to see the man
Whom it had slain, yet loath to leave him) with
A kind of unresolved unwilling pace,
Winding her waves one in another, like
A man that folds his arms or wrings his hands
For grief, ebbed from the body, and descends
As if it would sink down into the earth,
And hide itself for shame of such a deed.

D'AMVILLE. And, Soldier, who was this?

MONTFERRERS. O Charlemont!

BORACHIO. Your fear hath told you that, whereof my grief
Was loath to be the messenger.

CASTABELLA. O God!

[*Exit* CASTABELLA.]

D'AMVILLE. Charlemont drowned! Why how could that be, since
    It was the adverse party that received
    The overthrow?
BORACHIO. His forward spirit pressed into the front,
    And being engaged within the enemy
    When they retreated through the rising stream,
    In the violent confusion of the throng
    Was overborne, and perished in the flood.
    And here's the sad remembrance of his life,—*The Scarf.*
    Which, for his sake, I will forever wear.
MONTFERRERS. Torment me not with witnesses of that
    Which I desire not to believe, yet must
D'AMVILLE. Thou art a Scrichowle and dost come in the night
    To be the cursed messenger of death.
    Away! depart my house or, by my soul,
    You'll find me a more fatal enemy
    Then ever was Ostend. Be gone; dispatch!
BORACHIO. Sir, 'twas my love.
D'AMVILLE. Your love to vex my heart
    With that I hate?
    Hark, do you hear, you knave?
    O thou art a most delicate, sweet, eloquent villain! [*Aside.*]

BORACHIO. Was it not well counterfeited? [*Aside.*]

D'AMVILLE. Rarely. [*Aside.*] Be gone. I will not here reply.

BORACHIO. Why then, farewell. I will not trouble you.

    [*Exit.*]

D'AMVILLE. So. The foundation's laid. Now by degrees [*Aside.*]
    The work will rise and soon be perfected.
    O this uncertain state of mortal man!
BELFOREST. What then? It is the inevitable fate
    Of all things underneath the Moon.
D'AMVILLE. 'Tis true.
    Brother, for health's sake overcome your grief.
MONTFERRERS. I cannot, sir. I am incapable
    Of comfort. My turn will be next. I feel
    Myself not well.
D'AMVILLE. You yield too much to grief.
LANGUEBEAU. All men are mortal. The hour of death is uncertain. Age makes sickness
    the more dangerous, and grief is subject to distraction. You know not how soon you
    may be deprived of the benefit of sense. In my understanding, therefore,
        You shall do well if you be sick to set
        Your state in present order. Make your will.

D'AMVILLE. I have my wish. Lights for my Brother.
MONTFERRERS. I'll withdraw a while.
    And crave the honest counsel of this man.

BELFOREST. With all my heart. I pray attend him, sir.

    [*Exeunt* MONTFERRERS *and* SNUFFE.]

This next room, please your Lordship,

D'AMVILLE. Where you will.

    [*Exeunt* BELFOREST *and* D'AMVILLE.]

LEUIDULCIA. My Daughter's gone. Come son, Mistress Cataplasma, come, we'll up
    into her chamber. I'd feign see how she entertains the expectation of her husband's
    bedfellowship.
ROUSARD. 'Faith, howsoever she entertains it, I Shall hardly please her; therefore let
    her rest.
LEUIDULCIA. Nay, please her hardly, and you please her best.

    [*Exeunt.*]

SCENE II.

    [*Enter* 3 SERVANTS, *drunk, drawing in* FRESCO.]

1st SERVANT. Boy! fill some drink, Boy.
FRESCO. Enough, good Sir; not a drop more by this light.
2nd SERVANT. Not by this light? Why then put out the candles and we'll drink in the
    dark, and to it, old Boy.
FRESCO. No, no, no, no, no.
3rd SERVANT. Why then take thy liquor. A health, Fresco.

    [*Kneel.*]

FRESCO. Your health will make me sick, sir.
1st SERVANT. Then 'twill bring you of your knees, I hope, sir.
FRESCO. May I not stand and pledge it, sir?
2nd SERVANT. I hope you will do as wee do.
FRESCO. Nay then indeed I must not stand, for you cannot.
3rd SERVANT. Well said, old boy.
FRESCO. Old boy! you'll make me a young child anon; for if I continue this I shall
    scarce be able to go alone.
1st SERVANT. My body is a weak as water, Fresco.
FRESCO. Good reason, sir. The beer has sent all the malt up into your brain and left
    nothing but the water in your body.

[*Enter* D'AMVILLE *and* BORACHIO, *closely observing their drunkenness.*]

D'AMVILLE. Borachio, seest those fellows?
BORACHIO. Yes, my Lord.
D'AMVILLE. Their drunkenness, that seems ridiculous,
    Shall be a serious instrument to bring
    Our sober purposes to their success.
BORACHIO. I am prepared for the execution, sir.
D'AMVILLE. Cast off this habit and about it straight.
BORACHIO. Let them drink healths and drown their brains in the flood;
    I promise them they shall be pledged in blood.

    [*Exit.*]

1st SERVANT. You have left a damnable snuff here.
2nd SERVANT. Do you take that in snuff, sir?
1st SERVANT. You are a damnable rogue then——[*together by the ears.*]
D'AMVILLE. Fortune, I honour thee. My plot still rises
    According to the model of mine own desires.
    Lights for my Brother.——What have you drunk yourselves mad, you knaves?
1st SERVANT. My Lord, the Jacks abused me.
D'AMVILLE. I think they are the Jacks indeed that have abused thee. Dost hear? That
    fellow is a proud knave. He has abused thee. As thou goest over the fields by-and-by
    in lighting my brother home, I'll tell thee what shalt do. Knock him over the pate
    with thy torch. I'll bear thee out in it.
1st SERVANT. I will sing the goose by this torch.

    [*Exit.*]

D'AMVILLE. [*to* 2nd SERVANT.] Dost hear, fellow? Seest thou that proud knave.
    I have given him a lesson for his sauciness.
    He's wronged thee. I will tell thee what shalt do:
    As we go over the fields by and by
    Clap him suddenly o'er the coxcomb with
    Thy torch. I'll bear thee out in it.
2nd SERVANT. I will make him understand as much.

    [*Exit.*]

    [*Enter* LANGUEBEAU SNUFFE.]

D'AMVILLE. Now, Monsieur Snuffe, what has my brother done?
LANGUEBEAU. Made his will, and by that will made you his heir with this proviso, that
    as occasion shall hereafter moue him, he may revoke, or alter it when he pleases.

D'AMVILLE. Yes. Let him if he can.—I'll make it sure
    From his revoking. [*Aside.*]

[*Enter* MONTFERRERS *and* BELFOREST *attended with lights.*]

MONTFERRERS. Brother, now good night.
D'AMVILLE. The sky is dark; we'll bring you o'er the fields.
    Who can but strike, wants wisdom to maintain;
    He that strikes safe and sure, has heart and brain.

    [*Exeunt.*]

SCENE III.

    [*Enter* CASTABELLA *alone.*]

CASTABELLA. O Love, thou chaste affection of the Soule,
    Without the adulterate mixture of the blood,
    That virtue, which to goodness addeth good,—
    The minion of heaven's heart. Heaven! Is it my fate
    For loving that thou lovest, to get thy hate,
    Or was my Charlemont thy chosen Love,
    And therefore hast received him to thy self?
    Then I confess thy anger's not unjust.
    I was thy rival. Yet to be divorced
    From love, has been a punishment enough
    (Sweet heaven!) without being married unto hate
    Hadst thou been pleased, O double misery
    Yet, since thy pleasure hath inflicted it,
    If not my heart, my duty shall submit.

    [*Enter* LEUIDULCIA, ROUSARD, CATAPLASMA, SOQUETTE, *and* FRESCO
      with a lantern.]

LEUIDULCIA. Mistress Cataplasma, good night. I pray when your Man has brought you
    home let him return and light me to my house.
CATAPLASMA. He shall instantly wait upon your Ladyship.
LEUIDULCIA. Good Mistress Cataplasma! for my servants are all drunk, I cannot be
    beholding to 'em for their attendance.

    [*Exeunt* CATAPLASMA, SOQUETTE, *and* FRESCO.]

    O here's your Bride!
ROUSARD. And melancholic too, me thinks.
LEUIDULCIA. How can she choose? Your sickness will
    Distaste the expected sweetness of the night
    That makes her heavy.
ROUSARD. That should make her light.
LEUIDULCIA. Look you to that.
CASTABELLA. What sweetness speak you of?
    The sweetness of the night consists in rest.

ROUSARD. With that sweetness thou shalt be surely blest
    Unless my groaning wake thee. Do not moan.
LEUIDULCIA. She'd rather you would wake, and make her groan.
ROUSARD. Nay 'troth, sweet heart, I will not trouble thee.
    Thou shalt not lose thy maiden-head to-night.
CASTABELLA. O might that weakness ever be in force,
    I never would desire to sue divorce.
ROUSARD. Wilt go to bed?
CASTABELLA. I will attend you, sir.
ROUSARD. Mother, good night.
LEUIDULCIA. Pleasure be your bed-fellow.

    [*Exeunt* ROUSARD *and* CASTABELLA.]

    Why sure their Generation was asleep
    When she begot those Dormice, that she made
    Them up so weakly and imperfectly.
    One wants desire, the other ability,
    When my affection even with their cold bloods
    (As snow rubbed through an active hand does make
    The flesh to burn) by agitation is
    Inflamed, I could embrace and entertain
    The air to cool it.

    [*Enter* SEBASTIAN.]

SEBASTIAN. That but mitigates
    The heat; rather embrace and entertain
    A younger brother; he can quench the fire.
LEUIDULCIA. Can you so, sir? Now I beshrew your ear.
    Why, bold Sebastian, how dare you approach
    So near the presence of your displeased Father?
SEBASTIAN. Under the protection of his present absence.
LEUIDULCIA. Belike you knew he was abroad then?
SEBASTIAN. Yes.
    Let me encounter you so; I'll persuade
    Your means to reconcile me to his love.
LEUIDULCIA. Is that the way? I understand you not.
    But for your reconcilement meet m' at home;
    I'll satisfy your suite.
SEBASTIAN. Within this half-hour?

    [*Exit* SEBASTIAN.]

LEUIDULCIA. Or within this whole hour. When you will.—
    A lusty blood! has both the presence and spirit of a man. I like the freedom of his
      behavior.
    —Ho!—Sebastian! Gone?—Has set

My blood of boiling in my veins. And now,
Like water poured upon the ground that mixes
Itself with every moisture it meets, I could
Clasp with any man.

[*Enter* FRESCO *with a Lantern.*]

O, Fresco, art thou come?
If t'other fail, then thou art entertained.
Lust is a Spirit, which whosoever doth raise,
The next man that encounters boldly, lays.

[*Exeunt.*]

SCENE IV.

[*Enter* BORACHIO *warily and hastily over the Stage with a stone in either hand.*]

BORACHIO. Such stones men use to raise a house upon
But with these stones I go to mine one.

[*Enter two* SERVANTS *drunk fighting with their torches.*]

[D'AMVILLE, MONTFERRERS, BELFOREST, LANGUEBEAU SNUFFE.]

BELFOREST. Passion of me, you drunken knaves! You! put The lights out.
D'AMVILLE. No, my Lord; they are but in jest.
1st SERVANT. Mine's out.
D'AMVILLE. Then light it at his head,—that's light enough.—
'Fore God, they are out You drunken Rascals, back And light 'em.
BELFOREST. 'Tis exceeding dark. [*Exeunt Servants*].
D'AMVILLE. No matter;
I am acquainted with the way. Your hand.
Lets easily walk. I'll lead you till they come.
MONTFERRERS. My soul's oppressed with grief. It lies heavy at
My heart. O my departed Son, ere long
I shall be with thee!

[D'AMVILLE *thrusts him down into the gravel pit.*]

D'AMVILLE. Marry, God forbid!
MONTFERRERS. O, o, o!
D'AMVILLE. Now all the host of heaven forbid! Knaves! Rogues!
BELFOREST. Pray God he be not hurt. He's fallen into the gravel-pit.
D'AMVILLE. Brother! dear brother! Rascals! villains! knaves!

[*Enter the Servants with lights.*]

Eternal darkness damn you! come away!
Go round about into the gravel pit,
And help my Brother up. Why what a strange
Unlucky night is this! Is it not, my Lord?
I think that Dog that howled the news of grief,
That fatal Scrichowle ushered on this mischief.

[*Enter with the murdered body.*]

LANGUEBEAU. Mischief indeed, my Lord. Your Brother's dead!
BELFOREST. He's dead?
SERVANT. He's dead!
D'AMVILLE. Dead be your tongues! Drop out
    Mine eyeballs and let envious Fortune play
    At tennis with 'em. Have I lived to this?
    Malicious Nature, hadest thou borne me blind,
    Th'adst yet been something favorable to me.
    No breath? no motion? Prithee tell me, heaven,
    Hast shut thine eye to wink at murder; or
    Hast put this sable garment on to mourn
    At 's death?
    Not one poor spark in the whole spacious sky
    Of all that endless number would vouchsafe
    To shine?—You viceroys to the King of Nature,
    Whose constellations govern mortal births,
    Where is that fatal Planet ruled at his
    Nativity? that might have pleased to light him out,
    As well as into the world, unless it be
    Ashamed I have been the instrument
    Of such a good man's cursed destiny.—
BELFOREST. Passion transports you. Recollect yourself.
    Lament him not. Whether our deaths be good
    Or bad, it is not death, but life that tries.
    He lived well; therefore, questionless, well dies,
D'AMVILLE. I, 'tis an easy thing for him that has
    No pain, to talk of patience. Do you think
    That Nature has no feeling?
BELFOREST. Feeling? Yes.
    But has she purposed anything for nothing?
    What good receives this body by your grief?
    Whether is it more unnatural, not to grieve
    For him you cannot help with it, or hurt
    Yourself with grieving, and yet grieve in vain?
D'AMVILLE. Indeed, had he been taken from me like
    A piece of dead flesh, I should neither have felt it
    Nor grieved for it. But come hither, pray look here.
    Behold the lively tincture of his blood!
    Neither the Dropsy nor the Jaundies in it,

But the true freshness of a sanguine red,
For all the fog of this black murderous night
Has mixed with it. For any thing I know
He might have lived till doomsday, and have done
More good than either you or I. O Brother!
He was a man of such a native goodness,
As if Regeneration had been given
Him in his mother's womb. So harmless
That rather than have trod upon a worm
He would have shunned the way.
So dearly pitiful that ere the poor
Could ask his charity with dry eyes he gave 'em
Relief wi' tears—with tears—yes, faith, with tears.

BELFOREST. Take up the Corps. For wisdom's sake let reason fortify this weakness.

D'AMVILLE. Why, what would you have me do? Foolish Nature
Will have her course in spite of wisdom. But
I have even done. All these words were
But a great wind; and now this shower of tears
Has laid it, I am calm again. You may
Set forward when you will. I'll follow you
Like one that must and would not.

LANGUEBEAU. Our opposition will but trouble him.

BELFOREST. The grief that melts to tears by itself is spent;
Passion resisted grows more violent.

[*Exeunt.*]

[D'AMVILLE *remains.* BORACHIO *ascends.*]

D'AMVILLE. Here's a sweet Comedy. It begins with *O*
Dolentis and concludes with ha, ha, he!

BORACHIO. Ha, ha, he!

D'AMVILLE. O my echo! I could stand
Reverberating this sweet musical air,
Of joy till I had perished my sound lungs
With violent laughter. Lonely Night-Raven,
Thou hast seized a carcass.

BORACHIO. Put him out on's pain.
I lay so fitly underneath the bank,
From whence he fell, that ere his faltering tongue
Could utter double Oo, I knocked out's brains
With this fair Ruby, and had another stone,
Just of this form and bigness, ready; that
I laid in the broken skull upon the ground
For's pillow, against the which they thought he fell
And perished.

D'AMVILLE. Upon this ground I'll build my Manor house;
And this shall be the chiefest corner stone.

BORACHIO. It has crowned the most judicious murder that
    The brain of man was ere delivered of.
D'AMVILLE. I, Mark the plot. Not any circumstance
    That stood within the reach of the design
    Of persons, dispositions, matter, time, or place
    But by this brain of mine was made
    An Instrumental help; yet nothing from
    The induction to the accomplishment seemed forced,
    Or done of purpose, but by accident.
BORACHIO. First, my report that Charlemont was dead,
    Though false, yet covered with a masque of truth.
D'AMVILLE. I, and delivered in as fit a time
    When all our minds so wholly were possessed
    With one affaire, that no man would suspect
    A thought employed for any second end.
BORACHIO. Then the Precisian to be ready, when
    Your brother spake of death, to moue his Will.
D'AMVILLE. His business called him thither and it fell
    Within his office unrequested to it.
    From him it came religiously, and saved
    Our project from suspicion which if I
    Had moved, had been endangered.
BORACHIO. Then your healths,
    Though seeming but the ordinary rites
    And ceremonies due to festivals——
D'AMVILLE. Yet used by me to make the servants drunk,—
    An instrument the plot could not have missed.
    'Twas easy to set drunkards by the ears
    They'd nothing but their torches to fight with
    And when those lights were out———
BORACHIO. Then darkness did
    Protect the execution of the work
    Both from preventions and discovery.
D'AMVILLE. Here was a murder bravely carried through
    The eye of observation, unobserved.
BORACHIO. And those that saw the passage of it made
    The Instruments, yet knew not what they did.
D'AMVILLE. That power of rule Philosophers ascribe
    To him they call the Supreme of the stars
    Making their influences governors
    Of Sublunary Creatures when themselves
    Are senseless of their operations.

[*Thunder and lightning.*]

What!
Dost start at thunder? Credit my belief
'Tis a mere effect of nature—an exhalation hot

And dry involved within a watery vapor
In the middle region of the air; whose coldness,
Congealing that thick moisture to a cloud,
The angry exhalation, shut within
A prison of contrary quality,
Strives to be free and with the violent
Eruption through the grossness of that cloud,
Makes this noise we hear.
BORACHIO. 'Tis a fearful noise.
D'AMVILLE. 'Tis a brave noise, and methinks
Graces our accomplished project as
A peal of Ordnance does a triumph. It speaks
Encouragement. Now Nature shows thee how
It favored our performance, to forbear
This noise when we set forth, because it should
Not terrify my brother's going home,
Which would have dashed our purpose,—to forbear
This lightning in our passage least it should
Have warmed him of the pitfall.
Then propitious Nature winked
At our proceedings: now it doth express
How that forbearance favored our success.
BORACHIO. You have confirmed me. For it follows well
That Nature, since herself decay doth hate,
Should favor those that strengthen their estate.
D'AMVILLE. Our next endeavor is, since on the false
Report that Charlemont is dead depends
The fabric of the work, to credit that
With all the countenance we can.
BORACHIO. Faith, Sir,
Even let his own inheritance, whereof
Ye have dispossessed him, countenance the act.
Spare so much out of that to give him a
Solemnity of funeral. 'Twill quit
The cost, and make your apprehension of
His death appear more confident and true.
D'AMVILLE. I'll take thy counsel. Now farewell, black Night;
Thou beauteous Mistress of a murderer.
To honour thee that hast accomplished all
I'll wear thy colors at his funeral

[*Exeunt.*]

SCENE V.

[*Enter* LEUIDULCIA *into her chamber manned by* FRESCO.]

LEUIDULCIA. Thou art welcome into my chamber, Fresco. Prithee shut the door.——
——Nay, thou mistakest me.
    Come in and shut it.

FRESCO. 'Tis somewhat late, Madame.

LEUIDULCIA. No matter. I have somewhat to say to thee.
    What, is not thy mistress towards a husband yet?

FRESCO. Faith, Madame, she has suitors, but they will not suite her, me thinks. They
    will not come off lustily it seems.

LEUIDULCIA. They will not come on lustily, thou wouldst say.

FRESCO. I mean, Madame, they are not rich enough.

LEUIDULCIA. But I, Fresco, they are not bold enough. Thy Mistress is of a lively
    attractive blood, Fresco, and in truth she is of my mind for that. A poor spirit is
    poorer than a poor purse. Give me a fellow that brings not only temptation with him,
    but has the activity of wit and audacity of spirit to apply every word and gesture of a
    woman's speech and behavior to his own desire, and make her believe she's the suitor
    herself. Never give back till he has made her yield to it.

FRESCO. Indeed among our equals, Madame; but otherwise we shall be put horribly out
    of countenance.

LEUIDULCIA. Thou art deceived, Fresco. Ladies are as courteous as Yeomen's wives,
    and me thinks they should be more gentle. Hot diet and soft ease makes 'em, like
    wax always kept warm, more easy to take impression.—Prithee untie my shoe.—
    What, art thou shamefaced too? Go roundly to work, man. My leg is not gouty: 'twill
    endure the feeling I warrant thee. Come hither, Fresco; thine ear. Is dainty, I mistook
    the place, I missed thine ear and hit thy lip.

FRESCO. Your Ladyship has made me blush.

LEUIDULCIA. That shows thou art full of lusty blood and thou knowest not how to use
    it. Let me see thy hand. Thou shouldest not be shamefaced by thy hand, Fresco.
    Here's a brawny flesh and a hairy skin, both signs of an able body. I do not like these
    phlegmatic, smooth-skinned, soft-fleshed fellows. They are like candied suckets
    when they begin to perish, which I would always empty my closet of, and give 'em
    my chamber-maid.—I have some skill in Palmistry: by this line that stands directly
    against me thou shouldest be near a good fortune, Fresco, if thou hadest the grace to
    entertain it.

FRESCO. O what is that, Madame, I pray?

LEUIDULCIA. No less than the love of a fair Lady, if thou dost not lose her with faint-
    heartedness.

FRESCO. A Lady, Madame? Alas, a Lady is a great thing:
    I cannot compass her.

LEUIDULCIA. No? Why I am a Lady, Am I so great I cannot be compassed? Clasp my
    waist, and try.

FRESCO. I could find in my heart, Madame—

[SEBASTIAN *knocks within.*]

LEUIDULCIA. 'Uds body, my Husband! Faint-hearted fool! I think thou wert begotten between the North-pole and the congealed passage. Now, like an ambitious Coward that betrays himself with fearful delay, you must suffer for the treason you never committed. Go, hide thy self behind yond arras instantly.

[FRESCO *hides himself.*]

[*Enter* SEBASTIAN.]

Sebastian! What do you here so late?

SEBASTIAN. Nothing yet, but I hope I shall.—*Kisses her.*

LEUIDULCIA. Very very bold.

SEBASTIAN. And you very valiant, for you met me at full Carrier.

LEUIDULCIA. You come to have me moue your father's reconciliation. I'll write a word or two in your behalf.

SEBASTIAN. A word or two, Madame? That you do for me will not be contained in less than the compass of two sheets. But in plain terms shall we take the opportunity of privateness?

LEUIDULCIA. What to do?

SEBASTIAN. To dance the beginning of the world after the English manner.

LEUIDULCIA. Why not after the French or Italian?

SEBASTIAN. Fie! They dance it preposterously; backward!

LEUIDULCIA. Are you so active to dance?

SEBASTIAN. I can shake my heels.

LEUIDULCIA. Ye are well made for it.

SEBASTIAN. Measure me from top to toe you shall not find me differ much from the true standard of proportion.

[BELFOREST *knocks within.*]

LEUIDULCIA. I think I am accursed, Sebastian. There's one at the door has beaten opportunity away from us. In brief, I love thee, and it shall not be long before I give thee a testimony of it To save thee now from suspicion do no more but draw thy Rapier, chafe thy self, and when he comes in, rush by without taking notice of him. Only seem to be angry, and let me alone for the rest.

[*Enter* BELFOREST.]

SEBASTIAN. Now by the hand of Mercury.

[*Exit* SEBASTIAN.]

BELFOREST. What's the matter, Wife?

LEUIDULCIA. Ooh, Ooh, Husband!

BELFOREST. Prithee what ailest thou, woman?

LEUIDULCIA. O feel ray pulse. It beats, I warrant you. Be patient a little, sweet Husband: tarry but till my breath come to me again and I'll satisfy you.

BELFOREST. What ails Sebastian? He looks so distractedly.

LEUIDULCIA. The poor Gentleman's almost out on his wits I think. You remember the displeasure his Father took against him about the liberty of speech he used even now, when your daughter went to be married?

BELFOREST. Yes. What of that?

LEUIDULCIA. It has crazed him sure. He met a poor man in the street even now. Upon what quarrel I know not, but he pursued him so violently that if my house had not been his rescue he had surely killed him.

BELFOREST. What a strange desperate, young man is that!

LEUIDULCIA. Nay, husband, he grew so in rage, when he saw the man was conveyed from him, that he was ready even to have drawn his naked weapon upon me. And had not your knocking at the door prevented him, surely he'd done something to me.

BELFOREST. Where's the man?

LEUIDULCIA. Alas, here! I warrant you the poor fearful soul is scarce come to himself again yet.—If the fool have any wit he will apprehend me. [*Aside.*]—Do you hear, sir? You may be bold to come forth: the Fury that haunted you is gone.

[FRESCO *peeps fearfully forth from behind the Arras.*]

FRESCO. Are you sure he is gone?

BELFOREST. He's gone, he's gone I warrant thee.

FRESCO. I would I were gone too. H's shook me almost into a dead palsy.

BELFOREST. How fell the difference between you?

FRESCO. I would I were out at the back door.

BELFOREST. Thou art safe enough. Prithee tell 's the falling out.

FRESCO. Yes, Sir, when I have recovered my spirits. My memory is almost frighted from me.—Oh, so, so, so!—Why Sir, as I came along the street, Sir—this same Gentleman came stumbling after me and trod of my' heel.—I cried O. Do you cry, sirrah? says he. Let me see your heel; if it be not hurt I'll make you cry for something. So he claps my head between his legs and pulls off my shoe. I having shifted no socks in a sennight, the Gentleman cried foh! and said my feet were base and cowardly feet, they stunk for fear. Then he knocked my shoe about my pate, and I cried O once more. In the mean time comes a shag-haired dog by, and rubs against his shins. The Gentleman took the dog in shag-hair to be some Watch-man in a rug gown, and swore he would hang me up at the next door with my lantern in my hand, that passengers might see their way as they went, without rubbing against Gentlemen's shins. So, for want of a Cord, he took his own garters off, and as he was going to make a noise, I watched my time and ran away. And as I ran, indeed I bid him hang himself in his own garters. So he, in choler, pursued me hither, as you see.

BELFOREST. Why, this savors of distraction.

LEUIDULCIA. Of mere distraction.

FRESCO. Howsoever it savors I am sure it smells like a lie.

[*Aside.*]

BELFOREST. Thou mayest go forth at the back door, honest fellow; the way is private and safe.

FRESCO. So it had need, for your fore-door here is both common and dangerous.

[*Exit* Belforest.]

LEUIDULCIA. Good night, honest Fresco.
FRESCO. Good night, Madame. If you get me kissing of Ladies again!—

[*Exit* FRESCO.]

LEUIDULCIA. This falls out handsomely.
    But yet the matter does not well succeed,
    Till I have brought it to the very deed.

[*Exit.*]

SCENE VI.

[*Enter* CHARLEMONT *in Arms, a* MUSKETEER, *and a* SERGEANT.]

CHARLEMONT. Sergeant, what hour of the night is it?
SERGEANT. About one.
CHARLEMONT. I would you would relieve me, for I am
    So heavy that I shall have much ado
    To stand out my perdue.

[*Thunder and Lightning.*]

SERVANT. I'll even but walk
    The round, Sir, and then presently return.
SOLDIER. For God's sake, Sergeant, relieve me. Above five hours together in so foul a
    stormy night as this!
SERVANT. Why 'tis a music, Soldier. Heaven and earth are now in consort, when the
    Thunder and the Canon play one to another.

[*Exit* SERGEANT.]

CHARLEMONT. I know not why I should be thus inclined
    To sleep. I feel my disposition pressed
    With a necessity of heaviness.
    Soldier, if thou hast any better eyes,
    I prithee wake me when the Sergeant comes.
SOLDIER. Sir, 'tis so dark and stormy that I shall
    Scarce either see or hear him, ere he comes
    Upon me.
CHARLEMONT. I cannot force myself to wake.—

[*Sleeps.*]

[*Enter the Ghost of* MONTFERRERS.]

MONTFERRERS. Return to France, for thy old Father's dead,
    And thou by murder disinherited.
    Attend with patience the success of things,
    But leave revenge unto the King of kings.

    [*Exit.*]

    [CHARLEMONT *starts and wakes.*]

CHARLEMONT. O my affrighted soul, what fearful dream
    Was this that waked me? Dreams are but the raised
    Impressions of premeditated things
    By serious apprehension left upon
    Our minds, or else the imaginary shapes
    Of objects proper to the complexion, or
    The dispositions of our bodies. These
    Can neither of them be the cause why I
    Should dream thus; for my mind has not been moved
    With any one conception of a thought
    To such a purpose; nor my nature wont
    To trouble me with fantasies of terror.
    It must be something that my Genius would
    Inform me of. Now gracious heaven forbid!
    Oh! let my Spirit be deprived of all
    Fore-sight and knowledge, ere it understand
    That vision acted, or divine that act
    To come. Why should I think so? Left I not
    My worthy Father in the kind regard
    Of a most loving Uncle? Soldier, sawest
    No apparition of a man?
SOLDIER. You dream,
    Sir. I saw nothing.
CHARLEMONT. Tush! these idle dreams
    Are fabulous. Our boiling fantasies
    like troubled waters falsify the shapes
    Of things retained in them, and make 'em seem
    Confounded when they are distinguished. So,
    My actions daily conversant with war,
    The argument of blood and death had left
    Perhaps the imaginary presence of
    Some bloody accident upon my mind,
    Which, mixed confusedly with other thoughts,
    Whereof the remembrance of my Father might
    Be one presented, all together seem
    Incorporate, as if his body were
    The owner of that blood, the subject of
    That death, when he's at Paris and that blood

Shed here. It may be thus. I would not leave
The war, for reputation's sake, upon
An idle apprehension, a vain dream.

[*Enter the Ghost.*]

SOLDIER. Stand. Stand I say. No? Why then have at thee,
Sir. If you will not stand, I'll make you fall

[*Fires.*]

Nor stand nor fall? Nay then, the Devil's damn
Has broke her husband's head, for sure it is
A Spirit
I shot it through, and yet it will not fall.

[*Exit.*]

[*The Ghost approaches* CHARLEMONT.]

[*He fearfully avoids it.*]

CHARLEMONT. O pardon me, my doubtful heart was slow
To credit that which I did fear to know.

[*Exeunt.*]

ACT III.

SCENE I.

[*Enter the Funeral of* MONTFERRERS.]

D'AMVILLE. Set down the Body. Pay Earth what she lent.
But she shall bear a living monument
To let succeeding ages truly know
That she is satisfied what he did owe,
Both principal and use; because his worth
Was better at his death then at his birth.

[*A dead march. Enter the Funeral of* CHARLEMONT *as a Soldier.*]

D'AMVILLE. And with his Body place that memory
Of noble Charlemont his worthy Son;
And give their Graves the rites that do belong
To Soldiers. They were Soldiers both. The Father
Held open war with Sin, the Son with blood:
This in a war more gallant, that more good.

[*The first volley.*]

D'AMVILLE. There place their Arms, and here their Epitaphs
    And may these Lines survive the last of graves.

THE EPITAPH OF MONTFERRERS.

Here lye the Ashes of that Earth and fire,
whose heat and fruit did feed and warm the poor!
And they (as if they would in sighs expire,
and into tears dissolve) his death deplore.
He did that good freely for goodness sake
unforced, for generousness he held so dear
That he feared but him that did him make
and yet he served him more for love than fear.
So's life provided that though he did die
A sudden death, yet dyed not suddenly.

THE EPITAPH OF CHARLEMONT.

His Body lies interred within this mould,
Who died a young man yet departed old,
And in all strength of youth that Man can have
Was ready still to drop into his grave.
For aged in virtue, with a youthful eye
He welcomed it, being stil lprepared to die
And living so, though young deprived of breath
He did not suffer an untimely death,
But we may say of his brave blessed decease
He died in war, and yet he died in peace.

[*The second volley.*]

D'AMVILLE. O might that fire revive the ashes of
    This Phoenix! yet the wonder would not be
    So great as he was good, and wondered at
    For that. His lives example was so true
    A practice of Religion's Theory
    That her Divinity seemed rather the
    Description then the instruction of his life.
    And of his goodness was his virtuous Son
    A worthy imitator. So that on
    These two Herculean pillars where their arms
    Are placed there may be writ *Non ultra.* For
    Beyond their lives, as well for youth as age,
    Nor young nor old, in merit or in name,
    Shall ever exceed their virtues or their fame.

[The third volley.]

'Tis done. Thus fair complements make foul
Deeds gracious. Charlemont, come now when thou wilt
I've buried under these two marble stones
Thy living hopes, and thy dead father's bones.

[Exeunt.]

[Enter CASTABELLA *mourning to the monument of* CHARLEMONT.]

CASTABELLA. O thou that knowest me justly Charlemont's,
Though in the forced possession of another.
Since from thine own free spirit we receive it
That our affections cannot be compelled
Though our actions may, be not displeased if on
The altar of his Tomb I sacrifice
My tears. They are the jewels of my love
Dissolved into grief, and fall upon
His blasted Spring, as April dew upon
A sweet young blossom shaked before the time.

[Enter CHARLEMONT *with a* SERVANT.]

CHARLEMONT. Go see my Trunks disposed of. I'll but walk
A turn or two in the Church and follow you.

[Exit SERVANT.]

O! here's the fatal monument of my
Dead Father first presented to mine eye.
What's here?—'*In memory of* Charlemont?'
Some false relation has abused belief.
I am deluded. But I thank thee, Heaven.
For ever let me be deluded thus.
My Castabella mourning o'er my Hearse?
Sweet Castabella, rise. I am not dead,
CASTABELLA. O heaven defend me!

[Falls in a swoon.]

CHARLEMONT. I—Beshrew my rash
And inconsiderate passion.—Castabella!
That could not think—my Castabella!—that
My sudden presence might affright her sense.—
I prithee (my affection) pardon me. *[She rises.]*
Reduce thy understanding to thine eye.

Within this habit, which thy misinformed
Conceit takes only for a shape, Hue both
The soul and body of thy Charlemont.

CASTABELLA. I feel a substance warm, and soft, and moist,
Subject to the capacity of sense.

CHARLEMONT. Which Spirits are not; for their essence is
Above the nature and the order of
Those Elements whereof our senses are
Created. Touch my lip. Why turnest thou from me?

CASTABELLA. Grief above griefs! That which should woe relieve
Wished and obtained, gives greater cause to grieve.

CHARLEMONT. Can Castabella think it cause of grief
That the relation of my death proves false?

CASTABELLA. The presence of the person wee affect,
Being hopeless to enjoy him, makes our grief
More passionate than if we saw him not.

CHARLEMONT. Why not enjoy? Has absence changed thee?

CASTABELLA. Yes.
From maid to wife.

CHARLEMONT. Art married?

CASTABELLA. O! I am.

CHARLEMONT. Married?—Had not my mother been a woman
I should protest against the chastity
Of all thy sex. How can the Merchant or
The Mariners absent whole years from wives
Experience in the satisfaction of
Desire, promise themselves to find their sheets
Unspotted with adultery at their
Return, when you that never had the sense
Of actual temptation could not stay
A few short months?

CASTABELLA. O! do but hear me speak.

CHARLEMONT. But thou wert wise, and didst consider that
A Soldier might be maimed, and so perhaps
Lose his ability to please thee.

CASTABELLA. No.
That weakness pleases me in him I have.

CHARLEMONT. What, married to a man unable too?
O strange incontinence! Why, was thy blood
Increased to such a pleurisy of lust,
That of necessity there must a vein
Be opened, though by one that had no skill
To do it?

CASTABELLA. Sir, I beseech you hear me.

CHARLEMONT. Speak.

CASTABELLA. Heaven knows I am unguilty of this act.

CHARLEMONT. Why? Wert thou forced to do it?

CASTABELLA. Heaven knows I was.

CHARLEMONT. What villain did it?
CASTABELLA. Your Uncle D'amville.
    And he that dispossessed my love of you
    Hath disinherited you of possession.
CHARLEMONT. Disinherited? wherein have I deserved
    To be deprived of my dear Father's love?
CASTABELLA. Both of his love and him. His soul's at rest;
    But here your injured patience may behold
    The signs of his lamented memory.

[CHARLEMONT *finds his Father's Monument.*]

    H's found it When I took him for a Ghost
    I could endure the torment of my fear
    More easily than I can his sorrows hear.

[*Exit.*]

CHARLEMONT. Of all men's griefs must mine be singular?
    Without example? Here I met my grave.
    And all men's woes are buried in their graves
    But mine. In mine my miseries are borne.
    I prithee sorrow leave a little room
    In my confounded and tormented mind
    For understanding to deliberate
    The cause or author of this accident.—
    A close advantage of my absence made
    To dispossess me both of land and wife,
    And all the profit does arise to him
    By whom my absence was first moved and urged.
    These circumstances, Uncle, tell me you
    Are the suspected author of those wrongs,
    Whereof the lightest is more heavy then
    The strongest patience can endure to bear.

[*Exit.*]

SCENE II.

[*Enter* D'AMVILLE, SEBASTIAN, *and* LANGUEBEAU.]

D'AMVILLE. Now, Sir, your business?
SEBASTIAN. My Annuity.
D'AMVILLE. Not a denier.
SEBASTIAN. How would you have me live?
D'AMVILLE. Why turn Crier. Cannot you turn Crier?
SEBASTIAN. Yes.
D'AMVILLE. Then do so: ye have a good voice for it.

Ye are excellent at crying of a Rape.

SEBASTIAN. Sir, I confess in particular respect to yourself I was somewhat forgetful. General honesty possessed me.

D'AMVILLE. Go, thou art the base corruption of my blood;
And, like a tetter, grow'st unto my flesh.

SEBASTIAN. Inflict any punishment upon me. The severity shall not discourage me if it be not shameful, so you'll but put money in my purse. The want of money makes a free spirit more mad than the possession does an Usurer.

D'AMVILLE. Not a farthing.

SEBASTIAN. Would you have me turn purse-taker? 'Tis the next way to do it. For want is like the Rack: it draws a man to endanger himself to the gallows rather than endure it.

[*Enter* CHARLEMONT. D'AMVILLE *counterfeits to take him for a ghost.*]

D'AMVILLE. What art thou? Stay—Assist my troubled sense—
My apprehension will distract me—Stay.

[LANGUEBEAU SNUFFE *avoids him fearfully.*]

SEBASTIAN. What art thou? Speak.

CHARLEMONT. The spirit of Charlemont.

D'AMVILLE. O! stay. Compose me. I dissolue.

LANGUEBEAU. No. 'Tis profane. Spirits are invisible. 'Tis the fiend in the likeness of Charlemont. I will have no conversation with Satan.

[*Exit* SNUFFE.]

SEBASTIAN. The Spirit of Charlemont? I'll try that.

[*Strikes, and the blow returned.*]

'Fore God thou sayest true: thou art all Spirit.

D'AMVILLE. Go, call the Officers.

[*Exit* D'AMVILLE.]

CHARLEMONT. Thou art a villain, and the son of a villain.

SEBASTIAN. You lie.

[*Fight.*]

[SEBASTIAN *is down.*]

CHARLEMONT. Have at thee.

[*Enter the Ghost of* MONTFERRERS.]

Revenge, to thee I'll dedicate this work.
MONTFERRERS. Hold, Charlemont.
    Let him revenge my murder and thy wrongs
    To whom the Justice of Revenge belongs. *Exit.*
CHARLEMONT. You torture me between the passion of
    My blood and the religion of my soul.

    [SEBASTIAN *rises.*]

SEBASTIAN. A good honest fellow!

    [*Enter* D'AMVILLE *with Officers.*]

D'AMVILLE. What, wounded? Apprehend him. Sir, is this
    Your salutation for the courtesy
    I did you when we parted last? You have
    Forgot I lent you a thousand Crowns. First, let
    Him answer for this riot. When the Law
    Is satisfied for that, an action for
    His debt shall clap him up again. I took
    You for a Spirit and I'll conjure you
    Before I have done.
CHARLEMONT. No, I'll turn Conjurer. Devil!
    Within this Circle, in the midst of all
    Thy force and malice, I conjure thee do
    Thy worst.
D'AMVILLE. Away with him.

    [*Exeunt Officers with* CHARLEMONT.]

SEBASTIAN. Sir, I have got
    A scratch or two here for your sake. I hope
    You'll give me money to pay the Surgeon.
D'AMVILLE. Borachio, fetch me a thousand Crowns. I am
    Content to countenance the freedom of
    Your spirit when 'tis worthily employed.
    A God's name give behavior the full scope
    Of generous liberty, but let it not
    Disperse and spend itself in courses of
    Unbounded license. Here, pay for your hurts.

    [*Exit* D'AMVILLE.]

SEBASTIAN. I thank you, sir.—Generous liberty!—that is to say, freely to bestow my
abilities to honest purposes. Me thinks I should not follow that instruction now, i
having the means to do an honest office for an honest fellow, I should neglect i
Charlemont lies in prison for a thousand Crowns. Honesty tells me 'twere well done

to release Charlemont. But discretion says I had much a do to come by this, and when this shall be gone I know not where to finger any more, especially if I employ it to this use, which is like to endanger me into my Father's perpetual displeasure. And then I may go hang myself, or be forced to do that will make another save me the labor. No matter, Charlemont, thou gavest me my life, and that's somewhat of a purer earth then gold, fine as it is. 'Tis no courtesy, I do thee but thankfulness. I owe it thee, and I'll pay it. He fought bravely, but the Officers dragged him villainously. Arrant knaves! for using him so discourteously; may the sins of the poor people be so few that you shall not be able to spare so much out of your gettings as will pay for the hire of a lame starved hackney to ride to an execution, but go a foot to the gallows and be hanged. May elder brothers turn good husbands, and younger brothers get good wives, that there be no need of debt-books nor use of Sergeants. May there be all peace, but in the war and all charity, but in the Devil, so that prisons may be turned to Hospitals, though the Officers live of the benevolence. If this curse might come to pass, the world would say, *Blessed be he that curseth.*

[*Exit.*]

SCENE III.

[*Enter* CHARLEMONT *in prison.*]

CHARLEMONT. I grant thee, Heaven, thy goodness doth command
    Our punishments, but yet no further then
    The measure of our sins. How should they else
    Be just? Or how should that good purpose of
    Thy Justice take effect by bounding men
    Within the confines of humanity,
    When our afflictions do exceed our crimes?
    Then they do rather teach the barbarous world
    Examples that extend her cruelties
    Beyond their own dimensions, and instruct
    Our actions to be much more barbarous.
    O my afflicted soul! How torment swells
    Thy apprehension with profane conceit,
    Against the sacred justice of my God!
    Our own constructions are the authors of
    Our misery. We never measure our
    Conditions but with Men above us in
    Estate. So while our Spirits labor to
    Be higher than our fortunes, thou are more base.
    Since all those attributes which make men seem
    Superior to us, are Man's subjects and
    Were made to serve him. The repining Man
    Is of a servile spirit to deject
    The value of himself below their estimation.

[*Enter* SEBASTIAN *with the Keeper.*]

SEBASTIAN. Here. Take my sword.—How now, my wild Swaggerer? Ye are tame enough now, are you not? The penury of a prison is like a soft consumption. 'Twill humble the pride of your mortality, and arm your soul in complete patience to endure the weight of affliction without feeling it. What, hast no music in thee? The hast trebles and bases enough. Treble injury and base usage. But trebles and bases make Poor music without means. Thou wantest Means, dost? What? Dost droop? art dejected?

CHARLEMONT. No, Sir. I have a heart above the reach
    Of thy most violent maliciousness;
    A fortitude in scorn of thy contempt
    (Since Fate is pleased to have me suffer it)
    That can bear more than thou has power t' inflict.
    I was a Baron. That thy Father has
    Deprived me of. Instead of that I am
    Created King. I've lost a Signiorie
    That was confined within a piece of earth,
    A Wart upon the body of the world,
    But now I am an Emperor of a world,
    This little world of Man. My passions are
    My Subjects, and I can command them laugh,
    Whilst thou dost tickle 'em to death with misery.

SEBASTIAN. 'Tis bravely spoken and I love thee for it Thou liest here for a thousand crowns. Here are a thousand to redeem thee. Not for the ran-some of my life thou gavest me,—That I value not at one crown—'Tis none of my deed. Thank my Father for it. Tis his goodness. Yet he looks not for thanks. For he does it under hand, out of a reserved disposition to do thee good without ostentation.—Out of great heart you'll refuse it now; will you?

CHARLEMONT. No. Since I must submit myself to Fate
    I never will neglect the offer of
    One benefit, but entertain them as
    Her favors and the inductions to some end
    Of better fortune. As whose instrument,
    I thank thy courtesy.

SEBASTIAN. Well, come along. *Exeunt.*

SCENE IV.

[*Enter* D'AMVILLE *and* CASTABELLA.]

D'AMVILLE. Daughter, you do not well to urge me. I
    Have done no more than Justice. Charlemont
    Shall die and rot in prison, and 'tis just.

CASTABELLA. O Father, Mercy is an attribute
    As high as Justice, an essential part
    Of his unbounded goodness, whose divine
    Impression, form, and image man should bear!
    And, me thinks, Man should love to imitate

His Mercy, since the only countenance
Of Justice were destruction, if the sweet
And loving favor of his mercy did
Not mediate between it and our weakness.

D'AMVILLE. Forebear. You will displease me. He shall rot.

CASTABELLA. Dear Sir, since by your greatness you
Are nearer heaven in place, be nearer it
In goodness. Rich men should transcend the poor
As clouds the Earth, raised by the comfort of
The Sun to water dry and barren grounds.
If neither the impression in your soul
Of goodness, nor the duty of your place
As goodness substitute can moue you, then
Let nature which in Savages, in beasts
Can stir to pity, tell you that he is
Your kinsman.—

D'AMVILLE. You expose your honesty
To strange construction. Why should you so urge
Release for Charlemont? Come, you profess
More nearness to him then your modesty
Can answer. You have tempted my suspicion.
I tell thee he shall starve, and die, and rot.

[*Enter* CHARLEMONT *and* SEBASTIAN.]

CHARLEMONT. Uncle, I thank you.
D'AMVILLE. Much good do it you.—Who did release him?
SEBASTIAN. I.

[*Exit* CASTABELLA.]

D'AMVILLE. You are a villain.
SEBASTIAN. Ye are my Father. *Exit* Sebastian.
D'AMVILLE. I must temporize.—[Aside]
Nephew, had not his open freedom made
My disposition known, I would have borne
The course and inclination of my love
According to the motion of the Sun,
Invisibly enjoyed and understood.

CHARLEMONT. That shows your good works are directed to
No other end then goodness. I was rash,
I must confess. But—

D'AMVILLE. I will excuse you.
To lose a Father and, as you may think,
Be disinherited, it must be granted
Are motives to impatience. But for death,
Who can avoid it? And for his estate
In the uncertainty of both your lives

'Twas done discreetly to conferred upon
A known Successor being the next in blood.
And one, dear Nephew, whom in time to come
You shall have cause to thank. I will not be
Your dispossessor but your Guardian.
I will supply your Father's vacant place
To guide your green improvidence of youth,
And make you ripe for your inheritance.
CHARLEMONT. Sir, I embrace your generous promises.

[*Enter* ROUSARD *sick and* CASTABELLA.]

ROUSARD. Embracing! I behold the object that
    Mine eye affects. Deere Cousin Charlemont.
D'AMVILLE. My elder Son! He meets you happily.
    For with the hand of our whole family
    We interchange the indenture of our Loves.
CHARLEMONT. And I accept it. Yet not so joyfully
    Because ye are sick.
D'AMVILLE. Sir, his affection's sound
    Though he be sick in body.
ROUSARD. Sick indeed.
    A general weakness did surprise my health
    The very day I married Castabella
    As if my sickness were a punishment
    That did arrest me for some injury
    I then committed. Credit me, my Love,
    I pity thy ill fortune to be matched
    With such a weak, unpleasing bedfellow.
CASTABELLA. Believe me, Sir, it never troubles me.
    I am as much respectless to enjoy
    Such pleasure, as ignorant what it is.
CHARLEMONT. Thy Sex's wonder. Unhappy Charlemont!
D'AMVILLE. Come, let's to supper. There we will confirm
    The eternal bond of our concluded love.

[*Exeunt.*]

ACT IV.

SCENE I.

[*Enter* CATAPLASMA *and* SOQUETTE *with Needle-work.*]

CATAPLASMA. Come, Soquette, your work! let's examine your work. What's here? a Medlar with a Plum-tree growing hard by it; the leaves of the Plum-tree falling off; the gum issuing out of the perished joints; and the branches some of 'em dead, and some rotten; and yet but a young Plum-tree. In good sooth very pretty.

SOQUETTE. The Plum-tree, forsooth, grows so near the Medlar that the Medlar sucks and draws all the sap from it and the natural strength of the ground, so that it cannot prosper.

CATAPLASMA. How conceited you are! But here thou hast made a tree to bear no fruit. Why's that?

SOQUETTE. There grows a Savin-tree next it, forsooth.

CATAPLASMA. Forsooth you are a little too witty in that.

[*Enter* SEBASTIAN.]

SEBASTIAN. But this Honeysuckle winds about this white-thorn very prettily and lovingly, sweet Mistress Cataplasma.

CATAPLASMA. Monsieur Sebastian! in good sooth very uprightly welcome this evening.

SEBASTIAN. What, moralizing upon this Gentlewoman's needle-work? Let's see.

CATAPLASMA. No, sir. Only examining whether it be done to the true nature and life of the thing.

SEBASTIAN. Here ye have set a Medlar with a Bachelor's button of one side and a snail of the other. The Bachelor's button should have held his head up more pertly towards the Medlar: the snail of the other side should have been wrought with an artificial laziness, doubling his tail and putting out his horn but half the length. And then the Medlar falling (as it were) from the lazy Snail and ending towards the pert Bachelor's button, their branches spreading and winding one within another as if they did embrace. But here's a moral. A poppring Pear-tree growing upon the bank of a River seeming continually to look downwards into the water as if it were enamored of it, and ever as the fruit ripens lets it fall for love (as it were) into her lap. Which the wanton Stream, like a Strumpet, no sooner receives but she carries it away and bestows it upon some other creature she maintains, still seeming to play and dally under the Poppring so long that it has almost washed away the earth from the root, and now the poor Tree stands as if it were ready to fall and perish by that whereon it spent all the substance it had.

CATAPLASMA. Moral for you that love those wanton running waters.

SEBASTIAN. But is not my Lady Leuidulcia come yet?

CATAPLASMA. Her purpose promised us her company ere this Sirrie, your Lute and your Book.

SEBASTIAN. Well said. A lesson of the Lute, to entertain the time with till she comes.

CATAPLASMA. Sol, fa, mi, la.———Mi, mi, mi.———Precious! Dost not see *mi* between the two Crotchets? Strike me full there.———So——forward. This is a sweet strain, and thou fingerest it beastly. *Mi* is a large there, and the prick that stands before *mi* a long; always half your note.———Now———Run your division pleasingly with these quavers. Observe all your graces in the touch.———Here's a sweet cloze——strike it full; it sets off your music delicately.

[*Enter* LANGUEBEAU SNUFFE *and* LEUIDULCIA.]

LANGUEBEAU. Purity be in this House.

CATAPLASMA. 'Tis now entered; and welcome with your good Ladyship.

SEBASTIAN. Cease that music. Here's a sweeter instrument.

LEUIDULCIA. Restrain your liberty. See you not Snuffe?

SEBASTIAN. What does the Stinkard here? put Snuffe out. He's offensive.

LEUIDULCIA. No. The credit of his company defends my being abroad from the eye of Suspicion.

CATAPLASMA. Wilt please your Ladyship go up into the Closet? There are those Falls and Tyres I told you of.

LEUIDULCIA. Monsieur Snuffe, I shall request your patience. My stay will not be long.—

[*Exit with* SEBASTIAN.]

LANGUEBEAU. My duty, Madame.———Falls and Tyres! I begin to suspect what Falls and Tyres you mean. My Lady and Sebastian the Fall and the Tyre, and I the shadow. I perceive the purity of my conversation is used but for a property to cover the uncleanness of their purposes. The very contemplation of the thing makes the spirit of the flesh begin to wriggle in my blood. And here my desire has met with an object already. This Gentlewoman, me thinks, should be swayed with the motion, living in a house where moving example is so common.———Mistress Cataplasma, my Lady, it seems, has some business that requires her stay. The fairness of the evening invites me into the air. Will it please you give this Gentlewoman leave to leave her work and walk a turn or two with me for honest recreation?

CATAPLASMA. With all my heart, Sir. Go, Soquette: give ear to his instructions. You may get understanding by his company, I can tell you.

LANGUEBEAU. In the way of holiness, Mistress Cataplasma.

CATAPLASMA. Good Monsieur Snuffe!———I will attend your return.

LANGUEBEAU. Your hand, Gentlewoman.—
     The flesh is humble till the Spirit moue it.
     But when 'tis raised it will command above it.

[*Exeunt.*]

SCENE II.

[*Enter* D'AMVILLE, CHARLEMONT, *and* BORACHIO.]

D'AMVILLE. Your sadness and the sickness of my Son
    Have made our company and conference
    Less free and pleasing then I purposed it.
CHARLEMONT. Sir, for the present I am much unfit
    For conversation or society.
    With pardon I will rudely take my leave.
D'AMVILLE. Good night, dear Nephew.

[*Exit Charlemont.*]

    Seest thou that same man?
BORACHIO. Your meaning, Sir?
D'AMVILLE. That fellow's life, Borachio,
    Like a superfluous Letter in the Law,
    Endangers our assurance.
BORACHIO. Scrape him out.
D'AMVILLE. Wilt do it?
BORACHIO. Give me your purpose—I will do it.
D'AMVILLE. Sad melancholy has drawn Charlemont
    With meditation on his Father's death
    Into the solitary walk behind the Church.
BORACHIO. The Churchyard? 'Tis the fittest place for death.
    Perhaps he's praying. Then he's fit to die.
    We'll send him charitably to his grave.
D'AMVILLE. No matter how thou takest him. First take this.—

[*Gives him a Pistol.*]

    Thou knowest the place. Observe his passages
    And with the most advantage make a stand,
    That, favored by the darkness of the night,
    His breast may fall upon thee at so near
    A distance that he shall not shun the blow.
    The deed once done, thou mayest retire with safety.
    The place is unfrequented, and his death
    Will be imputed to the attempt of thieves.
BORACHIO. Be careless. Let your mind be free and clear.
    This Pistol shall discharge you of your fear.

[*Exit.*]

D'AMVILLE. But let me call my projects to account
    For what effect and end have I engaged

Myself in all this blood? To leave a state
To the succession of my proper blood.
But how shall that succession be continued?
Not in my elder Son, I fear. Disease
And weakness have disabled him for issue.
For the other,—his loose humor will endure
No bond of marriage. And I doubt his life,
His spirit is so boldly dangerous.
O pity that the profitable end
Of such a prosperous murder should be lost!
Nature forbid! I hope I have a body
That will not suffer me to lose my labor
For want of issue yet. But then it must be
A Bastard.—Tush! they only father bastards
That father other men's begettings. Daughter!
Be it mine own. Let it come whence it will
I am resolved. Daughter!

[*Enter Servant.*]

SERVANT. My Lord.
D'AMVILLE. I prithee call my Daughter.

[*Enter* CASTA.]

CASTABELLA. Your pleasure, Sir.
D'AMVILLE. Is thy Husband in bed?
CASTABELLA. Yes, my Lord.
D'AMVILLE. The evening's fair. I prithee walk a turn or two.
CASTABELLA. Come, Jaspar.

D'AMVILLE. No.
    We'll walk but to the corner of the Church;
    And I have something to speak privately.
CASTABELLA. No matter; stay.

[*Exit* SERVANT.]

D'AMVILLE. This falls out happily.

[*Exeunt.*]

SCENE III. *The churchyard.*

[*Enter* CHARLEMONT,—BORACHIO *dogging him in the Churchyard. The Clock strikes twelve.*]

CHARLEMONT. Twelve.
BORACHIO. 'Tis a good hour: 'twill strike one anon.
CHARLEMONT. How fit a place for contemplation is this dead of night, among the dwellings of the dead.—This grave.—Perhaps the inhabitant was in his life time the possessor of his own desires. Yet in the midst of all his greatness and his wealth he was less rich and less contented then in this poor piece of earth lower and lesser then a Cottage. For here he neither wants, nor cares. Now that his body savors of corruption
H' enjoys a sweeter rest then ever he did
Amongst the sweetest pleasures of this life
For here there's nothing troubles him.—And there
—In that grave lies another. He, perhaps,
Was in his life as full of misery
As this of happiness. And here's an end
Of both. Now both their states are equal. O
That man with so much labor should aspire
To worldly height, when in the humble earth
The world's condition's at the best, or scorn
Inferior men since to be lower than
A worm is to be higher than a King.
BORACHIO. Then fall and rise.

[*Discharges the pistol. Gives false fire.*]

CHARLEMONT. What villains hand was that?
Save thee, or thou shalt perish.

[*They fight.*]

BORACHIO. Zownes! unsaved
I think

[*Falls.*]

CHARLEMONT. What? Have I killed him? Whatsoever thou beest
I would thy hand had prospered. For I was
Unfit to live and well prepaid to die.
What shall I do? Accuse myself? Submit
Me to the law? And that will quickly end
This violent increase of misery.
But 'tis a murder to be accessory
To mine own death. I will not I will take

This opportunity to escape. It may
Be Heaven reserves me to some better end.

[*Exit* CHARLEMONT.]

[*Enter* LANGUEBEAU SNUFFE *and* SOQUETTE *into the Churchyard.*]

SOQUETTE. Nay, good Sir, I dare not In good sooth I come of a generation both by
  Father and Mother that were all as fruitful as Costard-mongers' wives.
LANGUEBEAU. Tush then a Timpanie is the greatest danger can be feared. Their
  fruitfulness turns but to a certain kind of phlegmatic windy disease.
SOQUETTE. I must put my understanding to your trust, Sir.
I would be loath to be deceived.
LANGUEBEAU. No, conceive thou shalt not. Yet thou shalt profit by my instruction too.
  My body is not every day drawn dry, wench.
SOQUETTE. Yet me thinks, Sir, your want of use should rather make your body like a
  Well,—the lesser 'tis drawn, the sooner it grows dry.
LANGUEBEAU. Thou shalt try that instantly.
SOQUETTE. But we want place and opportunity.
LANGUEBEAU. We have both. This is the back side of the House which the
  superstitious call Saint Winifred's Church, and is verily a convenient
  unfrequented place.—
Where under the close Curtains of the night—
SOQUETTE. You purpose in the dark to make me light.

[LANGUEBEAU SNUFFE *Pulls out a sheet, a hair, and a beard.*]

But what have you there?
LANGUEBEAU. This disguise is for securities sake, wench. There's a talk, thou
  knowest, that the Ghost of old Montferrers walks. In this Church he was buried. Now
  if any stranger fall upon us before our business be ended, in this disguise I shall be
  taken for that Ghost, and never be called to examination, I warrant thee. Thus we
  shall escape both preventions and discovery. How do I look in this habit, wench?
SOQUETTE. So like a Ghost that notwithstanding I have some foreknowledge of you,
  you make my hair stand almost on end.
LANGUEBEAU. I will try how I can kiss in this beard.—O fie, fie, fie I will put it off
  and then kiss, and then put it on. I can do the rest without kissing.

[*Enter* CHARLEMONT *doubtfully with his sword drawn; is upon them before they
  are aware. They run out divers ways, and leave the disguise.*]

CHARLEMONT. What have wee here? a Sheet! a hair! a beard!
  What end was this disguise intended for?
  No matter what I'll not expostulate
  The purpose of a friendly accident.
  Perhaps it may accommodate my 'escape.
  ——I fear I am pursued. For more assurance.
  I'll hide me here in the Charnel house,

This convocation-house of dead men's skulls.

[*To get into the Charnel house he takes hold of a Death's head; it slips and staggers him.*]

Death's head, deceivest my hold?
Such is the trust to all mortality.

[*Hides himself e in the Charnel house.*]

[*Enter* D'AMVILLE *and* CASTABELLA.]

CASTABELLA. My Lord, the night grows late. Your Lordship spake
 Of something you desired to moue in private.
D'AMVILLE. Yes. Now I'll speak it. The argument is love.
 The smallest ornament of thy sweet form
 (That abstract of all pleasure) can command
 The senses into passion and thy entire
 Perfection is my object, yet I love thee
 With the freedom of my reason. I can give
 Thee reason for my love.
CASTABELLA. Love me, my Lord?
 I do believe it, for I am the wife
 Of him you love.
D'AMVILLE. 'Tis true. By my persuasion thou wert forced
 To marry one unable to perform
 The office of a Husband. I was author
 Of the wrong.
 My conscience suffers under it, and I would
 Disburden it by satisfaction.
CASTABELLA. How?
D'AMVILLE. I will supply that pleasure to thee which he cannot.
CASTABELLA. Are ye a devil or a man?
D'AMVILLE. A man, and such a man as can return
 Thy entertainment with as prodigal
 A body as the covetous desire,
 Or woman ever was delighted with.
 So that, besides the full performance of
 Thy empty Husband's duty, thou shalt have
 The joy of children to continue the
 Succession of thy blood. For the appetite
 That steals her pleasure draws the forces of
 The body to an united strength and puts 'em
 Altogether into action, never fails
 Of procreation. All the purposes
 Of man aim but at one of these two ends
 Pleasure or profit; and in this one sweet
 Conjunction of our loves they both will meet.

    Would it not grieve thee that a Stranger to
    Thy blood should lay the first foundation of
    His house upon the ruins of thy family?
CASTABELLA. Now Heaven defend me! May my memory
    Be utterly extinguished, and the heir
    Of him that was my Father's enemy
    Raise his eternal monument upon
    Our ruins, ere the greatest pleasure or
    The greatest profit ever tempt me to
    Continue it by incest
D'AMVILLE. Incest? Tush!
    These distances affinity observes
    Are articles of bondage cast upon
    Our freedoms by our own objections.
    Nature allows a general liberty
    Of generation to all creatures else.
    Shall man
    To whose command and use all creatures were
    Made subject be less free then they?
CASTABELLA. O God!
    Is Thy unlimited and infinite
    Omnipotence less free because thou doest
    No ill?
    Or if you argue merely out of nature
    Do you not degenerate from that, and are
    You not unworthy the prerogative
    Of Nature's Masterpiece, when basely you
    Prescribe yourself authority and law
    From their examples whom you should command?
    I could confute you, but the horror of
    The argument confutes my understanding.—
    Sir, I know you do but try me in
    Your Son's behalf, suspecting that
    My strength
    And youth of blood cannot contain themselves
    With impotence.———Believe me, Sir,
    I never wronged him. If it be your lust,
    O quench it on their prostituted flesh
    Whose trade of sin can please desire with more
    Delight and less offence.———The poison of your breath,
    Evaporated from so foul a soul,
    Infects the air more than the damps that rise
    From bodies but half rotten in their graves.
D'AMVILLE. Kiss me. I warrant thee my breath is sweet.
    These dead men's bones lie here of purpose to
    Invite us to supply the number of
    The living. Come, we'll get young bones, and do it.
    I will enjoy thee. No? Nay then invoke

Your great supposed protector; I will do it.
CASTABELLA. Supposed protector! Are ye an Atheist? Then
    I know my prayers and tears are spent in vain.
    O patient Heaven! Why dost thou not express
    Thy wrath in thunder-bolts to tear the frame
    Of man in pieces? How can earth endure
    The burthen of this wickedness without
    An earthquake? Or the angry face of Heaven
    Be not enflamed with lightning?
D'AMVILLE. Conjure up
    The Devil and, his Damn: cry to the graves:
    The dead can hear thee: invocate their help.
CASTABELLA. O would this Grave might open and my body
    Were bound to the dead carcass of a man
    For ever, ere it entertain the lust
    Of this detested villain!
D'AMVILLE. Tereus-like
    Thus I will force my passage to———
CHARLEMONT. The Devil.

[CHARLEMONT *rises in the disguise, and frights* D'AMVILLE *away.*]

Now, Lady, with the hand of Charlemont
I thus redeem you from the arm of lust.
    ——My Castabella!
CASTABELLA. My dear Charlemont!
CHARLEMONT. For all my wrongs I thank thee, gracious Heaven,
    Thou hast made me satisfaction to reserve
    Me for this blessed purpose. Now, sweet Death,
    I'll bid thee welcome. Come, I'll guide thee home,
    And then I'll caste myself into the arms
    Of apprehension, that the law may make
    This worthy work the crown of all my actions,
    Being the best and last.
CASTABELLA. The last? The law?
    Now Heaven forbid! What have you done?
CHARLEMONT. Why, I have
    Killed a man; not murdered him, my Castabella.
    He would have murdered me.
CASTABELLA. Then Charlemont
    The hand of Heaven directed thy defense.
    That wicked Atheist! I suspect his plot.
CHARLEMONT. My life he seeks. I would he had it since
    He has deprived me of those blessings that
    Should make me love it. Come, I'll give it him.
CASTABELLA. You shall not. I will first expose myself
    To certain danger than for my defense
    Destroy the man that saved me from destruction.

CHARLEMONT. Thou canst not satisfy me better than
    To be the instrument of my release
    From misery.
CASTABELLA. Then work it by escape.
    Leave me to this protection that still guards
    The innocent Or I will be a partner
    In your destiny.
CHARLEMONT. My soul is heavy. Come, lie down to rest;
    These are the pillows whereon men sleep best.

[*They lie down with either of them a Death's head for a pillow.*]

[*Enter* LANGUEBEAU SNUFFE *seeking* SOQUETTE.]

LANGUEBEAU. Soquette, Soquette, Soquette! O art thou there?

[*He mistakes the body of* BORACHIO *for* SOQUETTE.]

Verily thou liest in a fine premeditated readiness for the purpose; Come kiss me, sweet Soquette.—Now purity defend me from the Sin of Sodom.—This is a creature of the masculine gender.—Verily the Man is blasted.—Yea, cold and stiff!—Murder, murder, murder;

[*Exit.*]

[*Enter* D'AMVILLE *distractedly: starts at the sight of a Death's head.*]

D'AMVILLE. Why dost thou stare upon me? Thou art not
    The soul of him I murdered. What hast thou
    To do to vex my conscience? Sure thou wert
    The head of a most dogged Usurer,
    Thou art so uncharitable. And that Bawd
    The sky there: she could shut the windows and
    The doors of this great chamber of the world,
    And draw the curtains of the clouds between
    Those lights and me, above this bed of Earth
    When that same Strumpet Murder and myself
    Committed sin together. Then she could
    Leave us in the dark till the close deed was done.
    But now that I begin to feel the loathsome horror of my sin, and, like a Lecher
        emptied of his lust, desire to bury my face under my eye-brows, and would steal
        from my shame unseen, she meets me
    In the face with all her light corrupted eyes
    To challenge payment of me.—O behold!
    Yonder's the Ghost of old Montferrers, in
    A long white sheet climbing yon lofty mountain
    To complain to Heaven of me.—
    Montferrers! pox of fearfulness! Tis nothing

But a fair white cloud. Why, was I borne a coward?
He lies that says so. Yet the countenance of
A bloodless worm might have the courage now
To turn my blood to water.
The trembling motion of an Aspen leaf
Would make me like the shadow of that leaf,
Lie shaking under it. I could now commit
A murder were it but to drink the fresh
Warm blood of him I murdered to supply
The want and weakness of mine own,
'Tis grown so colde and phlegmatic.
LANGUEBEAU. Murder, murder, murder!

[*Within.*]

D'AMVILLE. Mountains overwhelm me: the Ghost of old
    Montferrers haunts me.
LANGUEBEAU. Murder, murder, murder!
D'AMVILLE. O were my body circumvolved
    Within that cloud, that when the thunder tears
    His passage open, it might scatter me
    To nothing in the air!

[*Enter* LANGUEBEAU SNUFFE *with the* WATCH.]

LANGUEBEAU. Here you shall find
    The murdered body.
D'AMVILLE. Black Beelzebub,
    And all his hell-hounds, come to apprehend me?
LANGUEBEAU. No, my good Lord, we come to apprehend
    The murderer.
D'AMVILLE. The Ghost (great Pluto!) was
    A fool unfit to be employed in
    Any serious business for the state of hell.
    Why could not he have suffered me to raise
    The mountains of my sins with one as damnable
    As all the rest, and then have tumbled me
    To mine? But apprehend me even between
    The purpose and the act before it was
    Committed!
WATCH. Is this the murderer? He speaks suspiciously.
LANGUEBEAU. No verily. This is my Lord D'amville. And his distraction, I think,
    grows out of his grief for the loss of a faithful servant. For surely I take him to be
    Borachio that is slain.
D'AMVILLE. Hah! Borachio slain? Thou lookest like Snuffe, dost not?
LANGUEBEAU. Yes, in sincerity, my Lord.
D'AMVILLE. Hark thee?—Sawest thou not a Ghost?
LANGUEBEAU. A Ghost? Where, my Lord?—I smell a Foxe.

D'AMVILLE. Here in the Churchyard.

LANGUEBEAU. Tush! tush! their walking Spirits are mere imaginary fables. There's no
such thing *in rerum natura.* Here is a man slain. And with the Spirit of consideration
I rather think him to be the murderer got into that disguise then any such fantastic
toy.

D'AMVILLE. My brains begin to put themselves in order. I apprehend thee now.—'Tis
even so.—Borachio, I will search the Center, but I'll find the murderer.

WATCH. Here, here, here.

D'AMVILLE. Stay. Asleep? so soundly
So sweetly upon Death's Heads? and in a place
So full of fear and horror? Sure there is
Some other happiness within the freedom
Of the conscience then my knowledge ever attained to.—Ho, ho, ho!

CHARLEMONT. Ye are welcome, Uncle. Had you sooner come
You had been sooner welcome. I'm the Man
You seek. You shall not need examine me.

D'AMVILLE. My Nephew and my Daughter! O my dear
Lamented blood, what Fate has cast you thus
Unhappily upon this accident?

CHARLEMONT. You know, Sir, she's as clear as Chastity.

D'AMVILLE. As her own chastity. The time, the place,
All circumstances argue that unclear.

CASTABELLA. Sir, I confess it; and repentantly
Will undergo the self same punishment
That Justice shall inflict on Charlemont.

CHARLEMONT. Unjustly she betrays her innocence.

WATCH. But, Sir, she's taken with you and she must
To prison with you.

D'AMVILLE. There's no remedy.
Yet were it not my Sons bed she abused
My land should fly, but both should be excused.

[*Exeunt.*]

SCENE IV.

[*Enter* BELFOREST *and a* SERVANT.]

BELFOREST. Is not my wife come in yet?

SERVANT. No, my Lord.

BELFOREST. Me thinks she's very affectedly inclined
To young Sebastian's company of late.
But jealousy is such a torment that
I am afraid to entertain it. Yet
The more I shun by circumstances to meet
Directly with it, the more ground I find
To circumvent my apprehension. First,
I know she has a perpetual appetite,

Which being so oft encountered with a man
Of such a bold luxurious freedom as
Sebastian is, and of so promising
A body, her own blood corrupted will
Betray her to temptation.

[*Enter* FRESCO *closely.*]

FRESCO. Precious! I was sent by his Lady to see if her Lord were in bed. I should have done it slyly without discovery, and now I am blurted upon 'em before I was aware.

[*Exit.*]

BELFOREST. Know not you the Gentlewoman my wife brought home?

SERVANT. By sight, my Lord. Her man was here but now.
BELFOREST. Her man? I, prithee, run and call him quickly. This villain! I suspect him ever since I found him hid behind the Tapestry.———Fresco! thou art welcome, Fresco.———Leave us. Dost hear, Fresco? Is not my wife at thy Mistress's?
FRESCO. I know not, my Lord.
BELFOREST. I prithee tell me, Fresco——we are private——tell me:
Is not thy Mistress a good wench?
FRESCO. How means your Lordship that? A wench of the trade?
BELFOREST. Yes faith, Fresco; even a wench of the trade.
FRESCO. Oh no, my Lord. Those falling diseases cause baldness, and my Mistress recovers the loss of hair, for she is a Periwig-maker.
BELFOREST. And nothing else?
FRESCO. Sels Falls and Tyres and Bodies for Ladies, or so.
BELFOREST. So, Sir; and she helps my Lady to falls and bodies now and then, does she not?
FRESCO. At her Ladyship's pleasure, my Lord.
BELFOREST. Her pleasure, you Rogue? You are the Pander to her pleasure, you Varlet, are you not? You know the conveyances between Sebastian and my wife? Tell me the truth, or by this hand I'll nail thy bosom to the earth. Stir not you Dog, but quickly tell the truth.
FRESCO. O yes!

[*Speaks like a Crier.*]

BELFOREST. Is not thy Mistress a Bawd to my wife?
FRESCO. O yes!
BELFOREST. And acquainted with her tricks, and her plots, and her devises?
FRESCO. O yes! If any man, 'o Court, City, or Country, has found my Lady Leuidulcia in bed but my Lord Belforest, it is Sebastian.
BELFOREST. What dost thou proclaim it? Dost thou cry it, thou villain?
FRESCO. Can you laugh it, my Lord? I thought you meant to proclaim yourself cuckold.

[*Enter the Watch.*]

BELFOREST. The Watch met with my wish. I must request the assistance of your offices.

[FRESCO *runs away.*]

Is death, stay that villain: pursue him!

[*Exeunt.*]

SCENE. V.

[*Enter* LANGUEBEAU SNUFFE *importuning* SOQUETTE.]

SOQUETTE. Nay, if you get me any more into the Churchyard!
LANGUEBEAU. Why, Soquette, I never got thee there yet.
SOQUETTE. Got me there! No, not with childe.
LANGUEBEAU. I promised thee I would not, and I was as good as my word.
SOQUETTE. Yet your word was better than your deed.
But steal up into the little matted chamber of the left hand.
LANGUEBEAU. I prithee let it be the right hand. Thou *leftest* me before and I did not like that.
SOQUETTE. Precious quickly——So soon as my Mistress shall be in bed I'll come to you.

[*Exit* LANGUEBEAU SNUFFE.]

[*Enter* SEBASTIAN, LEUIDULCIA, *and* CATAPLASMA.]

CATAPLASMA. I wonder Fresco stays so long.
SEBASTIAN. Mistress Soquette, a word with you. [*Whispers.*]
LEUIDULCIA. If he brings word my Husband is in bed
    I will adventure one night's liberty
    To be abroad.———
    My strange affection to this man!———'Tis like
    That natural sympathy which even among
    The senseless creatures of the earth commands
    A mutual inclination and consent.
    For though it seems to be the free effect
    Of mine own voluntary love, yet I can
    Neither restrain it nor give reason for it.
    But now 'tis done, and in your power it lies
    To save my honour, or dishonor me.
CATAPLASMA. Enjoy your pleasure, Madame, without fear.
    I never will betray the trust you have
    Committed to me. And you wrong yourself
    To let consideration of the sin
    Molest your conscience. Me thinks 'tis unjust

That a reproach should be inflicted on
A woman for offending but with one,
When 'tis a light offence in Husbands to
Commit with many.

LEUIDULCIA. So it seems to me.———

Why, how now, Sebastian, making love to that Gentlewoman? How many mistresses
have you in faith?

SEBASTIAN. In faith, none; for I think none of 'em are faithful; but otherwise, as many
as clean shirts. The love of a woman is like a mushroom,—it grows in one night and
will serve somewhat pleasingly next morning to breakfast, but afterwards waxes
fulsome and unwholesome.

CATAPLASMA. Nay, by Saint Winifred, a woman's love lasts as long as winter fruit.

SEBASTIAN. 'Tis true—till new come in. By my experience no longer.

[*Enter* FRESCO *running.*]

FRESCO. Somebody's doing has undone us, and we are like to pay dearly for it.

SEBASTIAN. Pay dear? For what?

FRESCO. Will it not be a chargeable reckoning, think you, when here are half a dozen
fellows coming to call us to account, with every man a several bill in his hand that
we are not able to discharge.

[*Knock at the door.*]

CATAPLASMA. Passion of me! What bouncing's that?
Madame withdraw yourself.

LEUIDULCIA. Sebastian, if you love me, save my honour.

[*Exeunt.*]

SEBASTIAN. What violence is this? What seek you? Zownes!
You shall not pass.

[*Enter* Belforest *and the Watch.*]

BELFOREST. Pursue the Strumpet. Villain, give me way
Or I will make my passage through thy blood.

SEBASTIAN. My blood will make it slippery, my Lord,
'Twere better you would take another way.
You may hap fall else.

[*They fight. Both slain.* SEBASTIAN *falls first.*]

SEBASTIAN. I have it in faith.

[*Dies.*]

[*While* BELFOREST *is staggering enter* LEUIDULCIA.]

LEUIDULCIA. O God! my Husband! my Sebastian! Husband!
    Neither can speak, yet both report my shame.
    Is this the saving of my Honour when
    Their blood runs out in rivers, and my lust
    The fountain whence it flows? Dear Husband, let
    Not thy departed spirit be displeased
    If with adulterate lips I kiss thy cheek.
    Here I behold the hatefulness of lust
    Which brings me kneeling to embrace him dead
    Whose body living I did loathe to touch.
    Now I can weep. But what can tears do good
    When I weep only water, they weep blood.
    But could I make an Ocean with my tears
    That on the flood this broken vessel of
    My body, laden heavy with light lust,
    Might suffer shipwreck and so drown my shame.
    Then weeping were to purpose, but alas!
    The Sea wants water enough to wash away
    The foulness of my name. O! in their wounds
    I feel my honour wounded to the death.
    Shall I out-live my Honour? Must my life
    Be made the world's example? Since it must
    Then thus in detestation of my deed
    To make the example moue more forcibly
    To virtue thus I seal it with a death
    As full of horror as my life of sin.

[*Stabs herself.*]

[*Enter the* WATCH *with* CATAPLASMA, FRESCO, LANGUEBEAU SNUFFE,
    and SOQUETTE.]

WATCH. Hold, Madame! Lord, what a strange night is this!
LANGUEBEAU. May not Snuffe be suffered to go out of himself?
WATCH. Nor you, nor any. All must go with us.
    O with what virtue lust should be withstood!
    Since 'tis a fire quenched seldom without blood.

[*Exeunt.*]

ACT V.

SCENE I.

[*Music. A closet discovered. A Servant sleeping with lights and money before him.*]

[*Enter* D'AMVILLE.]

D'AMVILLE. What, sleepest thou?
SERVANT. No, my Lord. Nor sleep nor wake.
    But in a slumber troublesome to both.
D'AMVILLE. Whence comes this gold?
SERVANT. 'Tis part of the Revenue
    Due to your Lordship since your brother's death.
D'AMVILLE. To bed. Leave me my gold.
SERVANT. And me my rest.
    Two things wherewith one man is seldom blest.

[*Exit.*]

D'AMVILLE. Cease that harsh music. We are not pleased with it.

[*He handles the gold.*]

    Here sounds a music whose melodious touch
    Like Angels' voices ravishes the sense.
    Behold thou ignorant Astronomer
    Whose wandering speculation seeks among
    The planets for men's fortunes, with amazement
    Behold thine error and be planet struck.
    These are the Stars whose operations make
    The fortunes and the destinies of men.
    Yon lesser eyes of Heaven (like Subjects raised
    Into their lofty houses, when their Prince
    Rides underneath the ambition of their loves)
    Are mounted only to behold the face
    Of your more rich imperious eminence
    With unprevented sight Unmask, fair Queen.

[*Unpurses the gold.*

    Vouchsafe their expectations may enjoy
    The gracious favor they admire to see.
    These are the Stars the Ministers of Fate
    And Man's high wisdom the superior power
    To which their forces are subordinate.

[*Sleeps.*]

[*Enter the Ghost of* MONTFERRERS.]

MONTFERRERS. D'amville! With all thy wisdom thou art a fool.
    Not like those fools that we term innocents
    But a most wretched miserable fool
    Which instantly, to the confusion of
    Thy projects, with despair thou shalt behold.

[*Exit Ghost.*]

[D'AMVILLE *starts up.*]

D'AMVILLE. What foolish dream dares interrupt my rest
    To my confusion? How can that be, since
    My purposes have hitherto been borne
    With prosperous Judgment to secure success
    Which nothing lives to dispossess me of
    But apprehended Charlemont. And him
    This brain has made the happy instrument
    To free suspicion, to annihilate
    All interest and title of his own
    To seal up my assurance, and confirm
    My absolute possession by the law.
    Thus while the simple, honest worshipper
    Of a fantastic providence, groans under
    The burthen of neglected misery
    My real wisdom has raised up a State
    That shall eternize my posterity.

[*Enter* SERVANT *with the body of* SEBASTIAN.]

    What's that?
SERVANT. The body of your younger Son
    Slain by the Lord Belforest.
D'AMVILLE. Slain! You lie!
    Sebastian! Speak, *Sebastian!* He's lost
    His hearing. A Physician presently.
    Go, call a Surgeon.
ROUSARD. Ooh. [*Within.*]
D'AMVILLE. What groan was that?
    How does my elder Son? The sound came from
    His chamber.
SERVANT. He went sick to bed, my Lord.
ROUSARD. Ooh. [*Within.*]
D'AMVILLE. The cries of Mandrakes never touched the ear
    With more sad horror than that voice does mine.

[*Enter a* SERVANT *running.*]

SERVANT. Never you will see your Son alive——
D'AMVILLE. Nature forbid I ever should see him dead.

[*A Bed drawn forth with* ROUSARD.]

   Withdraw the Curtains. O how does my Son?
SERVANT. Me thinks he's ready to give up the ghost.
D'AMVILLE. Destruction take thee and thy fatal tongue.
   Dead! where's the Doctor?——Art not thou the face
   Of that prodigious apparition stared upon
   Me in my dream?
SERVANT. The Doctor's come, my Lord.

[*Enter* DOCTOR.]

D'AMVILLE. Doctor, behold two Patients in whose cure
   Thy skill may purchase an eternal fame.
   If thou'st any reading in *Hippocrates,*
   Galen, or *Avicenna;* if herbs, or drugs,
   Or minerals have any power to save,
   Now let thy practice and their sovereign use
   Raise thee to wealth and honour.
DOCTOR. If any root of life remains within 'em
   Capable of Physic fear 'em not, my Lord.
ROUSARD. Ooh.
D'AMVILLE. His gasping sighs are like the falling noise
   Of some great building when the ground-work breaks.
   On these two pillars stood the stately frame
   And architecture of my lofty house.
   An Earthquake shakes 'em. The foundation shrinks.
   Dear Nature, in whose honour I have raised
   A work of glory to posterity,
   O bury not the pride of that great action
   Under the fall and mine of itself.
DOCTOR. My Lord, these bodies are deprived of all
   The radical ability of Nature.
   The heat of life is utterly extinguished.
   Nothing remains within the power of man
   That can restore them.
D'AMVILLE. Take this gold, extract
   The Spirit of it, and inspire new life
   Into their bodies.
DOCTOR. Nothing can, my Lord.
D'AMVILLE. You have not yet examined the true state
   And constitution of their bodies. Sure

You have not. I'll reserve their waters till
The morning. Questionless, their urines will
Inform you better.
DOCTOR. Ha, ha, ha!
D'AMVILLE. Dost laugh.
Thou villain? Must my wisdom that has been
The object of men's admiration now
Become the subject of thy laughter?
ROUSARD. Ooh. *Dies.*
ALL. He's dead.
D'AMVILLE. O there expires the date
Of my posterity! Can Nature be
So simple or malicious to destroy
The reputation of her proper memory?
She cannot. Sure there is some power above
Her that controls her force.
DOCTOR. A power above
Nature? Doubt you that, my Lord? Consider but
Whence Man receives his body and his form.
Not from corruption like some worms and flies,
But only from the generation of
A man. For Nature never did bring forth
A man without a man; nor could the first
Man, being but the passive Subject not
The active Mover, be the maker of
Himself. So of necessity there must
Be a superior power to Nature.
D'AMVILLE. Now to myself I am ridiculous.
Nature thou art a Traitor to my soul.
Thou hast abused my trust. I will complain
To a superior Court to right my wrong.
I'll prove thee a forger of false assurances.
In yon Star chamber thou shalt answer it.
Withdraw the bodies. O the sense of death
Begins to trouble my distracted soul.

[*Exeunt.*]

SCENE II.

[*Enter* JUDGES *and* OFFICERS.]

1st JUDGE. Bring forth the malefactors to the Bar.

[*Enter* CATAPLASMA, SOQUETTE, *and* FRESCO.]

Are you the Gentlewoman in whose house
The murders were committed?

CATAPLASMA. Yes, my Lord.

1st JUDGE. That worthy attribute of Gentry which
    Your habit draws from ignorant respect
    Your name deserves not, nor yourself the name
    Of woman, since you are the poison that
    Infects the honour of all womanhood.

CATAPLASMA. My Lord, I am a Gentlewoman; yet
    I must confess my poverty compels
    My life to a condition lower than
    My birth or breeding.

2nd JUDGE. Tush, we know your birth.

1st JUDGE. But, under color to profess the Sale
    Of Tyres and toys for Gentlewomen's pride,
    You draw a frequentation of men's wives
    To your licentious house, and there abuse
    Their Husbands.——

FRESCO. Good my Lord her rent is great.
    The good Gentlewoman has no other thing
    To Hue by but her lodgings. So she's forced
    To let her fore-rooms out to others, and
    Herself contented to lie backwards.

2nd JUDGE. So.

1st JUDGE. Here is no evidence accuses you
    For accessories to the murder, yet
    Since from the Spring of lust, which you preserved
    And nourished, ran the effusion of that blood,
    Your punishment shall come as near to death
    As life can bear it Law cannot inflict
    Too much severity upon the cause
    Of such abhorred effects.

2nd JUDGE. Receive your sentence.
    Your goods (since they were gotten by that means
    Which brings diseases) shall be turned to the use
    Of Hospitals. You carted through the Streets
    According to the common shame of strumpets
    Your bodies whipped, till with the loss of blood
    You faint under the hand of punishment.
    Then that the necessary force of want
    May not provoke you to your former life
    You shall be set to painful labor whose
    Penurious gains shall only give you food
    To hold up Nature, mortify your flesh,
    And make you fit for a repentant end.

ALL. O good my lord!

1st JUDGE. No more. Away with 'em.

    [*Exeunt* CATAPLASMA, SOQUETTE, *and* FRESCO.]

[*Enter* LANGUEBEAU SNUFFE.]

2nd JUDGE. Now, Monsieur Snuffe! A man of your profession
    Found in a place of such impiety!
LANGUEBEAU SNUFFE. I grant you. The place is full of impurity. So much the more
    need of instruction and reformation. The purpose that carried me thither was with the
    Spirit of conversion to purify their uncleanness, and I hope your Lordship will say
    the law cannot take hold of me for that.
1st JUDGE. No, Sir, it cannot; but yet give me leave
    To tell you that I hold your wary answer
    Rather premeditated for excuse
    Then spoken out of a religious purpose.
    Where took you your degrees of Scholarship?
LANGUEBEAU SNUFFE. I am no Scholar, my Lord. To speak the sincere truth, I am
    Snuffe the Tallow-Chandler.
2nd JUDGE. How comes your habits to be altered thus?
LANGUEBEAU SNUFFE. My Lord Belforest, taking a delight in the cleanness of my
    conversation, withdrew me from that unclean life and put me in a garment fit for his
    society and my present profession.
1st JUDGE. His Lordship did but paint a rotten post,
    Or cover foulness fairly. Monsieur Snuffe,
    Back to your candle-making! You may give
    The world more light with that, then either with
    Instruction or the example of your life.
LANGUEBEAU SNUFFE. Thus the Snuffe is put out.

[*Exit* LANGUEBEAU SNUFFE.]

[*Enter* D'AMVILLE *distractedly with the hearses of his two Sons borne after him.*]

D'AMVILLE. Judgment! Judgment!
2nd JUDGE. Judgment, my Lord, in what?
D'AMVILLE. Your Judgments must resolve me in a case
    Bring in the bodies. Nay, I'll have it tried.
    This is the case, my Lord. By providence,
    Even in a moment, by the only hurt
    Of one, or two, or three at most, and those
    Put quickly out of pain too, mark me, I
    Had wisely raised a competent estate
    To my posterity. And is there not
    More wisdom and more charity in that
    Than for your Lordship, or your Father, or
    Your Grandsire to prolong the torment and
    The rack of rent from age to age upon
    Your poor penurious Tenants, yet perhaps,
    Without a penny profit to your heir?
    Is it not more wise? more charitable? Speak.
1st JUDGE. He is distracted.

D'AMVILLE. How? distracted? Then
    You have no Judgment. I can give you sense
    And solid reason for the very least
    Distinguishable syllable I speak.
    Since my thrift
    Was more judicious than your Grandsires, why
    I would feign know why your Lordship lives to make
    A second generation from your Father,
    And the whole fry of my posterity
    Extinguished in a moment. Not a Brat
    Left to succeed me.—I would feign know that.
2nd JUDGE. Grief for his children's death distempers him.
1st JUDGE. My Lord, we will resolve you of your question.
    In the mean time vouchsafe your place with us.
D'AMVILLE. I am contented, so you will resolve me.—[*Ascends.*]

    [*Enter* CHARLEMONT *and* CASTABELLA.]

2nd JUDGE. Now, Monsieur Charlemont, you are accused
    Of having murdered one Borachio, that
    Was servant to my Lord D'amville. How can
    You clear yourself? Guilty or not guilty?
CHARLEMONT. Guilty of killing him, but not of murder.
    My Lords, I have no purpose to desire
    Remission for myself.——

    [D'AMVILLE *descends to* CHARLEMONT.]

D'AMVILLE. Uncivil Boy!
    Thou wantest humanity to smile at grief.
    Why dost thou cast a cheerful eye upon
    The object of my sorrow—my dead Sons?
1st JUDGE. O good my Lord, let Charity forebear
    To vex the spirit of a dying Man.
    A cheerful eye upon the face of Death
    Is the true countenance of a noble mind.
    For honor's sake, my Lord, molest it not.
D'AMVILLE. Ye are all uncivil. O! is it not enough
    That he unjustly hath conspired with Fate
    To cut off my posterity, for him
    To be the heir to my possessions, but
    He must pursue me with his presence.
    And, in the ostentation of his joy,
    Laugh in my face and glory in my grief?
CHARLEMONT. D'amville, to show thee with what light respect
    I value Death and thy insulting pride,
    Thus, like a warlike Navy on the Sea
    Bound for the conquest of some wealthy land,

Passed through the stormy troubles of this life,
And now arrived upon the armed coast
In expectation of the victory
Whose honour lies beyond this exigent,
Through mortal danger, with an active spirit
Thus I aspire to undergo my death.

[*Leaps up the Scaffold.*]

[CASTABELLA *leaps after him.*]

CASTABELLA. And thus I second thy brave enterprise.
    Be cheerful, Charlemont. Our lives cut off
    In our young prime of years are like green herbs
    Wherewith we strow the hearses of our friends.
    For, as their virtue, gathered when thou are green,
    Before they wither or corrupt, is best;
    So we in virtue are the best for Death
    While yet we have not lived to such an age
    That the increasing canker of our sins
    Hath spread too far upon us.——
D'AMVILLE. A Boone, my Lords.
    I beg a Boone.
1st JUDGE. What's that, my Lord?
D'AMVILLE. His body when 'tis dead
    For an Anatomy.
2nd JUDGE. For what, my Lord?
D'AMVILLE. Your understanding still comes short of mine.
    I would find out by his Anatomy
    What thing there is in Nature more exact
    Then in the constitution of myself.
    Me thinks my parts and my dimensions are
    As many, as large, as well composed as his;
    And yet in me the resolution wants
    To die with that assurance as he does.
    The cause of that in his Anatomy
    I would find out.
1st JUDGE. Be patient and you shall.
D'AMVILLE. I have bethought me of a better way.
    —Nephew, we must confer.—Sir, I am grown
    A wondrous Student now of late. My wit
    Has reached beyond the scope of Nature, yet
    For all my learning I am still to seek
    From whence the peace of conscience should proceed.
CHARLEMONT. The peace of conscience rises in itself.
D'AMVILLE. Whether it be thy Art or Nature I
    Admire thee, Charlemont. Why, thou hast taught
    A woman to be valiant. I will beg

Thy life.—My Lords, I beg my Nephew's life.
I'll make thee my Physician. Thou shalt read
Philosophy to me. I will find out
The efficient cause of a contented mind.
But if I cannot profit in it then 'tis
No more good being my Physician,
But infuse
A little poison in a potion when
Thou givest me Physic, unawares to me.
So I shall steal into my grave without
The understanding or the fear of death.
And that's the end I aim at. For the thought
Of death is a most fearful torment; is it not?

2nd JUDGE. Your Lordship interrupts the course of law.

1st JUDGE. Prepare to die.

CHARLEMONT. My resolution's made.
But ere I die, before this honored bench,
With the free voice of a departing soul,
I here protest this Gentlewoman clear
Of all offence the law condemns her for.

CASTABELLA. I have accused myself. The law wants power
To clear me. My dear Charlemont, with thee
I will partake of all thy punishments.

CHARLEMONT. Uncle, for all the wealthy benefits
My death advances you, grant me but this:
Your mediation for the guiltless life
Of Castabella, whom your conscience knows
As justly clear, as harmless innocence.

D'AMVILLE. Freely. My Mediation for her life
And all my interest in the world to boot;
Let her but in exchange possess me of
The resolution that she dies withal.
—The price of things is best known in their want.
Had I her courage, so I value it:
The Indies should not buy it out of my hands.

CHARLEMONT. Give me a glass of water.

D'AMVILLE. Me of wine.———
This argument of death congeals my blood.
Cold fear, with apprehension of thy end,
Hath frozen up the rivers of my veins.—

[*A glass of wine given him.*]

I must drink wine to warm me and dissolve
The obstruction; or an apoplexy will
Possess me.—Why, thou uncharitable Knave,
Dost thou bring me blood to drink? The very glass
Looks pale and trembles at it.

SERVANT. 'Tis your hand, my Lord.

D'AMVILLE. Canst blame me to be fearful, bearing still
    The presence of a murderer about me?

CHARLEMONT. Is this water?

SERVANT. Water, Sir.—[*A glass of water.*]

CHARLEMONT. Come, thou clear emblem of cool temperance,
    Be thou my witness that I use no art
    To force my courage nor have need of helps
    To raise my Spirits, like those weaker men
    Who mix their blood with wine, and out of that
    Adulterate conjunction do beget
    A bastard valour. Native courage, thanks.
    Thou leadest me soberly to undertake
    This great hard work of magnanimity.

D'AMVILLE. Brave Charlemont, at the reflection of
    Thy courage my cold fearful blood takes fire
    And I begin to emulate thy death.
    —Is that thy executioner? My Lords,
    You wrong the honour of so high a blood
    To let him suffer by so base a hand.

JUDGES. He suffers by the form of law, my Lord.

D'AMVILLE. I will reform it. Down, you shag-haired cur.
    The instrument that strikes my nephew's blood
    Shall be as noble as his blood. I'll be
    Thy executioner myself.

1st JUDGE. Restrain his fury. Good my Lord, forebear.

D'AMVILLE. I'll butcher out the passage of his soul
    That dares attempt to interrupt the blow.

2nd JUDGE. My Lord, the office will impress a mark
    Of scandal and dishonor on your name.

CHARLEMONT. The office fits him: hinder not his hand,
    But let him crown my resolution with
    An unexampled dignity of death.
    Strike home. Thus I submit me.

    [*Ready for Execution.*]

CASTABELLA. So do I.
    In scorn of Death thus hand in hand we die.

D'AMVILLE. I have the trick on it, Nephew. You shall see
    How easily I can put you out of pain.—Ooh!

    [*As he raises up the Axe strikes out his own brains. Staggers of the Scaffold.*]

EXECUTIONER. In lifting up the Axe
    I think he's knocked his brains out.

D'AMVILLE. What murderer was he that lifted up
    My hand against my head?

JUDGE. None but yourself, my Lord

D'AMVILLE. I thought he was a murderer that did it.

JUDGE. God forbid!

D'AMVILLE. Forbid? You lie, Judge. He commanded it.
    To tell thee that man's wisdom is a fool.
    I came to thee for Judgment, and thou thinkest
    Thy self a wise man. I outreached thy wit
    And made thy Justice Murder's instrument
    In Castabella's death and Charlemont's.
    To crown my Murder of Montferrers with
    A safe possession of his wealthy state

CHARLEMONT. I claim the just advantage of his words.

JUDGE. Descend the Scaffold, and attend the rest.

D'AMVILLE. There was the strength of natural understanding.
    But Nature is a fool. There is a power
    Above her that hath overthrown the pride
    Of all my projects and posterity,
    For whose summing blood
    I had erected a proud monument,
    And struck 'em dead before me. For whose deaths
    I called to thee for Judgment. Thou didst want
    Discretion for the sentence. But yon power
    That struck me knew the Judgment I deserved,
    And gave it.—O! the lust of Death commits
    A Rape upon me as I would have done
    On Castabella.

    [*Dies.*]

JUDGE. Strange is his death and judgment. With the hands
    Of Joy and Justice I thus set you free.
    The power of that eternal providence
    Which overthrew his projects in their pride
    Hath made your griefs the instruments to raise
    Your blessings to a greater height then ever.

CHARLEMONT. Only to Heaven I attribute the work,
    Whose gracious motives made me still forebear
    To be mine own Revenger. Now I see
    That *Patience is the honest man's revenge.*

JUDGE. Instead of Charlemont that but even now
    Stood ready to be dispossessed of all
    I now salute you with more titles both
    Of wealth and dignity, then you were born to.
    And you, sweet Madame, Lady of *Belforest,*
    You have that title by your Father's death.

CASTABELLA. With all the titles due to me increase
    The wealth and honour of my Charlemont
    Lord of Montferrers, Lord D'amville Belforest,—

And for a cloze to make up all the rest—*Embrace.*
The Lord of Castabella. Now at last
Enjoy the full possession of my love,
As clear and pure as my first chastity.
CHARLEMONT. The crown of all my blessings!—I will tempt
My Stars no longer, nor protract my time
Of marriage. When those Nuptial rites are done
I will perform my kinsmen's funerals.
JUDGE. The Drums and Trumpets! Interchange the sounds
Of Death and Triumph. For these honored lives,
Succeeding their deserved Tragedies.
CHARLEMONT. Thus, by the work of Heaven, the men that thought
To follow our dead bodies without tears
Are dead themselves, and now we follow theirs.

[*Exeunt.*]

FINIS.

Lightning Source UK Ltd.
Milton Keynes UK
UKOW05f2347230614

233938UK00002B/287/P